ALSO BY STEVE MILLWARD:

From Blues To Rock: An Analytical History Of Pop Music – with David Hatch (Manchester University Press)

Changing Times: Music And Politics In 1964 (Matador)

Different Tracks: Music And Politics In 1970 (Matador)

FAST FORWARD

MUSIC AND POLITICS IN 1974

Steve Millward

Matador
9 Priory Business Park,
Wistow Road, Kibworth Beauchamp,
Leicestershire. LE8 0RX
Tel: 0116 279 2299
Email: books@troubador.co.uk
Web: www.troubador.co.uk/matador
Twitter: @matadorbooks

ISBN 978 1785891 588

British Library Cataloguing in Publication Data.
A catalogue record for this book is available from the British Library.

Printed and bound in the UK by TJ International, Padstow, Cornwall
Typeset in 12pt Bembo by Troubador Publishing Ltd, Leicester, UK

Matador is an imprint of Troubador Publishing Ltd

MIX
Paper from responsible sources
FSC www.fsc.org FSC® C013056

For Roy, Betty and Beverly

Contents

Preface

In October 1974 I started my first 'proper' job – a mundane enough experience but laden with memories of people, places and sounds. Even now I can barely listen to 'Killer Queen' or 'Let's Put It All Together' without thinking of my dingy Manchester flat, the 64 bus and the journey at some unearthly hour of the morning to the Education Offices. But to my delight I found that most of my co-workers were into music – not so much what was in the charts but exciting and diverse idioms like reggae and pre-war jazz. Earlier in the year I had been living in West Germany where the news from home arrived only sporadically. First the miners' strike, then a hung parliament – it was all very perplexing. In the summer I went off to hitchhike around North America, giving me plenty of opportunity to listen to music, and news, on car radios. The Watergate scandal was reaching its zenith; I watched Richard Nixon's resignation speech live on Canadian TV.

All this demonstrates that while 1974 was an eventful year for me, the picture I was left with was, in terms of both music and politics, incomplete. Perhaps that is why, for many years, I underestimated the significance of 1974. My inference – so wrong – was that the fervour had gone out of music and that what was left was sterile and going nowhere. The oil crisis and global recession; revolutions across Africa; governmental chaos in Britain; Watergate, Vietnam and the troubles in Northern Ireland; the Patty Hearst affair; the rise of the National Front; escalating football violence... it all seemed to conspire to deaden the senses and stifle creativity.

By the end of the year, however, something was clearly stirring.

You could hardly fail to notice the new pared-down, aggressive music that wantonly flouted the standards set so recently by the top rock bands. Basic – yes; ephemeral – certainly, but that was the whole idea. Though none but the most prescient knew it then, we were hurtling full-speed into the future. In retrospect, too, there was a good deal of high-quality folk, blues, classical music and even mainstream rock, where numerous bands and solo artists were able to come to terms with the burdensome legacy of the 1960s. It was also a vintage year for African-American music which, as ever, proved resilient in the face of adversity. Furthermore, across all of these fields there was no shortage of social and political comment.

1974 has, therefore, proved to be a fitting juncture at which to conclude this trilogy of books on music and politics. Like 1964, it signalled the start of a new era, but now grim reality had finally supplanted the last vestiges of innocent ideology – a process begun by the turbulent and traumatic events of 1970. In time, of course there would be further upheavals. 1984, for example – though perhaps not in the way foreseen by George Orwell – saw renewed tensions between governmental authority and the rights of individuals, and a concomitant reaction from musicians ranging from rappers to New Romantics. But that is a story still to be told.

As in *Changing Times* and *Different Tracks*, I have used parameters to define what constitutes music from the year in question. In this case, I include any item both recorded and released in 1974 plus any record made in 1973 (or earlier) but not issued until 1974 – for the obvious reason that its impact could date only from when it first became available. Similarly, I have omitted items made in 1974 but not released until later unless specific events from 1974 influenced their creation.

I should like to thank the people who have helped me write *Fast Forward*. Some have lent records, books or DVDs, others have given interviews, provided advice or given feedback – all of which I have made use of. They are: Carol Bushell, Jack Cooper, Geraldine

Crawford, Mark Dennis, Dave Driver, John Greenway, Les Hare, Beverly Howbrook, CP Lee, Chris Lee, Mary Millward, Matthew Millward, Tom Millward, Pete Newton, Kev Nolan, Lee Robinson, Helen Singer, Sid Toole and David K Williams. Finally I should like to express my gratitude to Chelsea Taylor and the team at Troubador for their continuing patience, guidance and support.

CHAPTER 1

Good Old Boys (and Girls)

As the early 1970s slipped imperceptibly into the mid-1970s, the optimism that had characterised the previous decade was also fading fast. The oil crisis of 1973 had resulted in runaway inflation and global recession. Petrol was rationed; energy shortages led to power cuts; firms ceased trading or went on to short-time working. There were fears, too, that basic commodities were becoming unaffordable or even unobtainable, exemplified by the great Japanese toilet paper panic. Even the TV shut down early.

The swinging sixties had, in fact, been dealt a mortal blow at the turn of decade. During 1970 popular protest grew more violent and the response from the authorities ever more brutal; acts of terrorism became commonplace. The break-up of The Beatles and the death of Jimi Hendrix served to exacerbate the growing sense of dislocation among the young: some espoused the new ways of living offered by vegetarianism, feminism and alternative religions. So by 1974 what most people even then regarded as a halcyon age should have been dead and buried. The trouble was that many of its major figures were not going away.

At the start of the year Richard Nixon was the President of the United States with Henry Kissinger as his Secretary of State. Leonid Brezhnev led the Soviet Union, Golda Meir, Israel; Willy Brandt was the West German Chancellor, Georges Pompidou the President of France. Former British Prime Minister Harold Wilson was about to return to office. Film directors Ingmar Bergman and Stanley Kubrick were still at the top; the leading actors included Steve McQueen, Sean Connery and Jane Fonda. Mary Quant and Laura Ashley continued to set high street fashion trends. Billie-Jean King and Jack Nicklaus dominated their respective sports and Muhammad Ali was on the verge of a sensational comeback; the successful football managers Alf Ramsey, Bill Shankly, Don Revie and Bill Nicholson were still in place. And in music, The Rolling Stones, The Who, James Brown, Stevie Wonder, Diana Ross, Bob Dylan, Joni Mitchell and Eric Clapton remained among the elite.

For these survivors the 364 days that followed were a tale of contrasting fortunes: some swam, some sank, others merely trod water as the trickle of change became first a stream, and then a torrent.

*****

The Arab oil embargo of 1973 meant that the leaders of the Western World were beset with problems on all fronts. Disrupted energy supplies, rampant inflation and industrial unrest made it impossible to ignore domestic issues; indeed the environment was so volatile that maintaining law and order was a pressing concern. Yet it was equally important to focus on international affairs. This was where the crisis had its roots and thus where a solution must be found.

It had all begun when, upset at America's support for Israel during the Yom Kippur War of October 1973, the Arab members of OPEC (Organisation of the Petroleum Exporting Countries) resolved to reduce production by 5% per month. In retaliation President Nixon increased aid to Israel in terms both of supplies and cash, a move that triggered the cessation of Arab oil exports to the US and, subsequently, to many of its allies.

Between October 1973 and March 1974, the price of oil quadrupled and although the embargo was then lifted, the consequences were felt for some time afterwards. Each affected country dealt with the situation in different ways. In West Germany, for example, a speed limit of 100 kph was introduced but then abandoned after public protest. A Sunday driving ban proved more acceptable but by then the pressure was taking its toll on Willy Brandt. Amid rumours of alcoholism and marital infidelity, he was constantly hounded by the media (the tabloid *Bild Zeitung* employed a photojournalist to shadow him wherever he went in the hope that he would say or do something unfortunate), and when it emerged that one of his assistants, Günter Guillaume, was an East German spy, Brandt resigned as Chancellor on 6 May, in favour of the Defence Minister, Helmut Schmidt.

In France, the year 1974 was even more turbulent. Rising prices and a drop in the standard of living sparked a series of demonstrations and disputes, the most serious of which was the postal workers' strike of 31 October. Following the decision to withdraw it from service the liner *France* was hijacked by its own crew, and a fraud scandal in Bordeaux caused a catastrophic drop in the export price of French wine. The new Charles de Gaulle Airport opened on 8 March but the celebrations were muted; five days earlier, the world's worst-ever air disaster had taken place near Paris when a Turkish Airlines DC-10 crashed near Paris, killing all of its 346 passengers. A few weeks later, on 2 April, President Pompidou died unexpectedly, at the age of 62. In the ensuing elections, the socialist François Mitterand was defeated by the candidate of the Right, Valéry Giscard d'Estaing. The margin of victory was, however, less than 2%, reflecting national doubts as to which way to turn in such uncertain times.

Those same anxieties were, no doubt, being felt all over Europe but were certainly expressed in the UK and Austria where national elections brought similarly close results. In Italy, however, the dilemma was moral, rather than political. Three years before, a law had been passed allowing divorce to take place in the civil court. Now religious leaders were campaigning to have the legislation repealed in the belief that the ending of a marriage was a matter for the Church rather than the State. It was therefore decided to hold a referendum on the issue with a 'Yes' vote signifying support for the repeal and

'No' indicating a vote to retain the new laws. The degree of sensitivity surrounding the referendum is illustrated by the action of the censors in banning coverage of the Eurovision Song Contest which took place on 6 April, some five weeks before the vote. The basis of their concern was that viewers might interpret the Italian entry, 'Si', sung by Gigliola Cinquetti, as endorsing the 'Yes' campaign. In the event, their fears were unjustified: the pro-divorce campaign polled 20% more of the vote than the Church and its supporters.

Meanwhile in the eastern Mediterranean a conflagration was imminent in the seemingly perennial trouble-spot of Cyprus. Tensions between the island's Greek and Turkish communities had come to a head in the late 1950s when it was still a British colony. Initially, the conflict stemmed from the desire on the Greek side for *enosis*, that is, the union of the island with Greece. Understandably, the British government rejected the notion – aside from any consideration of ownership, there was the Turkish population (smaller in number but still substantial) to consider. They, too, had entertained ideas of union with their 'home' country but now favoured *taksim,* partition.

During his rise to power the Greek Orthodox Archbishop of Cyprus, Makarios III, had been a proponent of enosis but by the time of his election as President of the island in December 1959 he favoured full independence. This was duly granted by Britain, perhaps seeing this as a neat solution, but in 1964 violence flared up again, prompted by the perceived bias of Makarios towards the Turks. Three years later there was a coup in Greece and a military junta came to power with enosis high on their agenda. From then on, the conflict in Cyprus acquired a new dimension – the division on the Greek side between the pro- and anti-enosis factions.

Makarios was firmly in the latter camp and thus became a target for the junta. Following various attempts to undermine him, they ordered a coup by the Cypriot National Guard and on 15 July 1974 the Cypriot government was overthrown and Makarios fled to London. Five days later, Turkey invaded Cyprus, with the apparent intention of protecting both the independence of the island and its Turkish citizens. Three days after that, the military junta fell and peace talks were convened immediately by the British Foreign Secretary, James Callaghan. The talks had the effect of partitioning the island but this seemingly equitable resolution masked the appalling nature of a ten-year conflict in which hundreds of Cypriots were displaced or lost their lives, atrocities were committed by both sides and sites of religious and cultural significance desecrated or destroyed. Memories of these tragic events are long and bitter: only in 2014 did talks finally begin on the reunification of Cyprus as a federal state.

Callaghan's diplomacy was effective but not on the same scale as Henry Kissinger's efforts to bring peace to the Middle East in the aftermath of the Yom Kippur War. Indeed the term 'shuttle diplomacy' was coined to describe the flurry of visits he made to all of the parties directly involved – Golda Meir, President Hafez al-Assad of Syria and President Anwar Sadat of Egypt – or to those with an indirect interest, such as Leonid Brezhnev. According to transcripts released in August 2004 by the US National Archive, Kissinger also held the fort when President Nixon was too drunk to take a phone call from the British Prime Minister, Edward Heath, on 11 October 1973, five days into the conflict.

Two weeks later the War was over and on 5 November Kissinger set off on his first round of visits. By February 1974, there was sufficient progress for the leading Arab states to plan the cessation of the oil embargo against the US; the following month, it was lifted. At the same time Kissinger was persuading Israel to return to Egypt and Syria some of the land it had gained in October and in the Six Day War of 1967. This move pleased both Arab countries: relations between the USA and Egypt immediately began to thaw, and at the end of May Syria ceased all hostilities. By then, however, Golda Meir was no longer Israeli Prime Minister. In the post mortems that followed the War it was said that Israel was insufficiently prepared for the Arab attacks. Though partially exonerated by the National Commission of

Inquiry, she had still attracted a good deal of blame and on 10 April, nine days after the publication of the Commission's interim report, she resigned. As for Kissinger, any joy he may have felt at his success in the Middle East was tempered by the fact that, on 4 January 1974, the War in Vietnam had restarted.

*****

One of the striking features of post-war popular culture is that pop music, produced – in theory – by the young for the young, has continued to be made and consumed by people well beyond their teenage years. At the time of writing The Rolling Stones, for example, are still playing to packed houses all around the world after 50 years of touring. Their audience will include septuagenarians who have followed them since they started out, plus representatives from each succeeding generation. And whatever their age, they all want to hear the old hits. Yet The Stones are untypical in that they have an extensive back-catalogue of excellent material to draw on. Most pop singers/rock bands soon run out of creativity yet in many cases they carry on undeterred for years, and often decades – a phenomenon satirised by Randy Newman in his 1999 song 'I'm Dead (But I Don't Know It)': 'I have nothing left to say, but I'm going to say it anyway'.

This was becoming a problem as early as 1974. In the UK, for example, many leading musicians had then been performing for over fifteen years, working their way from skiffle through rock and roll, British beat, R&B, blues, psychedelia and prog rock. For such artists, the well was beginning to run dry. There were, however, some American role models to give them at least a little inspiration. Elvis Presley's revival as a serious contender continued to gather momentum: first came a credible account of the Tony Joe White composition, 'I've Got A Thing About You Baby', and then, in November, a rampaging version of Chuck Berry's 'Promised Land' which made number fourteen on the US chart, his best result for nearly two years. But Presley's success was eclipsed by a man he had once employed on his Graceland estate.

Billy Swan was a music business veteran whose composition 'Lover Please' had been recorded by Bill Black, Presley's bassist, over ten years before – though it was Clyde McPhatter who made the American Top Ten with the song in spring 1962. Subsequently Swan wrote material for the likes of Waylon Jennings and Conway Twitty and produced Tony Joe White's debut album, *Black And White*, which included the classic 'Polk Salad Annie', a staple of Presley's live performances in the early 1970s. The guitarist on the album, Chip Young, owned his own studio, Youngun Sound, in Murfreesboro, Tennessee, and it was here that, in April 1974, Billy Swan made his first recording, 'I Can Help'.

Its swaying rhythm, catchy refrain – 'It'd sure do me good to do you good' – and retro organ sound proved a winning combination and the record shot to the top of the US singles chart on 23 November. But 'I Can Help' was just one of the many highlights of the album of the same name. Swan's compositions are naturally to the fore: 'I'm Her Fool', 'I'd Like To Work For You' and 'Queen Of My Heart' are all characterised by wry lyrics and memorable melodies while 'Lover Please' is treated to a dynamic arrangement and exultant guitar solo by Young. The covers, too, are excellent. 'The Ways Of A Woman In Love' recalls the Latin beat and expansive orchestrations of the Brill Building era and 'Shake, Rattle And Roll', though easy-paced, packs a punch. Best of all is the version of 'Don't Be Cruel'; taken at an unfamiliar, funereal pace it builds and releases tension through the upfront steady drumbeat and timely interjections from organ, guitar and piano.

Sadly, as far as the charts were concerned, *I Can Help* was Billy's swan song, yet it remains one of the most pleasurable releases of the year. It also reaffirmed that it was possible to make good records at the ripe old age of 31. Born just three months before Billy Swan, Carole King had already flown the flag for the more mature performer with her 1971 album *Tapestry*. In 1974 she was still going strong with her US number one album *Wrap Around Joy* and the two hits it spawned – the driving 'Jazzman' and the sophisticated yet touching 'Nightingale'.

King had reached the charts in 1962 with 'It Might As Well Rain Until September', but she spent the 1960s writing (with Gerry Goffin) hits for other people; Billy Swan, as we have seen, did not make his first recordings until 1974. So neither had the pressure of staying in the spotlight through the 1960s when trends were changing so rapidly that even the most successful performers were constantly faced with the dilemma of whether or not to continue in the same musical vein. In effect you were damned if you did and damned if you didn't. Those going down the latter route would be scorned for lack of adventure – a terrible accusation in a decade celebrated for its spirit of innovation. But at the same time efforts to adopt a new style – especially if an artist had already been pigeonholed by record companies, music critics and fans – could also provoke a negative reaction.

Bobby Darin was one of the stars of the late 1950s/early 1960s, notable for his sleek good looks, versatility and full-on singing style. Yet his transformation into a politically aware, folk-influenced singer/songwriter received only lukewarm enthusiasm. His beautiful version of Tim Hardin's 'If I Were A Carpenter' did at least make the charts in 1966 but the eponymous album from which it came sank without trace, as did all those that followed. An even worse fate, however, befell Ricky Nelson, who had had no fewer than 33 US hits between 1957 and 1964.

In 1972, now known as Rick Nelson, he appeared on the bill of a rock and roll revival concert at Madison Square Garden, New York, where the audience greeted his hippy-ish appearance and new songs with jeers and catcalls; following a rendition of The Rolling Stones' 'Honky Tonk Women', he was booed off the stage. Given the theme of the event, perhaps this should have been no surprise, but in disgust Nelson wrote the song 'Garden Party' which described his experience at the 'Garden', concluding, 'If memories are all I sang, I'd rather drive a truck'. It was therefore a matter of some irony that 'Garden Party' was Nelson's ticket back to the big time, hitting the charts in both the UK and the US, where it reached number six; the eponymous album made the Top 40, his first LP to do so for nine years.

Next came *Windfall*, recorded and released in 1974. This edition of Nelson's backing group, The Stone Canyon Band, included guitarist Dennis Larden who, as amply demonstrated here, was a writer of talent. His 'Legacy', for example, is pleasing, melodic country rock with lyrics that stay just on the right side of sentimentality; 'Don't Leave Me Here' and 'One Night Stand' are of similar quality – the latter, for instance, could easily have been by The Eagles. But 'Evil Woman Child' is, in contrast, a slice of high-energy funk with wah-wah guitar. Nelson's contributions are also varied: 'Someone To Love' is hard hitting blues-rock, 'Lifestream' a mellow country ballad and the title track, composed with Larden, has a Caribbean feel, not unlike Stephen Stills's 'Love The One You're With', but with better lyrics. Bassist J DeWitt White's 'How Many More Times' is gently jazzy while 'I Don't Want To Be Lonely Tonight' by long-time Nelson collaborator Thomas Baker Knight (he also wrote for acts varying from Frank Sinatra to The West Pop Art Experimental Band), is an out-and-out rocker. The musicianship of The Stone Canyon Band is first-class and Nelson's vocals are warm and relaxed, whatever the idiom.

But despite being, in Bruce Eder's words, 'as solid a piece of 70s music as any early rock and roller this side of Elvis Presley ever delivered' (*allmusic.com*), the album produced no windfall for Nelson. On the contrary, it barely made the US Top 200. Nelson was duly dropped by his record company, MCA, and before long was reduced to playing state fairs and theme parks.

★★★★★

Part of the fascination of 'Garden Party' lay in Nelson's reference to ex-Beatles John Lennon and George Harrison who, it therefore must be assumed, were present at the Madison Square Garden concert. The first allusion is transparent – 'Yoko brought her walrus', the second ('Mr Hughes hid in Dylan's shoes'), less so: Harrison, a friend and neighbour of Nelson's, used 'Mr Hughes' as an alias and was at that time considering an album of Dylan covers. That project failed to materialise and in the event Harrison had no albums out in 1972. Nor, for that matter, did his erstwhile colleagues Paul McCartney and Ringo Starr. Lennon, however, released the ferocious *Some Time In New York City*, a collaboration with Ono that spoke out unequivocally for feminism and civil rights.

Two years later the picture was very different for all four former Beatles. The stock of both Harrison and Lennon was falling fast. The former saw the universal acclaim he received for *All Things Must Pass* and *The Concert For Bangladesh* collapse into disdain for the perceived piety of his 1973 album *Living In The Material Word.* But at least it reached number one in America (and number two in the UK) and yielded a fine single, 'Give Me Love (Give Me Peace On Earth)'. The follow-up, *Dark Horse*, released in December 1974, garnered even worse reviews and despite reaching number four in the US it failed to chart at all in Britain. Earlier in the year Harrison had toured America (the first ex-Beatle to do so since the split), but with far from unqualified success. There was widespread unhappiness at the overuse/misuse of guest artist Ravi Shankar and Harrison himself contracted laryngitis, making his already limited voice sound feeble and strained. He had also lapsed into drug and alcohol abuse, the aftermath of the loss of his wife Pattie to Eric Clapton.

Lennon, too, was facing personal problems in 1974. While recording *Mind Games* towards the end of the previous year, he parted from Yoko Ono, not to be reunited with her until early 1975. *Walls And Bridges*, issued in September 1974, was his response, its title indicative of the barriers that must be crossed to secure a lasting relationship. Thus the longing expressed in '#9 Dream', the paranoia of 'Scared', the self-pitying 'Nobody Loves You (When You're Down And Out)' and the desperation of 'Whatever Gets You Thru The Night' reflect different aspects of his state of mind. But there is also an irrepressible energy about the record (and at, times, more than a hint of self-mockery) that lifts it away from the slough of despond. *Walls And Bridges* was to be Lennon's final album of originals for six years; the next, *Double Fantasy,* was issued on 17 November 1980, exactly three weeks before his death.

Paul McCartney, on the other hand, had no new albums out in 1974. He was no doubt content to bask in the critical and commercial triumph of *Band On The Run,* released the previous December. Moreover, both singles subsequently taken from the album were massive successes – the title track sold over a million in the US alone while the more complex – and exciting – 'Jet' was also a Top Ten hit on both sides of the Atlantic. Yet another big-selling single, 'Junior's Farm', came out in October; some odd lyrics and an edgy production conjure up a sinister atmosphere on what is ostensibly a simple song about the band's stay in Tennessee with the songwriter Curly Putman Jr. Ringo Starr was also coming off a successful year; 1973 had seen him achieve two consecutive US number ones with 'Photograph' and 'You're Sixteen'. His 1974 LP *Goodnight Vienna* entered the American chart on 7 December and reached number eight.

However, Starr has never reached the upper echelons of the album charts again, either in the US or the UK, and although McCartney has gone on to have many more hits, few have matched the quality of his output between the break-up of The Beatles and *Band On The Run.* Lennon, as we have seen, drew a line under his career with *Walls And Bridges*, while Harrison, after such a promising start to his solo album career, made the Top Ten only twice more after *Dark Horse.* 1974, therefore, signifies something of a watershed for the four ex-Beatles. At the start of the year, their standing as individuals equalled the popularity of their former band. No-one could have foreseen that, while their names remained legendary, they would soon become tangential to the direction pop music was about to take.

When The Beatles broke up in 1970, The Rolling Stones might reasonably have expected to be considered the greatest band in the world and certainly their first two albums of the decade, *Sticky Fingers* and *Exile On Main Street*, must by any yardstick count among their best. But with 1973's *Goat's Head Soup*, critics began to discern a decline into decadence and excess. As Keith Richards sank deeper into drug addiction and Mick Jagger took on the mantle of international jetsetter, the band seemed to forfeit their characteristic cutting edge.

Their 1974 release, *It's Only Rock 'N' Roll*, was a riposte to the band's detractors who, the title implied, were taking The Stones and their music far too seriously. The sleeve design underlines the point: the front depicts the band descending the red-carpeted staircase of a Greek temple, surrounded by garlanded female worshippers, but on the back cover everyone has vanished, leaving only graffiti and bare stone steps. It all conveys the message: rock music is transient – why over-analyse it? But at the same time the album's title indicates a return to basics after the experiments with funk and soul that characterised its predecessor.

As such it is, at best, a qualified success. 'Ain't Too Proud To Beg' may denote that, as only a rock 'n' roll band, The Stones must naturally be expected to do covers, but beyond that there seems to be little point in it; a number of other tracks are equally weak. But the record contains three classics: a title track that over the years has become the band's anthem; the vituperative and sinister 'Fingerprint File'; and 'Time Waits For No One' with its long, flowing guitar solo by Mick Taylor. Shortly afterwards, however, Taylor left the band, disgruntled at not getting more credit for his efforts to fill in for Richards during the latter's enforced absences. It was far from immediately apparent who would replace him, and so as 1974 came to an end, the future of The Rolling Stones – with two somewhat undistinguished recent albums and no lead guitarist – looked decidedly dim.

Like Keith Richards, Eric Clapton was struggling with heroin addiction in the early 1970s. After the spectacular success of his 1970 double album *Layla And Other Assorted Love Songs* he had dropped out of music and his return three years later at a concert at the Rainbow Theatre was understandably tentative. But by 1974, having kicked his habit, he was in a settled relationship with Pattie Boyd, now separated from her husband George Harrison. Perhaps this was what gave his album *461 Ocean Boulevard*, released in July, its sense of freshness and optimism, an impression enhanced by the cover picture of a relaxed and bearded Clapton outside the eponymous address in Golden Beach, Florida, a few miles from where the album was recorded.

Apart from bassist Carl Radle, the members of his band were, up to that point, largely unknown, yet their understated but accomplished contributions are crucial to the success of the record. Organist Dick Sims, for example, provides pithy punctuation in the reggae-flavoured 'Willie And The Hand Jive' and 'Get Ready' and George Terry's guitar integrates neatly with his employer's playing on 'Mainline Florida' and 'Steady Rollin' Man'. Drummer Jamie Oldaker is impressive throughout, never more so than when powering the cathartic fade-out to 'Let It Grow'. Clapton himself exudes confidence: to convert Blind Willie Johnson's anguished 'Motherless Children' into a high-speed rocker may, on the face of it, seem unwise, but the effervescence of the performance brings it off. His vocals, too, are expressive and assured and while his version of Bob Marley's 'I Shot The Sheriff' may lack the political bite of the original, its inclusion was a major factor in bringing reggae to a mass public.

461 Ocean Boulevard stands as one of the best albums of 1974. Tightly arranged yet free flowing, musicianly but uncluttered, its warm ambience perfectly evokes the sun-kissed environment in which it was made and, by extension, of summers across the globe. But it also represented the end for Clapton as a major creative force. Like the former Beatles, and the members of The Rolling Stones, he would become an elder statesman of rock, revered but irrelevant, and far distant from the political engagement that drove forward musical change in the 1970s.

★★★★★

In theory, 1973 should have been the year the Vietnam War ended. Talks begun in 1970 between US Secretary of State Henry Kissinger and North Vietnam's Le Duc Tho culminated in the Paris Peace Accords signed on 27 January 1973. On 29 March the last American troops left Vietnam, followed three days later by the remaining prisoners of war. His landslide victory in the presidential election the previous year had indicated to Richard Nixon that the American people wanted an end to the conflict but not at any price: the immediate troop withdrawal advocated by his Democratic opponent, George McGovern, was clearly considered incompatible with 'peace with honour'.

Now, with the signing of the Paris agreements, Nixon was able to claim he had achieved that hitherto elusive prize. At the same time he added that he would have no hesitation in resuming the offensive if the Communists reneged on the Peace Accords. It is doubtful, however, whether Nixon would have carried out such an action; public opinion was against it and antiwar demonstrations were continuing, though not with the same ferocity as before. The question was, in any case, rendered academic by the Case-Church Amendment of June 1973, legislation passed by the US Congress which in effect prevented any further military involvement in South-East Asia. But Nixon seems to have been tiring of the conflict before then. In April he appointed Graham Martin US Ambassador to South Vietnam; since Martin lacked the status of the heavy hitters who had previously occupied the post, this move was seen as further downgrading America's effort.

Yet still the War would not go away. The oil crisis of 1973 hit South Vietnam particularly hard and prices rocketed, further eroding the morale of a country now beginning to feel abandoned. Furthermore the Viet Cong took advantage of the autumn dry season to resume hostilities. In January 1974 President Nguyen Van Thieu of South Vietnam declared that the War was underway again and by spring Communist forces had recaptured all of the territory in the Mekong Delta lost at the time of the truce. The key now was what would happen in the dry season ahead.

By mid-August the US had a new President, Gerald Ford. The North Vietnamese had feared Richard Nixon and were thus emboldened by his departure. In the words of Frank Snepp, former CIA analyst and expert on the denouement of the Vietnam War, 'Hanoi suddenly saw the road to Saigon as being open'. Ford did little to disabuse them. One of the first actions carried out by Congress under his presidency was to trim the $1 billion limit Nixon had imposed on aid to South Vietnam to $700,000. Ford reassured Thieu that 'our support will be adequate' (quoted in Stanley Karnow, *Vietnam: A History*, p. 661), but in reality he was slowly distancing himself, and the US, from the War; in September he even introduced an amnesty for those who had evaded the draft. Should he have wanted to go in an alternative direction, his options were in any case much restricted by the midterm elections, held on 5 November. In the Senate the Democrats made four gains, in the House of Representatives, 49, thus taking their majority over the Republicans beyond the crucial two-thirds mark.

Meanwhile in Vietnam the Viet Cong commander Tran Van Tra was planning an endgame for the War. A series of swift attacks on strategic targets throughout South Vietnam would make it possible to enter the capital, Saigon – not in a single frontal assault but from five separate directions. This would be a meticulous, co-ordinated operation without the need for damaging artillery battles and wasteful attritional street skirmishes. Tra's ideas received a lukewarm welcome in Hanoi. Le Duc Tho, now back in charge of North Vietnamese policy in the South, preferred a more cautious build-up to the victory he expected to come in 1976. Eventually First Secretary Le Duan gave Tra permission (though with reduced forces) to implement one of the main objectives of his plan – the capture of a key road junction on Route 14 in Phuoc Long province, 60 miles north of Saigon, thus cutting off South Vietnamese forces from the Mekong Delta. After less than two weeks of fighting, the junction was taken on 26 December 1974. Just over four months later, the North Vietnamese Army entered Saigon, thus bringing to a conclusion a conflict that had lasted for 21 years.

*****

Several factors were critical to the demise of America's effort in Vietnam, but few would argue that student protest, which continued right up to the end of the War, was not one of them. Indeed, Nixon was perpetually fearful that the vehemence of the demonstrations across the country would destabilise his administration. But by 1974 most rock stars, though no doubt wanting the War to stop, had turned their attention away from politics towards more personal concerns or buried themselves in the seemingly endless search for instrumental proficiency. In a nutshell, it was no longer trendy to write songs about Vietnam: those who did seemed like relics from the sixties.

Some, nevertheless, retained their ardour; attacking injustice had become a habit they were not inclined to kick – it was by now an indelible part of their persona. Of these, Neil Young had the highest profile, both as a member of Crosby, Stills, Nash and Young (CSNY) and as a solo artist. *On The Beach*, released on 16 July 1974, was his sixth album and also one of his angriest. It is certainly possible, as Ian MacDonald did in an article for the British trade paper *New Musical Express* (17 August 1974), to perceive distinct autobiographical content in the record. The brisk 'Walk On', for instance, announces that it is time to forget past sorrows, an indication that Young is ready to face the future after a long period mourning the drug-induced deaths of his friends and colleagues Danny Whitten and Bruce Berry. 'Motion Pictures' presents a vision of his relationship with actress Carrie

Snodgrass: their idyllic life together is no more real than that of an on-screen celebrity couple. Yet there is no denying the political overtones of 'See The Sky About To Rain' – a warning that the Establishment will always win out in the end – nor of 'On The Beach' in which Young's grim analysis of his immediate environment is underscored by two emotive guitar solos and a wish to 'get out of town'.

But unlike so many of his contemporaries escape from reality was not an option for Young. Quite the opposite: he seemed to relish his battles with the individuals and institutions that antagonised him. The rock music industry itself was a favourite target: 'For The Turnstiles' attacks those making fortunes from concerts at the expense of audiences and 'Vampire Blues' parodies predictable, substandard musicianship and silly lyrics. In 'Revolution Blues' his fury spills over into violence: come the revolution, the Laurel Canyon celebs will be wiped out in their cars and, in an image redolent of the Manson Family, he visualises 'ten million dune buggies comin' down the mountains'. The closing 'Ambulance Blues' offers another bleak picture of contemporary society, where things are so bad as to be beyond redemption – 'an ambulance can only go so fast'. He also cannot resist a sideswipe at his old adversary, Richard Nixon ('I never knew a man could tell so many lies').

On The Beach entered the US album chart on 10 August, eventually reaching number sixteen. Its success was, however, partially eclipsed by that of Lynyrd Skynyrd, whose single 'Sweet Home Alabama' hit the Top 40 two weeks later. This catchy piece of hard rock celebrated the virtues of the state that Young had condemned as racist and dysfunctional in his 1972 song 'Alabama', itself a follow-up to his excoriation of the South, 'Southern Man', of two years earlier. 'Sweet Home Alabama' was a direct rebuttal to both and was a warning to Young that 'A Southern man don't need him around anyhow'.

None of this seemed to concern Young, whose demeanour at CSNY's appearance at Wembley Stadium on 14 September could hardly have been more jovial. Also featuring Jesse Colin Young, The

Band and Joni Mitchell, this massive event drew a crowd of 72,000. Though there would be many other big shows during the decade it is tempting to view this as the last hurrah for 1960s North American rock, or at least for what it had turned into by the end of the decade. None of the artists would, post-1974 – or, indeed, post-this concert – ever reach the heights of their previous output again. Indeed the concert itself had an air of finality.

Earlier in the year The Band had undertaken a two-month tour with Bob Dylan, his first for eight years. Coming straight after the release of his *Planet Waves* album, the project was a great success and led to the release in June of an acclaimed live set, *Before The Flood*. *Planet Waves* had been a grave disappointment aesthetically but returning to the road seemed to reignite Dylan's career; by the end of 1974 he had recorded the superlative *Blood On The Tracks*. Bill Graham, who had organised the tour, convinced CSNY – who had not played together for four years – that they should consider a similar venture. As Nash later told *The Wall Street Journal*, 'Many fans saw our tour as another shot at Woodstock, which they either had missed in '69 or wanted to revisit. The country's mood had shifted, too… kids were fed up with government manipulation. They realised that, in large numbers, they had power. Our band stood for keeping it real, which connected with them' (quoted by Dave Lifton for *ultimateclassicrock.com*). There were financial rewards, too: the 40 dates yielded over $11 million (though a mere $2 million went to the band).

The tour culminated with the Wembley event. Despite their experience with Dylan earlier in the year, The Band were growing tired of playing live; two years later they called it a day with an all-star concert at San Francisco's Winterland ballroom. For CSNY, the end came far sooner. This was to be the last time they appeared on stage together for thirteen years. The three-hour performance was far from flawless: their trademark harmonies often came unstuck, especially during the uptempo pieces. Nash's voice frequently sounded strained and off-note and it was far from clear how a song like 'Immigration Man' – about a delay he experienced going through US customs – was 'keeping it real' for the thousands of young Britons in the audience. The high point of the whole concert was, however, his 'Another Sleep Song', a duet with Mitchell whose eerie wordless vocals complemented the already haunting melody and moving lyrics. Nash also helped stir the anti-war emotions with 'Military Madness' and, presumably as a sop to the home crowd, was called on to make most of the announcements (many of which were, unfortunately, gauche and/or self-satisfied).

Crosby, in contrast, was under-employed, though Stills made his presence felt with a series of proficient guitar solos and an extended political rant on 'Word Game': 'American propaganda and South African lies will not force me to take up arms'. Young, who had drifted away from the band even before the concert (he travelled separately and was critical of his colleagues' lack of new material), was easily the most impressive of the four, in good voice, playing well and mixing recent compositions like 'Star Of Bethlehem' and 'Love Art Blues' with warhorses like his ferocious denunciation of the 1970 Kent State murders, 'Ohio', a rousing version of which closed the show.

Earlier in the day Joni Mitchell, accompanied by Tom Scott and The LA Express, had produced a set almost exclusively derived from her four most recent albums (the exception, 'Rainy Night House', appeared on her live double album with Scott, *Miles Of Aisles*, released in November). The setlist was hardly surprising since these records constituted as good a sequence of releases as any major rock artist had produced to date (or arguably ever has). From 1970's *Ladies Of The Canyon*, through *Blue* (1971) and *For The Roses* (1972), we can trace a growing profundity and expressiveness culminating in *Court And Spark*, issued on 1 January 1974. At the same time, Mitchell's lyrics had grown less political – a not-uncommon trajectory for early 1970s singer/songwriters – and more sophisticated musically, with a heavy jazz influence. This combination certainly appealed to the public taste, especially in the US where *Court And Spark* reached number two in the charts, as did *Miles Of Aisles.*

Lyrical and instrumental ideas come thick and fast but not so rapidly that they cannot be absorbed and within the overall sense of unity there is, paradoxically, considerable variety. The title track, with its compelling narrative and sweeping piano runs, and the sharply-observed 'People's Parties' both convey different aspects of isolation. Similarly, 'Trouble Child', the portrait of a psychiatric patient (possibly herself) – 'breaking like the waves at Malibu' – segues, via Chuck Findley's muted trumpet, into 'Twisted', a more jokey view of mental illness originally recorded by vocalese trio Lambert, Hendricks and Ross: here Mitchell all but matches their skill and exuberance, lifted by Max Bennett's supple bass and some dextrous drumming by John Guerin, her partner at the time. There are also different takes on freedom: 'Free Man in Paris' celebrates a trip to France with David Geffen and Robbie Robertson of The Band; in the more equivocal 'Help Me' she notes wryly and somewhat ruefully, 'We love our lovin' but not like we love our freedom'. If all of that were not enough, Mitchell displays her flair as an arranger both alone (the imaginative yet elegant 'Car On A Hill') and with Tom Scott, as on the spine-tingling climax to 'The Same Situation'.

September's Wembley concert may have started as an attempt to recapture Woodstock but in the event it signalled the end of an era – though perhaps the two were one and the same thing. Joni Mitchell and Neil Young were, however, not about to throw in the towel – each had many years of creativity to look forward to. Exactly the same was true of another songwriter who, like the two Canadians, had emerged exactly six years earlier.

*****

In 1974, both concept albums and political songs were passing out of fashion. It was typical of Randy Newman that he should go for both in one record. His reputation thus far was for seeing things from both sides, orientating especially to the derided, neglected and dispossessed.

Granted, his delivery was frequently sardonic, often downright comic, so his music required some concentration to get anything out of it; many listeners simply could not be bothered and as a result he tended to be seen as a 'cult' artist. The success of *Good Old Boys*, his first album to enter the US Top 40, therefore came as something of a shock, especially as it ventured into previously uncharted territory.

Originally intended to be the story of an archetypal white Southerner, Johnny Cutler, the finished album presents the thoughts and feelings of a range of characters from the South. It all begins with 'Rednecks', a song inspired by seeing the Governor of Georgia, Lester Maddox, humiliated on a New York chat show. The narrator, an unreconstructed Southern cracker, defends Maddox – 'he may be a fool but he's our fool' – and goes on to lambast hypocritical Northern liberals who may think they are superior to rednecks from the South but are equally, if less overtly, racist. Disarmingly, it is all delivered in cheery fashion, with a jaunty arrangement evocative of New Orleans jazz. In 'Kingfisher' (his nickname), we are introduced to another Southern populist, Huey P Long, Governor of Louisiana. An implacable opponent of the banks and oil companies, Long was assassinated in 1935, shortly after announcing he would run for President; in the song Newman assumes his larger-than-life persona and itemises, none too modestly, his achievements on behalf of the people. It is preceded by Long's own composition, 'Every Man A King', the motto of his 'Share Our Wealth' campaign which at his height attracted millions of supporters.

In 'Birmingham' the protagonist is fiercely proud of his hometown ('the greatest city in Alabam'') but, other than the fact that he lives there, cannot really say why. There are portraits of the happy and sad drunk in 'Rollin'' and 'Guilty' respectively and Newman returns to one of his favourite topics, the absurdities of love, in 'A Wedding In Cherokee County'. The strains of 'Old Man River' introduce 'Louisiana 1927', a stroke of devastating irony. For this song is about the Mississippi floods that laid waste to the region that year, not in the narrator's eyes a natural disaster but some sort of conspiracy ('they're tryin' to wash us away'), quite possibly involving President Coolidge whose visit emanates detachment, almost indifference. Fast forward nearly half a century and it is Richard Nixon who gets the brickbats for failing the poor: 'Mr President (Have Pity On The Working Man)' is a desperate, but at the same time comic, appeal for help – yet fated, one feels, not to succeed: 'Maybe you're cheating, maybe you're lying, maybe you have lost your mind'.

Using humour in rock music is like skating on thin ice and among those who fell through it in 1974 were the Canadian-American comedy duo Cheech and Chong. Following their appearance on Joni Mitchell's 'Twisted', they released their *Wedding Album.* Despite a clever cover design, it contains just one good track, 'Coming Attractions', which announces the upcoming contest for Mr Dope America; the categories ineligible to take part – presumably because they have an unfair advantage – include jazz musicians, beatniks and pre-med students. The rest of the record is, however, tedious, juvenile and unfunny.

John Stewart also hailed from the West Coast but stylistically was on another planet. A former member of influential folk group The Kingston Trio, Stewart had written hits for The Lovin' Spoonful ('Never Goin' Back') and The Monkees ('Daydream Believer'), both in 1968. His own records had not achieved the same commercial success but were favourites with the critics – none more so than the double album *The Phoenix Concerts*, recorded at the city's Symphony Hall in March 1974 and released in June. Stewart's emotionally-charged songs frequently reflect a yearning for the past: 'The Pirates Of Stone County Road', for example, is a poignant evocation of childhood and 'The Last Campaign Trilogy' recalls his time travelling with Robert Kennedy before his assassination in 1968. But at the same time he is acutely conscious of the pitfalls of nostalgia, as in 'Roll Away The Stone', 'You Can't Look Back' and 'Kansas' – 'you can't go back to Kansas 'cause that was yesterday'.

Yet there is humour – or rather, mordant wit – here, too, albeit behind a veil of trenchant social comment. 'Cody' tells the story of the derelict (with hair as 'dirty as the rivers of LA') who, though ostracised by dementia, still 'sang me a song about the great Montana sky', while 'Kansas Rain' includes the immortal line 'I was standing in line in the Bank of America – nobody spoke, they were in the House of God'. In 'Cops', he reminds us of the unwelcome fact that 'we love you when we need you and we hate you when we don't'.

Jackie Lynton was, like Stewart, both a veteran and something of a maverick. A fixture on the British scene from skiffle onwards, he was best known for his stint with the blues band Savoy Brown. In the late 1960s, he became a painter and decorator and worked on John Lennon's Weybridge home. *The Jackie Lynton Album* was his long-awaited chance to make it as a solo artist and certainly no-one could accuse him of lacking originality – or self-confidence. The record gets off to a promising start with the relaxed, country-flavoured 'Roll Me', but it is followed by 'The Last Say', the first of four Cockney monologues (two featuring animal characters) which, even if you have acquired the taste needed to enjoy them, could scarcely be listened to more than once. Furthermore there appears amidst the balance of the album – consisting mostly, it must be said, of very acceptable blues-rock – a mediocre poem, 'Thoughts'.

Certainly Lynton is to be admired for trying something different, but anyone attempting to offer the spoken word to a rock audience in 1974 should have deferred to the Poet Laureate, Sir John Betjeman, who made two albums during the year for Tony Stratton-Smith's adventurous Charisma label, accompanied on each occasion by an ensemble led by composer Jim Parker. The first, *Betjeman's Banana Blush*, was recorded in early spring, a couple of months before the poet's 68th birthday. Parker's orchestrations cleverly and sensitively follow the contours of Betjeman's verse, and provide the precise, period sound required by his frequently nostalgic narrative with its references to debs and Victrolas, congregation halls and slacks. The two poems mourning the death of his father, 'On The Portrait Of A Deaf Man' and 'A Child Ill', are harrowing, their impact much enhanced by Parker's unobtrusive arrangements, while on 'The Arrest Of Oscar Wilde At The Cadogan Hotel' the instrumental punctuation is as dramatic as the events it describes.

Betjeman delights in observing female demeanour. Here we have the 'Business Girls' having their baths in Camden Town, though 'all too soon the tiny breakfast, trolley-bus and windy street', and the stylish, self-possessed churchgoer of 'Lenten Thoughts'. On *Late Flowering Love*, such studies are to be found throughout an album which explores obsession and repressed sexuality as much as it does conventional courtship. Among the young women Betjeman puts on a pedestal are the beautiful Oxford undergraduate Myfanwy ('black-stockinged legs under navy-blue serge'), 'The Olympic Girl' ('Oh, would I were her racquet press'd with hard excitement to her breast'), and the calm, cool model Cecilia Green of 'A Russell Flint', in which the combination of crashing cymbals and steel guitar contrives to convey Betjeman's yearning. In 'Senex' he is barely able to control himself at the sight of an array of girls' bicycle saddles. 'Narcissus' is a comic account of an otherwise liberated mother determined to stop her young son from falling for his friend Bobby. But Betjeman reaffirms, too, that he is without equal in articulating the more distressing side of human relationships, from the lonely 'Eunice' to 'Late Flowering Lust' in which a lugubrious bassoon accompanies the story of an ageing couple losing the desire for each other, and for life.

On the mainstream British rock scene only Vivian Stanshall, formerly of the Bonzo Dog Doo Dah Band, could even begin to approach Betjeman in terms of idiosyncrasy, perception and wit. But his debut album *Men Opening Umbrellas Ahead*, completed in April 1974, sold only 5,000 copies, whereupon it was withdrawn and deleted by his record company, Warner Brothers. In retrospect, this seems an act of cultural vandalism, though perhaps it was not just the poor sales that pushed the executives over the edge. For the record is unremittingly explicit on the themes of sex, drugs and rock and roll. The seven-minute opener 'Afoju Ti Ole Riran (Dead Eyes)', for example, portrays show business people as dehumanised, akin to zombies, a sentiment driven home by a nagging riff interspersed with wah-wah guitar and flute. 'Redeye' and 'Bout Of Sobriety' lampoon the boorish behaviour and drinking habits endemic to rock stars; 'Strange Tongues' is a parody of prog. 'How The Zebra Lost Its Spots' takes Stanshall's penis as its subject but in the following 'Dwarf Succulents' his post-coital boasting is deflated by a partner who describes his performance as 'so-so'.

African rhythmic and melodic flavours surface occasionally on *Men Opening Umbrellas Ahead* and dominate the excellent associated single, 'Lakonga'/'Baba Tunde' – the first features a fine trumpet solo while on the latter Stanshall intones, in a manner reminiscent of both Dr John and Tom Waits, over a funky jazz undercurrent. Some of this may be due to the influence of Ghanaian conga player Reebop Kwaku Baah, who appeared on the album alongside fellow Traffic alumni Steve Winwood, Ric Grech and Jim Capaldi as well as percussionist Derek Quinn, drummer Gaspar Lawal and guitarist Bubs White. All seven of these musicians played on 'Summer Is Fading', a track from Capaldi's album, *Whale Meat Again*, which came out in August. Based on an idea by Stanshall, it was probably therefore recorded at the *Umbrellas* sessions, although the sleeve details do not say so.

Whatever the case, the rest of *Whale Meat Again* was made in the equally distinguished company of the Muscle Shoals Horns, pianist Barry Beckett, guitarists Jimmy Johnson and Pete Carr, bassist David Hood and drummer Roger Hawkins – the latter two also former members of Traffic. Such a line-up would normally be a guarantee of quality, but one can hardly blame the backing musicians for the failings of the principal. Indeed their talents transformed an ordinary song, 'It's All Right', into a record good enough to make the US singles chart. Carr contributes a fine solo to the title track but his playing is absolutely superb on 'Low Rider', an outstanding piece of music that also benefits from Capaldi's soulful vocals and a sparkling string arrangement by Harry Robinson.

But all this good work is sabotaged by 'I've Got So Much Lovin'', a clumsily-written, clichéd chunk of narcissism, the plot of which is as follows: Capaldi 'was down in LA trying to write myself a song', but he 'just could not relax – the radio was playing too strong'. So he 'went down to Sunset and found myself a pretty girl' – just like that! – but then, he *is* a famous rock star. The conquest was instant – 'And when we were through you know it felt so good'. The first question is: Who cares? The second, Was the bragging about LA and seducing pretty girls relevant to anyone but Capaldi himself? Both answers are in the negative. This sort of nonsense was, happily, doomed to oblivion, though there would be a few stages yet before the outbreak of revolution.

CHAPTER 2

Already Gone

According to the approval ratings published by Gallup since World War II, Richard M Nixon is the least popular of modern American Presidents. In the summer of 1974 his endorsement figure stood at 24%; only Harry S Truman had sunk lower in the nation's esteem with a rating of 22% in February 1952, but then Truman had enjoyed 87% approval in June 1945. Nixon's best, 67% in both November 1969 and January 1973, was no less than 23 points behind that of George W Bush (90% in September 2001) and only eleven points above John F Kennedy's *worst* rating of 56% in September 1963. Granted, Nixon had inherited an insoluble problem in the Vietnam War. Escalate aggression and forfeit yet more American lives, resources and respect; or withdraw and, in effect, lose the War – an equally unappealing prospect for the world's most powerful nation.

Vietnam was a continued source of anxiety, but in other areas of foreign policy he made considerable headway. His tough stance against the Russians during the latter stages of the Yom Kippur War arguably prevented a superpower conflict and in 1972 there were groundbreaking visits to China and to Russia, twice, for strategic arms limitation talks (SALT) with General Secretary Leonid Brezhnev. He was also the first US President to go to Israel. Nixon may have lacked the charisma of the Kennedys but to many Americans he represented a bulwark against unwelcome radical change. As 1974 began, his position seemed unassailable: just over a year before he had seen off George McGovern with one of the largest landslide victories in presidential election history. Though hostilities in Vietnam were about to resume, the US was slowly but surely disengaging from the conflict; relations with the major world powers were generally cordial and the end of the oil crisis was in sight. No-one could possibly have imagined that Nixon was, politically speaking, already a dead man.

But the labyrinthine trail to his demise had, in fact, run through his entire presidency; indeed it might be said that its origins date back to his narrow defeat by Kennedy in 1960. In the belief that Democratic vote fraud in Illinois and Texas had cost him the election, Nixon resolved that he would never again allow any opponent to get the better of him tactically. And in 1968, despite his victory over Hubert Humphrey, those opponents were everywhere. Nixon was the first President in 120 years to take office with both houses of Congress controlled by the opposition. This made him insecure not only about the present, but about the future – in particular, the presidential election of 1972, in which it was rumoured that Edward Kennedy, the younger brother of John and Robert, might stand as a candidate.

Nixon loathed both the Kennedy family and all who associated with them. In early 1969, within weeks of his inauguration, a programme of surveillance duly began on a number of individuals, some only tenuously linked with what turned out to be a hypothetical nemesis. These included Lawrence O'Brien, chairman of the Democratic National Committee (and, in Nixon's mind, a likely sponsor for Kennedy); billionaire Howard Hughes, actually a Republican supporter but who hedged his bets by maintaining a line to the Democrats through O'Brien's lobbying firm; and, of course, Edward Kennedy himself. Gradually Nixon became addicted to secret information that could discredit his enemies, real or imagined. On 9 September 1971, his special counsel Charles Colson sent a memo to his colleague John Dean identifying 20 such figures, including the chief of the National Security Council, Morton Halperin, and the actor Paul Newman. This was later supplemented by a vast and constantly changing Opponents List, divided into sections on politicians (with subdivisions for black Congressmen and Congresswomen), entertainers, business leaders, union officials and journalists.

In June 1971 former military analyst Daniel Ellsberg became a high-priority target when he made available to the *New York Times* a photocopy of the 'Pentagon Papers', the Defense Department's account of America's involvement in the Vietnam War. The document exposed all sorts of devious activities but, since it cut off at 1967, did not implicate Nixon. Nevertheless he was outraged by such a flagrant breach of national security. In order to prevent further leaks, the covert White House Special Investigations Unit was formed the following month; given their role it was no surprise that they became known as the White House Plumbers.

The head of the Unit, Egil Krogh, was well known to Nixon; he had, for example, organised his meeting with Elvis Presley in 1970 at which the President and the King discussed how to combat drug dealing. Now Krogh's task was to smear Ellsberg by raiding the office of his doctor, Lewis Fielding, to obtain his psychiatric records which, it was hoped, would reveal some serious character defects. In his book *Watergate* (p. 62), Fred Emery concludes that the President must have known of, and indeed authorised, this burglary. Not only did Nixon state, according to the testimony of Krogh's boss, John Ehrlichman, that Krogh 'should of course do whatever he considered necessary to get to the bottom of the matter', but, Emery goes on to note, 'since giving that testimony, Ehrlichman has concluded that it was Colson who intervened to get Nixon's direct approval for a break-in'.

In the event, the burglary was a failure, though it did not deter the Plumbers and Nixon's network of advisers – the 'President's Men' – from planning even more ambitious operations to bug, raid and discredit Nixon's opponents. Some of the more bizarre plans were proposed by G Gordon Liddy, a Plumber who had led the Fielding operation and in December 1971 took up a post with CRP (sometimes known as CREEP) – the Campaign to Re-elect the President.

Liddy's GEMSTONE project included the abduction of antiwar demonstrators to Mexico and sabotaging the Democrats with a series of actions ranging from the comic, such as disabling the air conditioning during their summer Convention, to the nefarious – the bugging of the Democratic National Committee offices at the Watergate Complex, New Hampshire Avenue Northwest, Washington, DC.

After two failed attempts, a team of five operatives, supervised by Liddy and White House Plumber E Howard Hunt, finally broke into the Watergate in the early hours of 17 June 1972. The intention was to install listening devices and photograph documents, but before they could complete the job the intruders were interrupted and arrested by police. With the presidential election only months away, the race was on to connect the Watergate break-in with the Republican Party and/or government officials. Early investigations revealed a link to the CRP, but at this stage Nixon remained untouched: in November, he secured an emphatic victory of McGovern, and in January 1973 – the month in which the Watergate burglars were convicted – his approval rating, as we have seen, was at a peak.

But on 21 March he made what proved to be a fatal error. In a meeting with John Dean, who in effect had managed the Watergate break-in, he made it abundantly clear that he knew all about the operation and the subsequent efforts to cover it up. There was much discussion, for instance, about Hunt and his demands for money to pay for the expenses incurred by the convicted Plumbers, particularly himself. Nixon was in no doubt that if this leaked out, thus exposing the whole Watergate conspiracy, there would be no question of his culpability: Dean would take the blame.

> *Nixon:* And then the thing blows cutting Bob [Haldeman, White House chief of staff] and the rest to pieces. You would never recover from that, John. (Quoted in Peter Woll, *American Government: Readings And Cases*, p. 396)

No doubt shaken by this conversation, Dean began to feed information to the Watergate prosecutors. On 30 April, he was dismissed by Nixon; two months later he began to testify before the Senate Watergate Committee and in October he confessed to paying out 'hush money' to Hunt and the other burglars.

The meeting with Dean (and every other conversation in Nixon's office for the previous two years) had been recorded and when in July 1973 former White House aide Alexander Butterfield informed the US Select Committee of this fact, it sparked huge interest in what the tapes might contain that was pertinent to Watergate. Nixon, as might be imagined, was reluctant to co-operate but when he did surrender nine of them in late October (albeit to the confidential confines of a grand jury), it was discovered that two were missing. Furthermore on another tape there was a gap of eighteen minutes, casting further suspicion on the President and his team. Now there were calls for his resignation including from a member of his own Party, Senator Edward Brooke of Massachusetts.

In spite of all of these damaging revelations, Nixon held firm. On 18 November 1973, the *Washington Post*, whose writers Bob Woodward and Carl Bernstein had done so much to bring the Watergate scandal to the public's attention, reported on a one-hour question and answer session conducted by the President with 400 Associated Press managing editors, at which he stated,

> In all of my years of public life I have never obstructed justice. People have got to know whether or not their President is a crook. Well, I'm not a crook.

In 1974 those claims would be put to the test with dramatic results.

*****

As we discovered in Chapter 1, many leading figures from the sixties were hanging on in 1974 – politicians, sports stars, actors and entertainers. Rock music was no exception; indeed the continued presence of the luminaries of the golden decade was seen by many to be stifling the potential for new ideas. Yet this was not to continue. For most of them, 1974 represented a decline – aesthetically, commercially, or both. In some cases, the year saw their last major success; others were already past their best. Despite below-par releases in 1974, both The Rolling Stones and Bob Dylan would soon make strong comebacks, though there was no way of knowing that at the time. And when an artist or band had no releases at all in the year, who could guess when the next one would be or if there were to be any at all?

Act	1974 album	
John Lennon	*Walls And Bridges*	Last new material for six years
Paul McCartney	None	
George Harrison	*Dark Horse*	Poor reviews, didn't make UK chart
Ringo Starr	*Goodnight Vienna*	US # 8, but last Top 20 album in US or UK
The Rolling Stones	*It's Only Rock And Roll*	Mixed reviews; Mick Taylor departs
Bob Dylan	*Planet Waves; Before The Flood* (live)	Poor sales after initial interest; mixed reviews
The Band	*Before The Flood*	See above
Joni Mitchell	*Court And Spark* *Miles Of Aisles*	Both # 2 US, but only one later album makes Top 10
CSNY	None	Farewell appearance Wembley 14.9.74
David Crosby	None	
Stephen Stills	None	
Graham Nash	*Wild Tales*	Three weeks on US chart, made #34
Neil Young	*On The Beach*	Career highlight and more to come

The Byrds		Disbanded 1973
The Beach Boys	None	
The Who	None	
Pink Floyd	None	
Eric Clapton	*461 Ocean Boulevard*	Last critically acclaimed album

The position of the sixties survivors can be summarised as follows: In the case of John Lennon, there were to be two more albums during his lifetime, the all-covers *Rock'n' Roll* (1975) and *Double Fantasy*. The latter was issued just before his murder in December 1980 and so inevitably became bound up with the universal anguish that followed, making it difficult to assess it dispassionately. Reviews on release were, however, mixed. The decline of Harrison and Starr was described in Chapter 1.

Eric Clapton never again reached the peak represented by *461 Ocean Boulevard*. For each act listed in *The Great Rock Discography*, compiler Martin C Strong includes album ratings based on the judgements of critics and fans as well as his own opinions. *461* receives a score of 8/10, unmatched by an any subsequent release: his next three, for example, are given 5/10, 5/10 and 6/10 respectively. Similarly, *Wild Tales* and all subsequent albums by Graham Nash (including those with David Crosby) are scored at 5/10 or lower. Joni Mitchell was to maintain the high quality of her output but, as noted in Chapter 1, was unable replicate the commercial success she attained in 1974; in fact, she seemed no longer to seek it. However the continued critical acclaim accorded to Neil Young was, at least in the latter part of the decade, more than matched by the sales of his records.

Like Neil Young, Pink Floyd still had triumphs to come, especially in what was left of the 1970s: *Wish You Were Here*, *Animals* and *The Wall* are considered (including by Strong) as among their very best. But for other major acts without an album release in 1974, the future was not so bright. The lack of new material by The Band may be explained by the fact that for much of the year they were on tour. At the same time, they were building their own studio, Shangri-La, in which they recommenced recording in 1975. Yet while there were to be some good records to come, notably 1998's *Jericho*, few would claim that any were of the calibre of their pre-1974 releases. David Crosby's solo career seemed to peter out even before 1974, while only one LP by Stephen Stills has made the US Top 20 on either side of the Atlantic since CSNY's Wembley concert in September of that year. Beset by internal wrangling and trapped by the overwhelming demand for their old music, The Beach Boys were in a creative drought which, arguably, has never ended; following 1973's *Holland*, no album of new material gets better than half-marks from Strong and 1992's *Summer In Paradise* receives an unprecedented 2/10. Exactly the same pattern is discernible for The Who: after the highs of *Who's Next* (1971, 10/10) and *Quadrophenia* (1973, 9/10), their ratings – except for greatest hits packages – plummet. And of the 20+ albums Paul McCartney has released since 1973's *Band On The Run*, none have been anywhere near as well-regarded.

So given this sudden vacuum what did the next generation of rock musicians have to offer?

★★★★★

At one time or other, most of the 1960s old guard listed above had made political and social comment in their music: indeed it might be said that, as they disengaged from what was happening in the world (and from the concerns of their fans), so the energy began to drain away. Most had turned inward to focus on their own relationships and experiences, but given the level of wealth and comfort they had attained by then, such narratives tend to betray a certain complacency and self-satisfaction. As we shall see, this provoked a musical revolution which was well underway by the end of 1974.

For most of the year – and indeed for the greater part of the rock audience – such stirrings were, however, invisible. From America's West Coast, for example, came a flood of beautifully made records in the singer/songwriter vein, some of which followed the tendency, popularised in 1970, of reaching back into the country's rich musical past. Little did the exponents of these apparently unquenchable sources realise that, as far as the future direction of rock was concerned, their records would soon be obsolescent.

All four of The Eagles – Glenn Frey, Bernie Leadon, Randy Meisner and Don Henley – were accomplished musicians, singers and composers. *On The Border*, released on 22 March 1974, was their third album, but the first to make the US Top 20; it was also their first to enter the UK album chart. Imbued with a distinct country flavour, it presents a pleasing variety of themes and moods. The opening 'Already Gone' is a lively rocker with a surging chorus and the twin lead guitars of Frey and guest musician Don Felder, shortly to join the band on a permanent basis. 'James Dean' ('too fast to live, too young to die') – written by Frey, Henley, John David Souther and Jackson Browne – benefits from more guitar fireworks, this time from Leadon, and an appropriately rock and roll feel. In contrast, 'Ol' 55' is a cantering song of the road, 'You Never Cry Like A Lover' a dramatic ballad and the title track a swamp-rock number that recalls Redbone's 1971 hit, 'The Witch Queen Of New Orleans'. The rich harmonies, touching lyrics and memorable melody of 'The Best Of My Love' propelled it to number one on the American singles chart.

Browne had contributed to a number of Eagles compositions, including their signature song, 'Take It Easy', which he himself recorded in 1973. Like them he had made his debut the previous year but not broken through until his third album came out in 1974. *Late For The Sky* made number nineteen in the US and is considered by many critics to be his best – it is, for instance, his only entry in the *Rolling Stone* poll for the 500 Greatest Albums of All Time, conducted in 2005. The striking cover picture of a white Chevrolet outside a house at dawn is based on the 1954 painting *Empire Of Light* by the Belgian surrealist René Magritte and sets the tone both for a specific track, 'The Late Show', a song of loneliness and longing, and, more generally, for a record in which disorientation permeates the superficial mood of elegance and tranquillity.

Typical are the bittersweet 'Fountain Of Sorrow' and 'Farther On', in which feelings of nostalgia are balanced with concerns for the future. Even the up-tempo 'Walking Slow' and 'The Road And The Sky' are tinged with melancholy, though the closing 'Before The Deluge' reverses the process by bringing some optimism to an otherwise apocalyptic vision. But perhaps most impressive is Browne's talent for using simple words to express profound emotion, as exemplified here by the title track and one of his most enduring pieces, 'For A Dancer'.

Late For The Sky may have brought Browne wide recognition but those inside the business had known about his talents for some time. Among those who covered his songs, often before he himself recorded them, were Nico, Joan Baez, Linda Ronstadt and Tom Rush who, as far back as 1967, had released a version of 'Shadow Dream Song' as the B-side of his excellent single, 'No Regrets'. Browne also had a close relationship with The Byrds, playing piano on their recording of Dylan's 'Just Like A Woman' and using former members David Crosby and Clarence White on his own debut. They in turn used his compositions 'Mae Jean Goes To Hollywood' and 'Jamaica Say You Will', the latter for 1971's *Byrdmaniax.* However they failed to save the record from critical opprobrium and within two years, despite an eleventh-hour reunion of the original band, The Byrds had broken up.

One of those founder members was Gene Clark, who survived that ill-fated project to make one of the finest albums of 1974, *No Other.* Yet at the time of its release it was considered a failure: a flop in both the US and UK, it was deleted by Asylum Records two years later. Perhaps the company's action was partly motivated by revenge.

The record cost over $100,000 to make, a huge amount for the time, especially for an album that contained only eight tracks. Producer Thomas Jefferson Kaye has referred to it as 'my Brian Wilson extravaganza' (quoted on sleeve note to the CD reissue) and it is indeed characterised by the lavish, imaginative arrangements typical of The Beach Boys at their peak. But equally remarkable are Clark's strange, often opaque, songs, delivered in his slightly strained voice, shallow in range but profound in emotional impact.

It opens deceptively with 'Life's Greatest Fool', orthodox country-rock albeit with a gospel flavour, but in 'Silver Raven' Clark begins to enter unchartered waters. Back in November 1929 Clarence Ashley had recorded this song as 'The Coo-Coo Bird', though its ancestry is long and complex. The English composer George Butterworth, for example, set it to music in 1912 as part of a selection of Sussex folk ballads which also included 'A Blacksmith Courted Me', the final line of which is 'Since I have lost my love, I will seek *no other*' [author's italics]. It is tantalising to think that Clark may have been inspired by Butterworth but the melody of 'Silver Raven' certainly resembles the Ashley version. Whatever the case, Clark gives the song a whole new meaning. Here, the bird becomes a harbinger of environmental disaster, floating over lilting, shifting musical undercurrents.

The title track is led by Clark's double-tracked vocals and features a Beatles-inspired ensemble sound incorporating elements of heavy rock, jazzy electric piano and Cuban percussion. Three ballads follow: in the big-production number, 'Strength Of Strings', the Beatles influence reappears in metaphysical concepts redolent of 'Tomorrow Never Knows', while both 'From A Silver Phial' and 'Some Misunderstanding' incrementally add layers of instrumental and lyrical elaboration. 'The True One' is a brief return to country-rock, before the epic 'Lady Of The North' in which the natural imagery is offset by a startling array of textures including cello, piano, wah-wah guitar and violin – the whole track, and album, ending with a touch of psychedelia.

After *No Other*, Clark's star began to wane and it was three years before he made his next album. In the meantime, however, another former Byrd had become a posthumous superstar in the world of country-rock. It would perhaps be an exaggeration to say that Gram Parsons invented the genre, but certainly he had propelled The Byrds in that direction when, in effect, he replaced Clark in 1968. His tenure with the band was brief but influential, though his ideas were more fully developed in his band The Flying Burrito Brothers and on his own albums *GP* and *Grievous Angel*. The latter was released in January 1974, four months after his death at the age of 26 from an overdose of morphine and alcohol.

Grievous Angel is rightly considered a classic of country-rock. For here Parsons exploits the strength and spirit of country music while integrating the dynamics and urgency of rock. 'Return Of The Grievous Angel', for instance, retains the melancholy of country without its sentimentality, and includes solos by giants from both idioms: Presley regular James Burton on guitar and top country fiddler Byron Berline who had also worked with The Flying Burrito Brothers. It also features – as does 'Hearts On Fire' and 'Love Hurts' – Emmylou Harris on what amounts to joint lead vocals. The intimacy between the two works well but understandably was not to the liking of Gretchen Parsons who allegedly had Harris's photo and name removed from the album cover.

The tracks on which Harris plays a less prominent role are just as successful. 'Brass Buttons', where she is absent altogether, is well-conceived and effortless, with an uncharacteristic warmth in the vocals; '$1000 Wedding' and 'Las Vegas' (co-written with Ric Grech) contain an attractive element of self-mockery; and on the otherwise exuberant 'I Can't Dance' Parsons contrives to inject an appropriate note of despair. Some of these songs were covers, others were by no means new; two were created spontaneously in the studio. That Parsons, already engaged in the difficult enough task of bringing together two disparate idioms, was able to create such a cohesive record is therefore all the more impressive.

But, as might be inferred from the circumstances of his death, Parsons's personal life was more chaotic. For a time he lived with The Byrds' producer Terry Melcher, another drug abuser and no stranger to the Los Angeles subculture. Melcher had got on the wrong side of Charles Manson and it was in his former residence, 10050 Cielo Drive, that the Manson Family slaughtered Sharon Tate and four others on 9 August 1969. In 1974 it was something of a surprise when Melcher, after over ten years in the business working with the elite of West Coast rock, emerged with his own, eponymous, debut album.

For the album cover, designed by Dean Torrence of Jan and Dean, Melcher is dressed all in white – an indication, perhaps, of rebirth after past traumas. But his sullen expression suggests, too, that there are scores still to settle, and indeed the record is a *tour de force* of regret, self-pity and barely concealed resentment. Melcher's surprisingly strong voice has echo applied throughout, adding drama and placing him firmly centre-stage; but his full-on approach means that any possible sense of irony in the material he covers is obliterated. All of this points up the autobiographical content of the album.

Owing to his position in the industry Melcher was able to surround himself with a constellation of West Coast musicians, including three ex-Byrds, Ry Cooder, pianist Larry Knechtel of 'Bridge Over Troubled Water' fame and drummers Jim Keltner and Hal Blaine. But of all the illustrious names it is Jimmie Haskell who makes the most telling contribution with a sparse but beautiful string arrangement on the stand-out track, Jackson Browne's 'These Days'; here Melcher harmonises with his mother, Doris Day, which gives an extra poignancy to the line, 'Please don't confront me with my failures, I have not forgotten them'. 'These Bars Have Made A Prisoner Out Of Me' loses the wryness intended by composers Dan Penn and Spooner Oldham to become a statement of fact, while his treatment of Roger McGuinn and Jacques Levy's reflective 'Just A Season' (which Melcher had produced for The Byrds) emphasises its more negative aspects. His own 'Beverly Hills' and 'The Old Hand

Jive' are both embittered accounts of how things have gone downhill in LA and the Dylan songs he chooses to cover are among his most acerbic: '4th Time Around', 'Positively 4th Street' and 'Like A Rolling Stone'.

There was no political content whatsoever in *Terry Melcher* but – rather like the Browne, Clark and Parsons records in varying degrees – its pessimistic outlook, at times bordering on misanthropy, was emblematic of a country staring failure in the face. The economic outlook was gloomy, unemployment was rising and civil rights were far from embedded; the Vietnam War was likely to end in ignominy. And perhaps worst of all, the President of the United States, for the first time in over 100 years, was heading for impeachment.

★★★★★

At the beginning of 1974, not many people seriously believed that the Watergate scandal would ruin Richard Nixon. His contention that it was all the work of subordinates, an operation planned and carried out without his knowledge, was widely accepted, especially among those who had endorsed him at the election only fourteen months earlier. But the nagging question remained. If Nixon was so blameless, why was he so reluctant to release all of the White House tapes which, it must follow, would exonerate him? Nixon's first line of defence was that making the tapes public would compromise national security. Instead he offered on two occasions to produce edited versions, a suggestion which unsurprisingly met with a lukewarm response. At other times he refused point blank to hand them over. On 21 January 1974, for example, Watergate special prosecutor Leon Jaworski was rebuffed when he requested 22 more tapes from Nixon's lawyer, James St Clair.

However the tapes he had already supplied were beginning to prove fruitful for the prosecutors. On 1 March, a group of President's Men including Ehrlichman, Colson, Haldeman and former attorney-general John Mitchell were charged with conspiracy to obstruct justice. As Emery (*op. cit.*, p.427-8) relates,

> The indictment was a long document listing all the alleged crimes in the Watergate cover-up, and it carried a pregnant phrase, little noticed at the time, linking those indicted "with persons known and unknown".

One of these persons was, of course, Nixon; indeed it later transpired that the grand jury had wanted to indict the President, too, but were deterred by the prosecutors.

The following month, following a subpoena from the House Judiciary Committee for a further 42 tapes, Nixon released a consignment of edited transcripts, claiming that they 'will at last, once and for all, show that what I knew and I did in regard to the Watergate break-in and cover-up were just as I have described them to you from the beginning' (quoted in Emery, p. 429). One of Nixon's actions was to excise the swear-words he had used in conversation. Though these were normally very mild, 'My mother would turn over in her grave if she knew I used such language' (*ibid.).* In their place he inserted the phrase 'expletive deleted', which duly entered the vernacular when the transcripts were published. Though Nixon's other censorship notation – 'material unrelated to presidential action deleted' – did not, understandably, do likewise, it did have the effect of arousing suspicion – what *was* this material?

At this point, contrary to his intention in providing the transcripts, Nixon's support began to crumble. That their President frequently swore was an unpleasant surprise for the 'silent majority' (a term he himself had coined five years earlier) and caused almost as much revulsion as the removal of potentially incriminating evidence. Leading figures in the Republican Party denounced him as did conservative newspapers like the *Chicago Tribune*. And naturally the prosecutors continued to press for more tapes. One of these contained a conversation between Nixon and Haldeman which took place on 23 June 1972, an extract from which is as follows:

> *Haldeman:* You know the Democratic break-in thing, we're back in the problem area because the FBI is not under control...
> *Nixon:* When you get in [to the CIA] people, say, "Look, the problem is that this will open the whole Bay of Pigs thing, and the President just feels that..." without going into the details – don't, don't lie to them to the extent to say there is no involvement, but just say this is a comedy of errors... they should call the FBI in and [unintelligible] don't go any further into this case – period. (Quoted in Woll, *op. cit.,* p. 373)

The President's instruction that the CIA should halt the FBI investigation into Watergate would be catastrophic for Nixon, since it proved that he was unquestionably involved in a conspiracy to obstruct justice: in time this recording became known as the 'smoking gun tape'. Knowing this, Nixon refused to surrender it to Jaworski, but was forced to do so by a Supreme Court ruling of 24 July enforcing the subpoena. At exactly the same time, the House Judiciary Committee were discussing whether Nixon had been aware of the Watergate break-in and, if so, whether to impeach him. It should be noted that impeachment does not equate to removal from office – it is simply the process by which formal charges are made against a government official. Indeed both cases of presidential impeachment – Andrew Johnson in 1868, Bill Clinton 130 years later – have led to acquittal.

However, the televised debates on Nixon's impeachment made that outcome impossible. Articles were drafted which left the public, the politicians and the President in no doubt as to the conclusion the Watergate investigations were leading to: Article I – Obstruction of Justice; Article II – Abuse of Power; Article III – Defiance of Subpoenas. The subsequent release of the 'smoking gun tape' was the final straw. Rather than face impeachment and the lost cause of a tortuous trial in the Senate, Richard M Nixon became the first US President in history to resign.

*****

Millions of people remember where they were when President Kennedy was assassinated. But for the next generation Nixon's resignation was equally momentous. Many can recall with absolute clarity the live broadcast of 8 August 1974 in which he made the announcement that he was to hand over the presidency to Gerald Ford the following day. I watched it with the children of my parents' friends, Bill and Maureen Johnston, at their home in Toronto, Canada. Like viewers throughout the world, I greeted it with disbelief. In the middle of a hitchhiking expedition across North America, I had been following the denouement of the Watergate saga only intermittently and had not realised how perilous Nixon's position had become. But that wasn't the shock. Rather, it was that this man, a hate figure for young people in my circle for over six years, but who, nevertheless, seemed completely invincible, was suddenly gone. With its headline 'The Quitter', *Rolling Stone* venomously threw back in his face the words Nixon had uttered in that televised address:

> I have never been a quitter. To leave office before my time is completed is abhorrent to every instinct in my body. But as President, I must put the interests of America first. Therefore I shall resign the Presidency, effective at noon tomorrow.

Yet in the circumstances Nixon took the correct decision. In effect he left office without anyone knowing the full extent of his culpability. And despite assertions that he would promote a new style of leadership ('I believe that truth is the glue that holds government together'), President Ford granted Nixon a full pardon for his actions exactly one month after he had resigned. Within a year he was making public appearances again and by the end of the decade he had become an elder statesman of American politics with best-selling memoirs and no fewer than nine further books to come.

For a number of reasons, it is difficult to evaluate Nixon's role in the Watergate scandal with complete certainty. Firstly, the full facts have not come to light and probably never will do. Were the comments that damned him actually conclusive proof of his knowledge and endorsement of the break-in and the resultant cover-up? Moreover in these days of hacking and cyber-attacks, have governments not carried out far more damaging operations against their opponents than a bungled burglary? It is sometimes tempting to think that Nixon's worst crime was to get caught. On the other hand, of course, his misdemeanours may have been far more extensive than was appreciated then, or now. It was also not hard to believe that someone who conducted the Vietnam War in the manner Nixon did could have been guilty of such monumentally flawed judgements.

Whatever the case, it took America some time to recover. Compared with his larger-than-life predecessor, Gerald Ford was an unspectacular President. At first that seemed a good thing: his arrival provided a welcome opportunity for reassessment, not just of the horribly failed security policy, but the country's economic and social wellbeing which, now that Watergate was slipping from the headlines, was again becoming a cause for concern. Under Ford, however, it was about to get worse.

★★★★★

On the same day, 12 September 1974, that Neil Young was bidding his own acidic farewell to Nixon with a stirring version of 'Ohio' at CSNY's Wembley concert, the West Coast band Little Feat were playing live (to a much smaller audience) at Ultrasonic Studios for WLIR-FM, Hampstead, New York. Their set, as might be expected, largely derived from their fourth album, *Feats Don't Fail Me Now*, issued the previous month. Yet such was the band's inventiveness and energy that they were already transforming its content. Sometimes this was for purely musical reasons: the taut 'Rock And Roll Doctor', with its irresistible drum beat to the fore, was, for example, taken slower for added funk. Elsewhere the adjustments enhanced meaning. The studio version of 'The Fan' uses varied instrumental effects and tricky time changes to reflect the story of a young female admirer debauched by a rock star; at Hampstead the band added a folky introduction to symbolise her naivety.

For the finale, they integrated their classic, 'Dixie Chicken', into the medley of 'Cold, Cold, Cold' and 'Tripe Face Boogie' which had closed the album. The result was a free flowing improvisation which, though featuring diverse guitar sounds and a long piano solo, retained its momentum to the end. Indeed the whole show was notable for the way in which all the instrumental textures knitted together into a cogent and coherent whole. Such virtues were shared by Little Feat's label-mates and fellow Californians The Doobie Brothers. Indeed in early 1975 the two bands co-headlined The Warner Brothers Music Tour, an eighteen-date European showcase for the company's roster.

But whereas Little Feat's music was a sophisticated blend of rock, funk and blues, The Doobies just concentrated on doing the simple things well. Technical proficiency without self-indulgence; attractive, undemanding material; a well-constructed and exciting stage-act – it all added up to a successful formula, and like clockwork they released one album every year between 1971 and 1978. The 1974 edition was *What Were Once Vices Are Now Habits* (a somewhat disingenuous title given their reputation for efficiency). Issued on 1 February, it reached number four on the US chart, their highest position to date. Almost all the tracks are up-tempo rockers, of which 'Road Angel' with its pulsating guitar battle is the most impressive. Even when they threaten to go in another direction – as on the reflective 'Another Park, Another Saturday' or the prog-like 'Daughter Of The Sea', the lure of returning to their comfort zone is too strong. The one exception is the lilting 'Black Water' which incorporates dobro, country fiddle and a superb *a cappella* interlude.

Little Feat and The Doobie Brothers belong firmly in that category of early 1970s West Coast rock described earlier in this chapter – immaculately executed and beautifully produced, their work was firmly rooted in America's rich musical tradition. Unfortunately all of that was insufficient to weather the storm that was brewing during 1974, and by the end of the decade they had passed out of fashion. The same fate almost befell another band in a not dissimilar mould, Steely Dan, but their urbane, harmonically complex music was often more akin to jazz than rock and thus perhaps more immune to changes of taste. They also survived the loss of stellar guitarist Jeff 'Skunk' Baxter to The Doobie Brothers, but not before he had appeared on *Pretzel Logic*, released on 20 February.

This turned out to be Steely Dan's best-selling record so far – their first to chart in Britain (where it was named Album of the Year by the *New Musical Express*) and a Top Ten hit in the US – something of a paradox given that it illustrates their ability to avoid the obvious. Very few bands of the period, for example, would open an album with a low-key piece like 'Rikki Don't Lose That Number', especially with an intro consisting of an out-of-tempo flourish on the flapamba (a type of marimba) and a quote from a ten-year-old hard bop classic; the chorus, too, does not arrive until over a minute into the track. But both narrative and melody are enticing – so much so that when issued as a single (minus the flapamba), it made number four in the US. As with most of the tracks that follow, the lyrics consist of direct speech, in this case an admonition to a potential girlfriend, and this gives them an accessibility sometimes lacking on the band's other records. Their legendary penchant for arresting chord changes is also employed judiciously: in 'Barrytown', for example, the switch from verse to chorus is exhilarating. And for the jazz aficionados, there is, as well as the quote from Horace Silver's 'Song For My Father' at the start of 'Rikki', a delightful pastiche of Duke Ellington's 'East St Louis

Toodle-Oo'; (Charlie) 'Parker's Band' is , however, an up-tempo rock number!

Little Feat, The Doobie Brothers and Steely Dan proved that good quality rock music could still have wide appeal in 1974, a fact underlined by the success of releases like Steve Miller's flamboyant 'The Joker' – the first American number one of the year – and Maria Muldaur's sensuous 'Midnight At The Oasis', a summer hit on both sides of the Atlantic. The Carpenters' 'I Won't Last A Day Without You' demonstrated the exact reverse – that an ultra-commercial act can still produce something worthwhile; but this touching record, for once shorn of the duo's customary blandness, failed to make the US Top Ten, their worst result for two years. Similarly, Dolly Parton's *Jolene*, despite the inclusion of both the magnificent title track and the future smash 'I Will Always Love You', failed to trouble the national album chart compilers.

In contrast, Carly Simon's *Hotcakes*, though seemingly overshadowed by the simultaneous release of label-mate Bob Dylan's *Planet Waves*, comfortably outsold it. It also yielded the huge hit single 'Mockingbird', recorded with her then husband, James Taylor, and contained such quintessential examples of middle-of the-road rock as the heartfelt 'Haven't Got Time For The Pain' and the relaxed ballad, 'Mind On My Man'. Canadian singer/songwriter Gordon Lightfoot also hit the jackpot when, on 22 June, his album *Sundown* reached the top of the American album chart. This was something of a surprise since Lightfoot's downbeat vocal style could make the happiest of songs sound gloomy, but here, propelled by the catchy title track – itself a US number one single a week later – his reflective, evocative compositions were a welcome diversion for a nation heading towards the nadir of the Watergate scandal. There is, for example, a pleasingly rustic feel to the gently rolling 'Somewhere USA' while 'Carefree Highway' (another hit single) is a potent blend of nostalgia and romance. But Lightfoot is not totally immune from his environment; in 'Too Late For Prayin'', he suggests 'Let's pray for the ones they call the children of today'.

Sundown's cover photo has Lightfoot sitting cross-legged in a barn wearing denims and a pair of sandals. At the other end of the sartorial spectrum Randy Edelman wears a grey peaked cap, long tweed overcoat, white flares and white shoes on the front of his album, *Prime Cuts,* heralding a much more contemporary singer/songwriter album. Edelman had become well-known for his score to *Executive Action*, the 1973 film which presents its own somewhat bizarre version of the Kennedy assassination. Edelman's approach is just as idiosyncratic and when it works, the results are startling. 'Pistol Packing Melody', for example, is a song about writing a song – this one; effectively it is an ode, almost an anthem, to the music of the past with a dramatic transition from wistful verse to walloping chorus. 'Stan The Pantsman' is a bold piece of social commentary, excoriating the millionaires who rip off the public. But 'I Am A Dancer' and 'You Are The Sunlight – I Am The Moon' sail too close to sentimentality and pretentiousness.

All of these records, with the exception of *Jolene* and *Sundown*, were made by West Coast performers and/or recorded in California. The epicentre of American rock was about to shift 3,000 miles to the east, leaving most of them high and dry, if not commercially, then certainly in terms of fashion. Few in number are the artists from that part of the world whose work has remained entirely unaffected by the vicissitudes of rock trends.

That guitarist Ry Cooder is one of them stems from the fact that he has pretty much bypassed contemporary styles to focus on what is now described as World Music; initially, that meant the American tradition, and 1974's *Paradise And Lunch* finds him mixing and matching country blues, jazz and gospel, with just a touch of R&B. Genres collide to delightful effect on Blind Blake's 'Ditty Wah Ditty' on which Cooder duets with the legendary jazz pianist Earl Hines while the spiritual 'Jesus On The Mainline', first recorded in the early 1950s by Mississippi Fred McDowell, profits from a robust horn arrangement and just a touch of parody. 'Mexican Divorce', by

Burt Bacharach and Bob Hilliard, prefigures Cooder's next project, the Tex-Mex influenced *Chicken Skin Music* of 1976. *Paradise And Lunch* also features a strong supporting cast including arranger Nick DeCaro, who worked on the Gordon Lightfoot and Randy Edelman albums discussed above; Lenny Waronker, who produced *Sundown*, Randy Newman's *Good Old Boys* and records by Little Feat and The Doobie Brothers; and a distinguished backing group including drummer Jim Keltner, percussionist Milt Holland and veteran jazz bassist Red Callender.

Such musicians formed part of a larger circle of West Coast session players drawn from both rock and jazz who, despite their high status as individuals in their respective fields, were sufficiently versatile to work on recordings by a wide variety of artists. Tom Waits has benefited from such accompaniment on the sixteen albums he released between 1973 and 2011, although it is his own powers as a composer, singer and pianist that are exclusively responsible for his longevity. *The Heart Of Saturday Night*, released in October 1974, was his second album, but the first to define his unique style. (His debut, *Closing Time*, contained 'Ol' 55', covered by The Eagles for *On The Border*; in typically mordant manner, he called their version 'antiseptic'.)

Even before the record reaches the turntable there are strong hints as to what that style might be: the cover design, based on Frank Sinatra's *In The Wee Small Hours*, depicts a nocturnal urban scene with Waits – standing on a seedy-looking street corner, tie loosened, eyes closed, smoking a cigarette – about to be approached by a blonde young woman in a long purple dress. But nothing could prepare the first-time listener for his voice – gravelly and expressive in the manner of Louis Armstrong (or even Captain Beefheart) but endowed with a sensitivity all of its own. The songs, too, are stunning. 'Diamonds On My Windshield' and 'The Ghosts Of Saturday Night' are in the stream-of-consciousness manner characteristic of beat poetry while the imagery employed in 'New

Coat Of Paint' – 'we'll laugh at that old bloodshot moon in that burgundy sky' – verges on surrealism. Almost all the tracks evoke the late-night, low-life landscape of the city, making it tantamount to a concept album; in placing it at number 335, *Rolling Stone: The 500 Greatest Albums Of All Time* described the content as 'growling, jazzy beatnik gutter tales' (p. 189). But equally affecting are bluesy, boozy ballads such as 'San Diego Serenade' and 'Please Call Me, Baby', both poignant tales of lost love which land firmly on the right side of sentimentality. Though Waits was to go from strength to strength, few would argue that the seeds of his success are not readily apparent on *The Heart Of Saturday Night.*

★★★★★

The privations brought about by the oil crisis meant that many Americans started 1974 in a sombre mood. There were, however, some positive news stories around the corner. On 10 January, for example, Secretary of State James Schlesinger announced a new policy of 'limited strategic strike options' which meant that extensive procedures aimed at deterrence would be enacted before the launch of any large-scale nuclear attack. On 30 January, President Nixon seemed to have drawn a line under the Watergate affair when, in his State of the Union address, he stated that, 'One year of Watergate is enough'. And, on 8 February, the crew of *Skylab 4* – a mission involving a final trip to America's first space station – arrived back safely after a record 84 days in orbit. Four days earlier, however, a sequence of events began which would plunge the nation into shock, outrage and sheer panic.

Randolph Apperson Hearst was at that time one of the richest men in America. His father was the newspaper magnate William Randolph Hearst on whom Orson Welles and Herman Mankiewicz based the film *Citizen Kane.* Hearst Sr bequeathed none of his vast media holdings to his four sons but young Randolph did inherit his father's business acumen to amass a fortune of $2 billion. So, when his daughter Patty was abducted from her apartment in Berkeley, California, on 4 February, it was big news. But perhaps more alarming than the kidnap itself was the identity of the perpetrators, a previously unknown revolutionary group called the Symbionese Liberation Army (SLA).

In fact the Army consisted of just ten individuals: Rich Little; Joe Remiro and his girlfriend Angela Atwood; Willie Wolfe; Bill and his wife Emily Harris; Camilla Hall and her girlfriend Patricia Soltysik; Nancy Ling Perry; and Donald DeFreeze. All except Remiro and DeFreeze were white, middle-class young people who had become radicalised – or, perhaps, more accurately, had radicalised themselves – on the turbulent college campuses of the late 1960s/early 1970s when the ideals of the peace movement were transmuting into furious, uncompromising protest.

Through Little, they came into contact with Remiro, a former member of Vietnam Veterans Against the War, who was involved with an education program called the Black Cultural Association (BCA). The plight of the country's African-American prison population appealed to the nascent SLA since it was another glaring example of governmental oppression of 'the people' (often to be cited in future communications as the object of their dedication). So when DeFreeze, who had been a participant in the BCA, escaped from prison on 5 March 1973, he was sheltered in turn by Little, Wolfe, Soltisyk and Perry. During the next six months, the SLA coalesced as a group; their first operation took place on 6 November 1973 when they murdered an African-American school superintendent, Marcus Foster. Given the SLA's agenda, it was an odd choice of victim, especially as Foster had initially opposed the student ID card scheme to which they took so much exception. But now he had agreed to implement it in watered-down form and it cost him his life.

In their Communiqué Number One, the SLA (Western Regional Youth Unit) admitted responsibility for the murder, which perplexed the FBI somewhat since they had never heard of them; their name also made them sound far bigger than they actually were. On 10 January 1974, Little and Remiro were stopped by police and after an exchange of gunfire they were arrested for Foster's murder. Just over three weeks later, Hearst was kidnapped.

On 8 February, Randolph Hearst read out a communiqué from the SLA which stated they had 'served an arrest warrant' on his daughter and concluded with their oft-repeated slogan, 'Death to the Fascist Insect that Preys upon the Life of the People'. The SLA wanted to exchange Hearst for Little and Remiro but when this was refused, they demanded that her father fund the distribution of free groceries to the poor of California. This was followed by the first in a chilling series of taped messages from Hearst herself:

> Mom, Dad, I'm OK… these people are perfectly willing to die for what they're doing. I would hope that you will do what they say, Dad, and do it quickly.

The food donation program duly began, and though it was on a smaller scale than they had demanded, it was still a huge propaganda coup for the SLA.

Then came another message from Hearst:

> I have been given the choice of one: being released in a safe area, or two: joining the forces of the Symbionese Liberation Army and fighting for my freedom and the freedom of all oppressed people. I have chosen to stay and fight. I have been given the name Tania after a comrade who fought alongside Che in Bolivia.

Much to the disgust of the authorities and, in particular, the Governor of California, Ronald Reagan, posters began to appear everywhere, picturing an armed Hearst in front of an SLA flag and bearing the legend 'We love you, Tania'. Support for both Hearst and the SLA started to erode, however, when on 15 April they shot two civilians during the robbery of the Hibernia Bank in San Francisco. CCTV pictures clearly showed Hearst holding a rifle and shouting at bank staff and customers.

The SLA then moved operations to Los Angeles, but after a botched attempt at shoplifting in a sporting goods store, they were traced to a property on East 54th Street. On 17 May, in a shootout with police which culminated in the destruction of the house by fire, DeFreeze, Atwood, Wolfe, Perry, Hall and Soltysik were all killed. More members were recruited and there was another bank raid in which another innocent bystander was killed, but sixteen months later Hearst was arrested. She immediately renounced the SLA and the clinical psychologist Margaret Singer, who in the past had also interviewed Charles Manson, claimed that her case was an example of the Stockholm syndrome whereby the kidnapped victim comes to identify with his/her kidnappers. But Hearst was still given seven years, later commuted to 22 months by President Jimmy Carter.

★★★★★

Back in 1974 at the height of the Hearst affair, the poet Patti Smith released her first single, the traditional murder ballad, 'Hey Joe'. Eight years earlier, as the Summer of Love was approaching, Jimi Hendrix had made his own debut with an incendiary version of the same song. But Smith injected a whole new meaning with her spoken introduction:

> Honey, the way you play guitar makes me feel so,
> Makes me feel so masochistic
> The way you go down low deep into the neck
> And I would do anything, and I would do anything and Patty Hearst,

You're standing there in front of the Symbionese
Liberation Army flag with your legs spread
I was wondering will you get it every night
From a black revolutionary man and his women or whether you really
did

And now that you're on the run what goes on in your mind
Your sisters they sit by the window
You know your mama doesn't sit and cry and your daddy
Well you know what your daddy said

Patty, you know what your daddy said
Patty, he said, he said, he said
Well, sixty days ago she was such a lovely child
Now here she is with a gun in her hand...

Thus it was with curious symmetry that, from the ashes of the hippie dream, the phoenix called punk now began to rise.

CHAPTER 3

Let's Put It All Together

The year 1974 represented a peak in the history of African-American music. New idioms were emerging as others reached maturity, and the more traditional forms enjoyed a revival of interest. Some of the big stars of the 1960s were still around and producing music of high quality. And female artists – so often second-class citizens in white genres such as glam, heavy metal and prog-rock – took a leading role in every sphere. Songwriters continued to take politicians to task on issues of equality and civil rights while more domestic subjects were tackled with a new and unflinching realism. At the same time, many leading performers were happy just to combine dance and romance. It all made for a rich and varied diet with plenty to satisfy both mind and body.

As ever in American music, regional variations were significant. Music made in one part of the country could sound very different from that made in another even if the idiom was, in theory, the same. In the South, traditions were slow to change and the studios in Memphis and Muscle Shoals were still famous for the emotionally-charged soul music which had been created there in the early 1960s. In contrast, the big, cosmopolitan cities thrived on innovation and setting new trends. Disco, for instance, began in New York; Philadelphia specialised in heavily orchestrated, glossy pop; and Los Angeles was, as we saw in Chapter 2, a major centre for rock music. The principal African-American idiom of the period, funk, was all-pervasive and thus not really tied to one location. However, certain cities had their own variant, especially New Orleans where the music seems to have orginated.

There were casualties, too, of the changes in fashion, illustrated most graphically by the decline in the fortunes of Detroit where during the 1960s the Motown label had turned out hit after hit. But in 1972 Motown had moved to LA and as a consequence, though it had recording facilities there, lost its distinctive quality. The cramped Detroit basement studio had somehow contrived to produce a sound that was instantly recognisable and massively successful. Yet the company's big stars such as Stevie Wonder and Marvin Gaye had tired of that sound and wanted greater creative freedom to develop their music. For them, LA offered an attractive environment with spacious, comfortable studios such as The Record Plant, founded in New York but with recently-opened premises on the West Coast.

The following table is a general guide to the locations important to the African-American music of 1974. It is not intended to be comprehensive since it focuses primarily on those artists discussed later in this chapter, and book. Production staff and session musicians are included since they made a key contribution to a studio's (and by extension a city's) individual sound. Producers also frequently wrote the material to be recorded, managed the artists and/or ran the studio and record label concerned. In some cases – notably Stevie Wonder, Barry White and James Brown – the artists produced their own records, and those of others. Most African-American acts were solo singers or vocal groups and thus needed the services of session musicians to a greater extent than, say, in rock which was still dominated by the culture of the band. Some individuals performed the role of composer, producer, arranger *and* studio musician on the same record. In Stevie Wonder's case, he was the artist, too.

City	Studios	African-American artists with 1974 releases recorded there	Producers/arrangers/ session musicians
New York City	The Record Plant, A&R, Sound Ideas, Media Sound, Electric Lady, The Hit Factory	James Brown, The Fatback Band, Gloria Gaynor, Al Downing, Stevie Wonder, The Stylistics, Kool and The Gang, BT Express, Billy Cobham	Meco Monardo, Tony Bongiovi, Jay Ellis, Harold Wheeler, Steve Metz, Van McCoy, Trade Martin, Dave Matthews, Lowell Dorn, Carlos Ward, Terrell Woods
Los Angeles	The Record Plant, Westlake, A&M, MCA, Whitney, ABC, The Sound Factory, Quantum, Motown Recording Studios, RCA	Stevie Wonder, Barry White, Bobby Bland, Rufus ft Chaka Khan, The Isley Brothers, Billy Preston, Johnny Bristol, The Commodores, Minnie Riperton, Syreeta, The Jackson Five, Eddie Kendricks, The Hues Corporation	Gene Page, Bob Monaco, Steve Barri, James Carmichael, HB Barnum, Arthur Wright, Frank Wilson, John Florez, Leonard Caston, Hal Davis, Michael Omartian, Joe Sample, Dean Parks, Larry Carlton, William Salter, Wilton Felder, Max Bennett, James Gadson
Sausalito, California	The Record Plant	Betty Davis	Buddy Miles, Cordell Dudley, Larry Johnson, Mike Clark
Memphis, Tennessee	Stax, Hot Buttered Soul, Royal	Shirley Brown, Inez Foxx, Margie Alexander, Veda Brown, The Staple Singers, Isaac Hayes, The Soul Children, Ann Peebles, Hot Sauce, Al Green	Homer Banks, Carl Hampton, Jim Stewart, Willie Mitchell, Al Jackson, The Memphis Horns, Bobby Manuel, Michael Toles, Marvell Thomas, Lester Snell, the Hodges Brothers, Archie Turner, Howard Grimes

Muscle Shoals, Alabama	Fame	Bobby Womack, Millie Jackson, Candi Staton, The Staple Singers, The Soul Children	Rick Hall, Bobby Womack, The Muscle Shoals Rhythm Section (including Pete Carr, Barry Beckett, Roger Hawkins)
New Orleans	Sea-Saint	The Meters, Labelle	Allen Toussaint, The Meters
Miami	Criteria, TK	Millie Jackson, KC and The Sunshine Band, George McCrae, Betty Wright, Latimore	Harry Casey, Richard Finch, Steve Alaimo, Willie Clarke, Timmy Thomas, Ron Bogdon, Robert Furgeson
Philadelphia	Sigma Sound, Omega Sound	The Three Degrees, The Tymes, Harold Melvin and The Blue Notes, The Intruders, Billy Paul, People's Choice, The O'Jays, The Trammps, William DeVaughn, Blue Magic	Kenny Gamble, Leon Huff, Bobby Martin, Thom Bell, John Davis, Billy Jackson, MFSB (including Norman Harris, Ronnie Baker, Vince Montana, Earl Young, Larry Washington)
Chicago	Curtom, Paragon, Sound Studios, PS Studios	Curtis Mayfield, The Chi-Lites, The Ohio Players, Fenton Robinson, Oscar Brown Jr	Curtis Mayfield, Eugene Record, Bruce Iglauer, Phil Upchurch

The second dimension to be considered in analysing the African-American music is that of style. As noted above, this was almost always a function of location, though the links are not always straightforward. The foundations of African-American music – jazz, blues and gospel – were laid in the South; but following the mass migration northwards in the early 20th century these musical forms spread throughout the country and were remade and remodelled.

Most of the jazz discussed in this book (Chapter 6) was made in New York or Los Angeles while the blues artists referred to are mainly from Chicago. Later styles show the same pattern: soul was developed in the South but variants cropped up everywhere, notably in Detroit. But when Motown relocated, its erstwhile blend of lavish arrangements, catchy compositions and well-groomed performers was re-invented in Philadelphia. Disco, too, derived from soul.

The taut, edgy music known as funk can be traced back to the syncopated rhythms of New Orleans jazz and R&B but, to all intents and purposes, was invented by James Brown in the late 1960s. Inverting the conventional roles allotted to the ensemble, Brown made bass and drums tantamount to lead instruments, with guitar and horns adding the punctuation. He also shifted the rhythmic emphasis from the second and fourth beat of the bar to the first and third – especially the first, so that it became known as the 'rhythm of the one'. This gave funk an immediacy and intensity that other forms lacked and it wasn't long before it was ubiquitous, sometimes – as with Brown, George Clinton and Sly Stone – suffusing the whole of an artist's work.

The third dimension of African-American music, subject-matter, was as varied as location and style. Although the conventional love song maintained its popularity, a small but significant number of songwriters described relationships with a new and frequently disturbing frankness. Others followed the tried and tested formula of using the personal as a metaphor for the political, while funk proved a suitable vehicle for overt social comment, its terseness ideal for blunt statements of dissatisfaction. And in 1974 there was plenty for African-Americans to be dissatisfied about.

★★★★★

In the ten years since the Civil Rights Act had been signed with such great optimism, progress towards equality of opportunity for African-Americans had been slow. Indeed, some observers believed that things had got worse. Safeguarding equality under the law has never guaranteed that attitudes will change – at least not immediately – and this piece of legislation, though undoubtedly a landmark in the country's history, was no different. To begin with, some states, including California, tried to block some of its provisions, and it was no coincidence that just over a year later there was a six-day riot in the African-American neighbourhood of Watts, Los Angeles. As in so many comparable cases, the trouble was sparked by a single instance of conflict between police and one individual, but the ensuing eruption of violence reflected the pent-up anger of a whole community. In 1967, further disturbances took place in Detroit, with even more tragic results: the death toll of 43 surpassed that in Watts by nine, while the total of 1,189 injured was 157 greater.

At the time when the Act was passed, there was a division in the African-American community between the non-violent, integrationist approach of Martin Luther King and the more militant Black Nationalism symbolised by Malcolm X. The publication in 1967 of *Black Power* by Stokely Carmichael with Charles V Hamilton seemed to provide a platform whereby these opposing ideologies could be reconciled. While Carmichael understood and respected King's teachings, he felt that the time was right for more proactive tactics and, alongside the assertive and at times aggressive rhetoric came the call for African-Americans to empower themselves through self-help rather than relying on whites to offer them charity. Meanwhile the Black Panther Party, founded the previous year by Huey P Newton and Bobby Seale, were putting some of Carmichael's theories into practice. Initially known as the Black Panther Party for Self-Defense, the Panthers' immediate priority was to encourage African-Americans to retaliate against police brutality. To this end, they built up an arsenal of weaponry and the paramilitary discipline and uniform (leather jacket, black beret) to go with it. At the same time, the Panthers offered a range of social provision, including free medical care and legal services and free breakfasts for schoolchildren. As far as the authorities were concerned, the combination of self-defence and self-help represented a challenge that needed to be met with force and the repression that resulted set off a cycle of violence that culminated in the killing, incarceration or exile of key figures in the Party and ultimately the destruction of the Party itself.

Clearly, therefore, the Civil Rights Act had not brought the peaceful transition to a just and stable society its architects had hoped for. The problem was merely compounded when in order to hasten progress, the government felt it necessary to introduce a series of corrective measures, none of which were contained in the Act. One was the imposition of bussing – that is, transporting children from their local area to another in order to achieve integration between white and African-American children. While the Act required desegregation of schools, it had said nothing about integration – indeed proponents of the Act such as Hubert Humphrey had specifically denied that the latter was a consequence of the former. Yet within four years the two terms were being used interchangeably and the courts were enforcing bussing, moving from a position – in the Act – where race should not be relevant to education to a position where it was the determining factor.

Irrespective of the effectiveness of bussing in terms of educational outcomes for children (and this was much disputed), such examples of what was called 'affirmative action' were not universally popular in either the white or African-American communities and led to turmoil in some of the country's big cities that had certainly not evaporated by 1974. In Boston, for example, the Schools Committee was accused of violating the Civil Rights Act by continuing to practise segregation and US District Judge W Arthur Garrity agreed, ruling on 21 June that the city should initiate a program of bussing and 're-destricting' in order to facilitate it. The result was an explosion of racial violence. When the school year began in September, buses carrying African-American children into white areas had to be escorted by police cars, motorcycles and, in one case, a helicopter on the lookout for snipers who might fire at the buses; police had to be called to the schools themselves to break up fights and were greeted by a hail of bricks and bottles.

Meanwhile on 25 July the Supreme Court ruled that Detroit need *not* re-district to aid bussing arrangements. Yet this decision, while diametrically opposite to that made in Boston, was equally unhelpful in easing racial tensions. As Lewis M Killian noted one month later,

> While a ruling requiring interdistrict bussing might have been of dubious benefit to black pupils, the antibussing ruling surely strengthened the formidable division between increasingly black central cities and white suburbs. (*The Impossible Revolution, Phase II: Black Power And The American Dream*, p. 152)

Killian's analysis is particularly important to us since it was carried out in 1974 itself. Like many commentators, he paints a pessimistic picture of developments since the Civil Rights Act, noting that 'the black power movement has lapsed into disorganization and inactivity' (*ibid.*). Given the controversy surrounding just one issue – bussing – this is perhaps hardly surprising: it would seem that whatever position you took, you were likely to face ferocious opposition, including from your own side of the racial divide. And, of course, as we have seen, leadership was in any case in short supply. The economic outlook was, according to Killian, just as bleak:

> The American economy is in a state of uncertainty that baffles even erstwhile optimistic economists, with inflation reaching a crisis level, while unemployment remains at about five percent – and double that for blacks. In 1974 the nation seems closer to the brink of another depression than at any time since the 1930s and black workers can be pretty sure that the rule of "last hired, first fired" will continue to apply to them. (*ibid.*)

The issue of equal opportunities in employment had also required supplementary action, even though the Civil Rights Act had declared that all were equal under the law. By 1971 quotas were in place to ensure that employers maintained a racially-mixed workforce, but as may be inferred from the above passage from Killian, these had not worked especially well. Thomas Sowell, an implacable critic of social engineering, contends that they had had the opposite effect to that intended:

> Those blacks with less education and less job experience – the truly disadvantaged – have been falling farther and farther behind their white counterparts under affirmative action... Black male high school dropouts with less than six years of work experience earned 79 percent of the income of white male high school dropouts with less than six years of work experience in 1967 (before affirmative action quotas) and this *fell* to 69 percent by 1978 (after affirmative action quotas). (*Civil Rights: Rhetoric Or Reality?* p. 51-52)

Sowell, like Killian, refers to the backlash against quotas and inevitably there were complaints from individuals who felt they had fallen foul of the system. In February 1974, for example, the Supreme Court heard the case of William De Funis, a white student who believed he had been refused a place at Washington University Law School because of an admissions quota scheme giving preferential treatment to African-American applicants.

Both writers also note that the increased political representation of African-Americans since the Civil Rights Act did not bring commensurate benefits to the community. There were still too few leading African-American politicians to form a powerful front, even assuming they were of one mind when it came to resolving the key problems. And of course once elected they were obliged to try to serve the interests of *all* their constituents, of whom African-Americans would only be a part. Where deprivation was prevalent across every section of the community, this task was, admittedly, more straightforward, since the whole question of universal welfare reform was bound up with the struggle for civil rights.

On the face of it the accession of Richard Nixon to the presidency seemed unlikely to take this agenda very far forward. His opponent in the 1968 election, Hubert Humphrey, had received 85% of the African-American vote, a clear indication of how Nixon's record on civil rights was regarded. Once in office, he did not change his views but recognised that something needed to be done about social welfare. Dona Cooper Hamilton and Charles V Hamilton note that

> HR Haldeman's diary reveals Nixon's negative views about blacks as he discussed welfare reform, an issue high on his domestic agenda, with Haldeman and John Ehrlichman, chief members of the White House staff. Nixon said, "The *whole* problem is really the blacks. The key is to devise a system that recognises this while not appearing to". (*The Dual Agenda*, p. 177)

In pursuit of that objective Nixon came up with the Family Assistance Plan (FAP), which was intended to sweep aside a whole range of fragmented and uncoordinated support programs in favour of direct cash payments to those in need. However, as the Hamiltons relate, the FAP was supported by no-one: conservatives found it too liberal, liberals too conservative; trade unions felt it would erode the minimum wage, the National Welfare Rights Organisation considered just about every provision detrimental to the recipient, and of course Democrats were reluctant to endorse a plan to help the poor devised by Republicans. The FAP therefore foundered and with it Nixon's interest in welfare reform.

So by 1974, the tenth anniversary of the Civil Rights Act, the picture was one of conflict, confusion and chaos. Some African-Americans had benefited from the legislation but many – especially the disaffected and disadvantaged – had not, and the decline in the economy threatened worse to come. The government, supported by the courts, had tried to enforce the law by affirmative action but in so doing set off a chain of violence that set the civil rights movement back ten years. Its leadership – already bereft of Martin Luther King, Malcolm X and Fred Hampton, all of whom had been assassinated, and Stokely Carmichael, living in Guinea – now suffered further blows when Bobby Seale left the Black Panther Party and his co-founder Huey P Newton fled to Cuba. Yet despite the mayhem, some individuals continued to press the case for equality, whether through their actions, their writings, their speeches – or their music.

*****

Prior to 1964, the songbook of overt African-American political protest would have been one of the shortest ever written. With a tiny number of honourable exceptions – Big Bill Broonzy, JB Lenoir and Oscar Brown Jr among them – social and/or political comment had been disguised in allegory including, during earlier eras, in spirituals. But in 1964 two records heralding a new era appeared within six months of each other. 22 December saw the release of Sam Cooke's 'Shake', its B-side the stirring and prophetic 'A Change Is Gonna Come'. In June, five days before the Civil Rights Act became law, The Impressions' 'Keep On Pushing' entered the US singles chart. It was written by the group's leader, Curtis Mayfield, and marked the first in a series of inspirational compositions which included 'People Get Ready', 'We're A Winner' and 'Move On Up'. But Mayfield was equally astute in his analysis of the racial divide plaguing America and apportioned blame to all sides, as in 1970's apocalyptic '(Don't Worry) If There's A Hell Below We're All Going To Go'.

The year 1974 was one of Mayfield's busiest yet, involving no fewer than three albums. His most high-profile assignment was composing the soundtrack to the film *Claudine* starring Dihann Carroll and James Earl Jones. An unsentimental portrait of life in the ghetto, it drew praise for the quality of the acting and for avoiding the gratuitous violence of the blaxploitation films then in vogue. Mayfield's soundtrack contained the vigorous 'On And On', an American Top Five hit for Gladys Knight and The Pips in July. But the two albums under his own name provide a more accurate indicator of the direction in which he was heading.

The first, *Sweet Exorcist*, amounts to a barometer of the civil rights movement. That the majority of the compositions are personal rather than political perhaps symbolises the waning enthusiasm for confrontation. Moreover there is a sense of retreat in 'To Be Invisible', an urge to escape 'a world that seems not for me'. 'Power To The People', despite its belligerent title, concedes that much has been achieved – though protection is still needed for the 'sick and hungry' and 'those who may live in fear'. Yet in the brooding 'Kung Fu', Mayfield articulates the anger still present in the African-American community, using the interface between percussion and strings to symbolise continued racial tension and underline the song's unequivocal message:

> My mother bore me in a ghetto
> There was no mattress for my bed
> No, she couldn't name me Jesus
> I wasn't white enough, she said

Released as a single, 'Kung Fu' made the US Top 40 in August, but it was the last Mayfield record to do so. His take on funk, mellow yet imaginative, was perhaps too sophisticated for the genre's hardcore aficionados and as he moved closer to disco, his campaigning spirit seemed to evaporate. His second album of 1974, *Got To Find A Way*, signalled the start of the process. The positive sentiments suggested by the title are unceremoniously dispelled by 'Cannot Find A Way' and though some residual hope is evident in 'Prayer', he concludes that 'we are just people in people's hands'.

Mayfield's insight into the issues confronting African-Americans over the previous decade was matched only by James Brown, a very different character musically but equally inspirational. Like Mayfield, Brown evinced a strong sense of pride in his race and culture, encapsulated in his 1968 single 'Say It Loud – I'm Black And I'm Proud'. His creed of self-reliance corresponded to Black Panther ideology but he also had respect for authority and, in particular, the value of education as a means of escaping poverty and disadvantage. By 1974 he was in his forties but showed no signs of decline – indeed his output of two double albums in the year exceeded Mayfield's. He also remained a formidable live performer and made a successful appearance at the 'Rumble in the Jungle' festival in Zaïre.

Unlike Mayfield, however, he was out of favour as a film composer. Having contributed the soundtrack to the 1973 blaxploitation movie *Black Caesar*, Brown recorded material for the sequel, *Hell Up In Harlem.* When the producers rejected it as more of the same, he decided to release it anyway; no doubt much to his delight it became one of his best-selling recordings and his only certified gold album. Much of the reputation of *The Payback* rests on its glorious title track – seven-and-a-half minutes of full-strength funk, sparsely arranged, intense and unrelenting. The lyrics, written by Brown's long-term collaborator Fred Wesley, concern personal revenge, but are easy to interpret as a metaphor for African-American retaliation against continued oppression. Other songs – 'Shoot Your Shot', 'Forever Suffering' and 'Time is Running Out Fast' – are equally ambiguous, but there is no mistaking the message of the closing 'Mind Power'. Here Brown expresses some sympathy with those who get involved in crime to combat poverty – he had done the same himself – but in the end, 'You have to have mind power to deal with starvation'. For Brown, this means strength of character and self-advancement by legal means – education and work.

Another two-album set, *Hell,* followed at the end of June. Given Brown's rebuff by the producers of *Hell Up In Harlem*, its title might seem provocative; at first sight, however, the record seems to be about the various experiences of hell suffered by various individuals (including the President of the United States), but beyond the cover design and the title track the concept breaks down. We are then left with a mixture of remakes – 'Lost Someone', 'I Can't Stand It "76"' and the umpteenth 'Please Please Please', this time Afro-Cuban style; standards – 'When The Saints Go Marching In', 'Stormy Monday' and 'These Foolish Things Remind Me Of You' – and some outstanding new material, including 'Coldblooded', another object-lesson in funk, and the hypnotic 'Papa Don't Take No Mess'. But with the exception of 'Hell' ('It's hell down here and we've got to make a change') and the supercharged 'Sayin' It And Doin' It', it is hard to find any tracks with political import.

That was soon to change with the single 'Funky President (People It's Bad)', released in October. Hailing the new President (Ford), Brown exhorts America to deal with economic depression ('ain't no funking jobs to be found') and bounce back – 'we got to get over before we go under'. His tongue (perhaps) in his cheek, he even puts himself forward as a mayor ('so I can change things around here') or a governor. As such it typifies the equilibrium in Brown's work between deference to authority and desire for change.

By this stage Brown had been in the music business for 20 years and had become a figure of considerable standing in the African-American community. Any pronouncements he might make, verbally or through his music, therefore commanded respect. Much the same can be said of The Staple Singers who, while lacking the superstardom enjoyed by Brown, had an additional moral authority derived from their gospel background. Formed in 1948, they were led by patriarch Roebuck 'Pops' Staples and included his daughters Mavis, Cleotha and Yvonne. During the 1950s they had made a series of fine recordings including the brooding 'This May Be The Last Time' in 1955. Ten years later The Rolling Stones turned it into their smash hit 'The Last Time', demonstrating to The Staples that – although no royalties accrued to them – their music had commercial potential. Thereafter they crossed over into mainstream pop and won widespread acclaim for their releases on the Stax label. But in 1974 Stax was running into financial trouble and The Staples' *City In The Sky* was their last for the company.

As might be expected, there are several reaffirmations of their Christian faith, none more exuberant than the Mack Rice number, 'Who Made The Man'. Rice, who with Luther Ingram had written The Staples' big hit, 'Respect Yourself', also contributes to 'My Main Man', another gospel piece with an uplifting message. However his 'If It Ain't One Thing It's Another' (co-composed with Eddie Floyd) is much less positive while 'Something Ain't Right' is a graphic portrait of ghetto life – 'I'm sick and tired of seeing my brothers uptight'. The songs by the team of Homer Banks, Raymond Jackson and Carl Hampton are on the same lines: 'Blood Pressure' is an expression of frustration at the state of the world, 'Washington We're Watching You' a promise of vigilance. Osbie McClinton's 'Back Road Into Town' tells a depressing tale of discrimination, and even the title track, ostensibly a vision of salvation, complains of 'too many people tellin' too many lies'. This already strong material is delivered by The Staples with verve and, at times, ferocity, much aided by the top-flight Muscle Shoals musicians, among them Jimmy Johnson, Barry Beckett, David Hood and Roger Hawkins.

In spite of their high profile with African-Americans, neither Mayfield nor Brown nor The Staple Singers made the US Top 40 with their 1974 album releases. Stevie Wonder, on the other hand, spent two weeks at number one in September with *Fulfillingness' First Finale* and thus became the first African-American to make it to the top of the album charts for seventeen months and the only one to do so in 1974. Compared with its politically-charged predecessor, *Innervisions*, it is rather low-key, although the cover design does feature images of Martin Luther King and John F Kennedy and the second side opens with his vitriolic verdict on Nixon's presidency, 'You

Haven't Done Nothin''. An ominous, rumbling riff sets the mood for Wonder's invective while the dramatic entrance of horns and backing vocals (The Jackson Five, no less) turns up the heat still further. By a happy coincidence, 'You Haven't Done Nothin'' (backed by another excoriation of the political elite, 'Big Brother'), was issued as a single two days before Nixon's resignation and rose to the number one spot on 2 November.

The follow-up, 'Boogie On Reggae Woman', also came from *Fulfillingness' First Finale* and was another huge hit – though it could hardly have been more of a contrast. With its burbling bass, gospel piano and joyous harmonica, it is one the great feel-good records of the era. But other than the haunting 'Creepin'' and the Latin-flavoured 'Bird Of Beauty' (sung partly in Portuguese 'to enable me to speak to my people of Mozambique and the beautiful people of Brazil'), the rest of the album is pervaded by empty philosophising and undemanding love songs. As such it resembles the albums Wonder produced in 1974 for his ex-wife, Syreeta Wright, and for Minnie Riperton, both of whom appeared on *Fulfillingness' First Finale.*

Ballads and big productions dominate *Stevie Wonder Presents Syreeta* and love is everywhere: love of partner, love of family, love of God. There is, too, the trace of a sub-plot – the breakdown in the couple's brief marriage – but any rancour that may have entailed is buried under an avalanche of sentimentality, from the self-satisfied 'Cause We've Ended As Lovers' to the sickly 'When Your Daddy's Not Around'. To make matters worse, 'Your Kiss is Sweet' is repetitive and infantile, while 'Universal Sound Of The World' lacks both focus and substance. Only the anthem-like opener, 'I'm Goin' Left', has any sense of urgency but even here the message is equivocal – an indication of political direction or merely an expression of independence?

Despite its title Minnie Riperton's *Perfect Angel* displays a little more grit, thanks largely to the prominence of Michael Sembello's guitar. But the material – this time mainly by Riperton and her husband, Richard Rudolph – follows the Wonder/Wright template. Thus, for example, the swaying 'Reasons' contemplates the meaning of life and 'It's So Nice (To See Old Friends)' and 'Our Lives' are sugary and superficial. 'Lovin' You' – a lullaby to daughter Maya – was apparently added at the last moment in response to Wonder's challenge to the couple to come up with their most embarrassing song. In the end, the simplicity of the sentiments and Riperton's vocal gymnastics proved a winning combination and released as a single it climbed to the top of the US chart (and number two in the UK) in early 1975.

But perhaps the most impressive track on *Perfect Angel* is 'The Edge Of A Dream', a tribute to Martin Luther King and a vision of what he had been working for. It was a timely reminder that, in the stormy landscape of contemporary race relations, King's doctrine of non-violence was more relevant than ever.

*****

Jesse Jackson, according to his own testimony, had been the last person to speak to Martin Luther King who, after being shot at the Lorraine Motel, Memphis, on 4 April 1968, died in Jackson's arms. A veteran of the Selma-Montgomery marches of 1965, Jackson had joined King's Southern Christian Leadership Conference (SCLC) shortly afterwards and created a good impression with his eloquence and drive. But these qualities did not endear him to King's successor, Ralph Abernathy, and in1971 Jackson left the SCLC to form Operation PUSH (People United to Save Humanity), the purpose of which was to pressurise companies into hiring African-Americans by threatening to boycott their goods if they did not.

Though an ordained minister, Jackson had not run for political office by 1974. He was, however, continually lobbying politicians, particularly Richard Daley, the Mayor of Chicago. On 21 September, for instance, the *Chicago Tribune* reported that Jackson had met with Daley and given him a four-point plan for 'relieving the plight of blacks in Chicago' including a free-meal program and a conference aimed at reducing unemployment. Jackson also orchestrated a national campaign to get Gerald Ford to appoint the African-American senator, Edward Brooke, as his Vice-President. In short, Jackson was trying to effect the transition of the civil rights movement to electoral politics.

On the West Coast, and at the same time, the Black Panthers had begun to move in the same direction. This was a radical step since a culture of violence governed the Party – rooted, to be sure, in its policy of self-defence but now applied indiscriminately to settle any form of dispute, whether with the authorities, other African-American organisations, or among the Panthers themselves. The problem was that the Party had attracted a large group of young people for whom violence was already a way of life and who jumped at the chance of taking up a role in a respected, and feared, paramilitary movement. Some, such as the charismatic Bunchy Clark, brought valuable energy and commitment to the Party, but all too often brutal, summary justice was meted out at the slightest provocation, particularly to women, who were regarded, and treated, as inferior.

Much of the blame for this can be traced back to the leader of the Party, Huey P Newton, an intellectually gifted but violent individual who not only tolerated but encouraged displays of machismo. But on 6 August 1974 Newton, accused of shooting a seventeen-year-old prostitute, Kathleen Smith, absconded to Cuba, creating what, given the prevailing Panther culture, could easily have been a fatal crisis. For power now passed to the Chairman of the Party who in fact was *not* a man but a woman – Elaine Brown.

Though raised in a poverty-stricken neighbourhood of North Philadelphia, Brown came from a distinguished family. Her grandfather was Emmett Scott, the first African-American to serve in a presidential Cabinet, that of Woodrow Wilson. Scott's children, too, were high achievers: they included the engineer Emmett Scott Jr, the writer Clarissa Scott Delaney and the neurosurgeon Horace Scott, Brown's father. But her mother, Dorothy Brown, was of much lower social class and was abandoned by Horace when she became pregnant, and received no financial support with which to bring up their daughter.

Brown moved to California in the mid-1960s and found work as a waitress in a strip club. It was there that she met the novelist Jay Kennedy who introduced her to left-wing politics and, in particular, civil rights. In 1967, prompted by a neighbour, she carried out voluntary work at the Jordan Downs Housing Project in Watts – scene of the horrendous rioting two years before. From there Brown came into contact with the Black Congress, an umbrella group comprising numerous African-American organisations in the Los Angeles area and, immersing herself in political and historical reading, began to write articles for their newspaper. That November she attended a Black Congress Executive Committee meeting addressed by Earl Anthony, of the newly-formed Black Panther Party. Anthony was appealing for funds to assist the defence of their leader, Huey Newton, charged with murdering a police officer. Five months later and following the assassination of Martin Luther King, Brown joined the Panthers.

Shortly afterwards, she released an album, *Seize The Time*, which includes what came to be the Party's anthem, 'The Message'. Brown's semi-operatic voice carries the sombre melody through an arrangement, by jazz musician Horace Tapscott, that builds from a sparse introduction to full-blown orchestration. There was no follow-up until 1973 when Brown recorded *Until We're Free* for Motown's Black Forum label. The gospel-flavoured title piece works well but on tracks like 'I Know Who You Are' Tapscott's settings are too lavish and Brown's strong but stentorian singing locks the record into one emotional dimension.

Whatever her shortcomings as a recording artist, Brown rose through the ranks of the Black Panthers. By 1971, she was a member of the Party's Central Committee, replacing Eldridge Cleaver as Minister of Information; in 1973 she stood for election to Oakland City Council, garnering a creditable 30% of the vote. Part of her success lay in the fact that she gained the trust and respect of Huey

Newton, with whom she had an on-off relationship. However this did not prevent her falling foul of the Panthers' predilection for brutality: on one occasion, after failing to get the Party's newspaper out on time, she received a flogging at the hands of Bobby Seale.

Brown was under no illusions about the magnitude of the task facing her in August 1974:

> A woman in the Black Power movement was considered, at best, irrelevant. A woman asserting herself was a pariah. A woman attempting the role of leadership was, to my proud black Brothers, making an alliance with the "counter-revolutionary, man-hating, lesbian, feminist white bitches." It was a violation of some Black Power principle that was left undefined. If a black woman assumed a role of leadership, she was said to be eroding black manhood, to be hindering the progress of the black race. She was an enemy of black people. I knew I would have to muster something mighty to manage the Black Panther Party. (Elaine Brown – *A Taste Of Power: A Black Woman's Story*, p. 357)

The fact that the 'something mighty' involved more emphasis on politics and community support rather than an increased level of violence was an impressive achievement. Reversing the seemingly unassailable 'Black Power principle', she also appointed women in key roles within the Party and, in the process, restored its financial stability. Under her leadership, the level of student attainment at the Panthers' Liberation School increased dramatically. By the time Newton came back from Cuba in 1977, Brown had made a second bid for election to Oakland City Council (this time getting 44% of the vote) and successfully managed the campaign of Lionel Wilson to become the city's first African-American mayor.

But things went rapidly downhill within months of Newton's return. After hearing that he had authorised the beating-up of Regina Davis, the administrator of the Liberation School, Brown quit the

Black Panthers. Membership began to dwindle and when, in 1982, it emerged that Newton had been embezzling the school's funds to feed his drug habit, it signalled the end for the Party. Newton was murdered in 1989; Brown continues to campaign on political, social and environmental issues.

★★★★★

Elaine Brown's rise to the top of the Black Panther Party was symptomatic of a new assertiveness among African-American women. To a large extent, the women's movement of the early 1970s had passed them by, partly because, as Brown points out, it was seen as a white initiative. More effective were the growing number of positive role models in a range of fields including entertainment and, specifically, music. While women had always played a leading role in African-American music, the stereotype of polite female subservience was ubiquitous in their songs, if not always in their personalities. The class of '74 were a separate breed.

Take, for example, Betty Davis. *They Say I'm Different* lived up to its name with a candour and sexual aggression never before seen from a female singer, and seldom since. In 1989 her former husband, Miles Davis, wrote:

> If Betty were singing today she'd be something like Madonna… She was the beginning of all that when she was singing as Betty Davis. She was just ahead of her time. (*Miles: The Autobiography*, p. 280)

She had introduced Miles to Sly Stone and to Jimi Hendrix (whose alleged affair with Betty led to their divorce) and there are elements of both artists in her work, which combined grinding funk with histrionic rock guitar. She also adopted their sartorial style – on the cover of *They Say I'm Different* she appears as a sci-fi warrior with a flamboyant, though skimpy, metallic costume and Afro hairdo.

But her lyrics copy no-one. 'Git In There' and 'Don't Call Her No Tramp' exude belligerence, 'Your Mama Wants You Back' is seething and sinister and 'He Was A Big Freak' itemises her partner's proclivities. The highlight, however, is 'Shoo-B-Doop And Cop Him' in which her predatory growling prefigures an orgasmic explosion of sound with wailing guitar and wild female backing singers.

Although there was no-one quite like Betty Davis, Yvonne Fair was in a similar mould. Her 'Funky Music Sho Nuff Turns Me On' was written by Barrett Strong and Norman Whitfield and had been previously recorded by The Temptations and Edwin Starr. But on Fair's pounding version, egged on by Marvin Gaye's interjections, she positively spits out the lyrics. It was only a short step from Davis and Fair to Tanya Winley's 'Vicious Rap', released the following year and a good candidate for the first-ever rap record.

Even orthodox soul singers were emboldened to make frank statements about their relationships. Though not liberated in the sense of championing independence from men (invariably just the opposite), such artists now had the freedom to express their emotions without the constraint of moral taboos. Millie Jackson epitomised the trend with *Caught Up*, a concept album describing a love triangle from the points of view of both wife and mistress. On the first side, Jackson plays the part of the latter and gives full rein to feelings of jealousy, spite and loathing. She opens with a full-blooded rendition of '(If Loving You Is Wrong) I Don't Want To Be Right' – originally written for Luther Ingram by Homer Banks, Raymond Jackson and Carl Hampton – followed by 'The Rap', six minutes of spoken narrative on the vicissitudes of being in love with a married man. Among the low-points are 'when the holidays roll around', since 'he has to stay home and play the part of the good and faithful husband'. As the narrative unfolds, the music ebbs and flows, and we finally come to the only advantages of her situation. 'When you're going with a married man, he can come over two or three times a week and give you a little bit' putting you ahead of the wife – 'cause once you marry one you don't get it but once a week'; in addition, 'you don't have to wash anybody's funky drawers but your own'. There is then a searing reprise of 'I Don't Want To Be Right' with wonderfully emotive playing by drummer Roger Hawkins and organist Barry Beckett; and the suite ends with entreaties to the wife ('All I Want Is A Fighting Chance') and the husband ('I'm Tired Of Hiding').

Side two, the wife's response, is equally feisty. Assuming the marriage is over, she begins with 'It's All Over But The Shouting' – 'but the shouting's gonna be done by me!' 'It's Easy Going' quashes any prospect of reconciliation and the Bobby Womack composition 'I'm Through Trying To Prove My Love To You' administers the coup de grace: 'I let you take my heart but I just can't let you take my soul'. In any case, she, too, has found someone new and now just wants to reminisce – cue Bobby Goldsboro's coming-of-age melodrama 'Summer (The First Time)'.

Written by Homer Banks and Carl Hampton, The Soul Children's *Friction* follows exactly the same theme as *Caught Up*, but with both a male and female lead singer, J Blackfoot and Shelbra Bennett, the group were able to pursue it from both perspectives. All bar one track are ballads with impassioned vocals from the principals. Blackfoot's input includes the chronicle of a souring marriage, 'What's Happening Baby' ('even the kids can see a change in you') and the agonising 'Just One Moment', while Bennett weighs in with the exquisite and moving 'I'll Be The Other Woman', and 'Love Makes It Right' – an extraordinary piece in which an apparently devout mother disapproves of her daughter's feelings for a married man on the basis that 'what God has joined together let no man put asunder' but then reassures her, 'If you really love him, love makes it right'!

Alongside these remarkable, riveting albums were a number of singles occupying similar territory. The songwriting team of Henderson Thigpen, James Banks (brother of Homer) and Eddie Marion came up with 'Woman To Woman' for Shirley Brown; it was Banks's idea to begin it with an extended rap in which Brown phones her rival to warn her off any attempt to steal her man. What results is a soul classic in which Brown's spoken and sung contributions are both utterly convincing. Subsequent Brown singles such as 'It Ain't No Fun'/'I've Got To Get On Without You' and 'It's Worth A Whippin'' are equally candid but, as the titles suggest, less triumphant. In Candi Staton's 'As Long As He Takes Care Of Home' (written, like *Caught Up*'s 'I'm Tired Of Hiding' and 'It's Easy Going', by Phillip Mitchell), the protagonist professes indifference to the attention her partner is attracting from another woman – 'if I were a man I would get some too' – provided he is 'taking care of business, taking care of home'.

But of all the 1974 releases proclaiming the new assertive, and raunchy, image of the African-American female singer, none was more influential than Labelle's 'Lady Marmalade'. To see a song about prostitution – especially one sung by women – become such a huge hit was a new experience in itself, never mind the group's spectacular space-age stage outfits. But it was the combination of the surging, imaginative production and the barely-controlled frenzy of Labelle's performance that turned the record into an immortal party anthem.

★★★★★

Written by Bob Crewe and Kenny Nolan, 'Lady Marmalade' was the opening track on Labelle's album *Nightbirds*, which otherwise was dominated by group member Nona Hendryx's compositions, such as the socially conscious 'Are You Lonely', the enigmatic ballad 'Nightbird', and 'Space Children', an engaging mix of rock, reggae, philosophy and sci-fi. *Nightbirds* was made in New Orleans under the supervision of Allen Toussaint and the backing musicians included the city's premier R&B group, The Meters, who, two months earlier, had released their own Toussaint-produced album, *Rejuvenation*.

In effect, *Rejuvenation* defines the New Orleans branch of funk: relaxed and buoyant, it is looser in feel than the tense, tight music pioneered by James Brown. Rock, soul, R&B, and aspects of jazz knit together on numbers like 'People Say', in which the rolling rhythm is punctuated by stabbing horns. Mardi Gras chants and an infectious hambone beat enliven 'Hey Pocky A-Way' while 'Africa' features the ferocious drumming, rooted in the city's marching bands, of Joseph Modeliste. But this music is devoid of egotism: even on the eleven-minute jam, 'It Ain't No Use', the emphasis, in accordance with New Orleans tradition, is on collective rather than individual improvisation.

Other varieties of funk to proliferate during the year included the vibrant 'Mighty Mighty', Earth, Wind & Fire's first hit; The Commodores' 'Machine Gun' with its rapid-fire clavinet; the persistent, insistent 'Do It ('Til You're Satisfied)' by BT Express; and The Ohio Players' rock-influenced 'Fire' which developed from a studio jam. Others blended funk with the new musical trend, disco. The Fatback Band's 'Keep On Steppin'' lays down an irresistible groove, distilling rhythm and melody into a simple, mesmeric five-note riff, while on 'Hollywood Swinging,' by Kool and The Gang, despite the prominence of guitar and bass, the beat is heavier. There are also echoes of Manu Dibango's 'Soul Makossa', an all-pervasive influence on the nascent disco scene since it hit the US singles chart in July 1973.

But disco really broke through in 1974, thanks largely to two more instrumentals. On 'Love's Theme' by The Love Unlimited Orchestra, conducted by Barry White, the synthesis of swirling strings and funky guitar conjures up visions of the good life – glamour with a beat – and it duly made number one on 9 February. MFSB's 'TSOP (The Sound Of Philadelphia)' employed the same techniques and achieved the same result, reaching the top spot on 16 March. Written by Kenny Gamble and Leon Huff, it heralded a vintage year for their label, Philadelphia International Records (PIR). For example The Three Degrees, who had sung back-up on 'TSOP', had a huge hit with 'When Will I See You Again', a Gamble-Huff composition with a Motownesque arrangement fronted by percussion and strings. A US number two, it reached number one in the UK, where the group also had hits with the brisk, catchy 'Year Of Decision' and 'Get Your Love Back' in which the interplay between lead singer Sheila Ferguson and the other two Degrees recalls The Supremes. The Intruders' '(Win Place Or Show) She's A Winner', with its racetrack sound effects, also performed better in Britain. At the start of the year, 'The Love I Lost (Part 1)' by Harold Melvin and The Blue Notes was riding high in both the US and UK; it was the first record to feature the disco style of drumming – played here by Earl Young – whereby hi-hat and snare knit together for additional propulsion. The rolling, soulful 'Satisfaction Guaranteed (Or Take Your Love Back)' was a fine follow-up but charted in the UK only, and the high-energy 'Love Shop' by People's Choice and Derek and Cyndi's elegant ' You Bring Out The Best In Me' were, inexplicably, hits in neither country.

Though most of PIR's output was of the boy-meets-girl variety, there were occasional forays into more socially aware territory. The O'Jays led the way with 'Put Your Hands Together' ('we've got to pray for all the people sleeping in the street') and 'For The Love Of Money', a Temptations-like slice of psychedelic soul which itemises the horrors of materialism. William DeVaughn's 'Be Thankful For What You Got' conveys the same message but more gently, with congas, vibes and organ enhancing the reflective feel.

Philly's non-PIR acts were flourishing, too. The Trammps, for instance, came up with the stomping 'Where Do We Go from Here?' and an up-tempo treatment of James F Hanley's 1934 composition 'Zing Went The Strings Of My Heart' with, just to underline its modernity, a plethora of 'it's alrights', 'huhs' and 'sock-it-to-mes'. The Tymes took a smoother approach but beefed up their sound with touches of rock and soul; the bright and breezy 'You Little Trustmaker' was a hit on both sides of the Atlantic, though the catchy 'Ms Grace' (written by Johanna Hall and her husband, future Congressman John) made number one in the UK but got nowhere in the States.

However in 1974 the biggest vocal group in Philadelphia, and indeed the US, were The Stylistics. Their formula of soaring falsetto voice (Russell Thompkins) plus sentimental ballad was not unique, even in their home town. Eddie Holman's 'Hey There Lonely Girl' pioneered it back in 1969, its reappearance in the UK chart in October 1974 serving as a reminder. The unjustly neglected 'Sideshow' by Blue Magic (with vocalist Ted 'Wizard' Mills) was in the same vein. But The Stylistics had the advantage of a supporting cast well placed to exploit their talents: producer Thom Bell, arranger/conductor Van McCoy and writers Hugo Peretti and Luigi Creatore, for whose New York-based Avco Records the group recorded. The year began with the uncharacteristically animated 'Rockin' Roll Baby' but with 'You Make Me Feel Brand New', a number two hit in both the US and UK, they hit their stride. Written by Thom Bell and Linda Creed, it veers close to saccharine but is redeemed by the clever juxtaposition of Thompkins and the deeper-voiced Airrion Love. The follow-up, 'Let's Put It All Together', fared less well commercially but is the better record: the group's performance of this simple but poignant ballad (by Peretti, Creatore and David Weiss) is immaculate, McCoy's orchestration – with glockenspiel to the fore – subtle but effective.

While the falsetto of Russell Thompkins was at one end of the romantic spectrum, the gruff baritone voice of LA-based Barry White was at the other; Thompkins symbolised innocence and purity, White exuded macho sexuality. And 1974 was the zenith of both their careers. White released only two singles during the year but both were enormous, in every sense. 'Can't Get Enough Of Your Love, Babe' opens with a melodramatic monologue on the subject of love (or 'lurve' as it became in the parodies that followed) but swiftly hits a crisp but relentless disco beat while White's voice (doubled tracked for extra emotional impact) thunders over the shimmering string arrangement. 'Can't Get Enough Of Your Love, Babe' reached the top of the American singles chart on 21 September; 'You're The First, The Last, My Everything', the similar but even more insistent follow-up, made only number two but went one better in the UK on 7 December.

Meanwhile, over in New York, Meco Monardo and Tony Bongiovi had formed the Disco Corporation of America, with Gloria Gaynor as one of their first signings. Together with Jay Ellis and Harold Wheeler, they produced her cover version of The Jackson Five's 'Never Can Say Goodbye', thus creating one of the classic records of the disco era. Another DCA production, Al Downing's 'I'll Be Holding On', was equally danceable if not quite as successful. By the end of a breathless year, disco was sufficiently well-established to spawn a pastiche – the Bob Crewe and Kenny Nolan composition 'Get Dancing', by Disco Tex and The Sex-O-Lettes – just in time for the Christmas party season.

★★★★★

At a time of so many new developments in African-American music, there was still a place for the long-established performers – and styles. Bobby Bland, for example, had been in the business for a quarter of a century but could still turn out majestic, brooding records like 'Ain't No Love In The Heart Of the City' and 'I Wouldn't Treat A Dog (The Way You Treated Me)', while Don Covay, whose career had begun in 1957 as a support act for Little Richard, released the pulsating dance-floor filler, 'It's Better To Have And Don't Need (Than Need And Don't Have)'. Billy Preston's tenure with Richard came five years later but by 1974, having worked with a wide range of artists including The Beatles, was a popular solo attraction: his gospel-flavoured 'Nothing From Nothing', a US number one in October, positively exudes *joie de vivre*.

Two other R&B survivors from the early sixties were still at the top of their game. Isaac Hayes was now a noted film composer and the soundtrack to *Truck Turner* (in which he also played the starring role) is one of his most compelling. Originally intended as a studio warm-up, Bobby Womack's driving, soulful remake of his 1962 hit, 'Looking For A Love', became the centrepiece of a whole album, *Looking For*

A Love Again, though new compositions like the complex yet funky 'You're Welcome, Stop On By' and the pacy, incisive 'I Don't Wanna Be Hurt By Ya Love Again' are equally impressive.

The 17 May edition of NBC's *The Midnight Special* saw the one-off reunion of Shirley and Lee, whose 'Let The Good Times Roll' was one of the big rock and roll hits of 1956. Twelve years later, Shirley Goodman went on to make the outstanding soul single 'Kid Games And Nursery Rhymes'/'Too Much, Too Soon' in the company of Brenton Wood; now in 1974 she again switched styles successfully by recording, under the name Shirley & Company, the disco smash 'Shame, Shame, Shame'.

Oscar Brown Jr, as noted above, was one of the few African-American singers of the early 1960s to make overt political comment in his songs. The funk-flavoured *Fresh*, produced by soul veteran Jerry Butler, is his withering critique of contemporary society, from the horrors of 'Ghetto Scene' to 'Bull "Bleep"', an attack on censorship inspired by the 'expletive deleted' sections of the Watergate transcripts. Charles Bevel's 'Sally B White' lambasts the upwardly-mobile protagonist for betraying her race and 'Let's Get Drunk (And Be Somebody)' is an uproarious satire on binge drinking.

The Isley Brothers, who emerged at the same time as Brown, offered a very different but equally stimulating blend of past and present. *Live It Up*, released on 20 August, builds on their groundbreaking *3 + 3* album of the previous year and if anything is even more exciting: the title track, powered by a heavy beat, howling guitar and dramatic chord changes, fairly flies off the turntable. 'Midnight Sky (Part I and II)' is not far behind, while contrast comes from the ballads 'Lover's Eye' and 'Hello It's Me', both of which showcase the plaintive, impassioned voice of Ronald Isley.

The Isleys' former label, Motown, continued to churn out the hits despite its relocation to LA, though it was now espousing disco with releases like The Jackson Five's 'Dancing Machine', featuring a scintillating Arthur Wright arrangement, and the dynamic 'Boogie

Down' by Eddie Kendricks. The 'old' Motown sound was, however, still in evidence. The UK re-issue of Jimmy Ruffin's 1966 hit 'What Becomes Of The Brokenhearted' did even better business second time around and former label stalwart Johnny Bristol recaptured some of the magic of the halcyon days with his album *Hang On In There Baby.* There was also something of Barry White about it, with its spoken introductions and tough-but-tender lyrics, but the nine songs, all by Bristol himself, have an appeal of their own. The mixture of intimacy and urgency that permeates the title track – a Top Ten hit in both the US and UK – is, for example, completely absorbing, while the boy-band favourite 'Love Me For A Reason' and the nod to women's liberation, 'Woman, Woman', show other sides of his personality.

Southern soul music was also alive and well, particularly when in the hands, or voice, of female singers. Even the ailing Stax Records released a crop of classics, including Margie Alexander's 'Keep On Searching', a lively ballad written and produced by Clarence Carter; Veda Brown's ultra-slow and anguished 'Don't Start Lovin' Me (If You're Gonna Stop)'; 'Funny' by Hot Sauce, featuring the searing vocals of Rhonda Washington; and Inez Foxx's 'Circuit's Overloaded', written by the team responsible for Shirley Brown's 'Woman To Woman'.

Stax's place on the pantheon was, however, being usurped by the rival Memphis label Hi Records, as the Ann Peebles album *I Can't Stand The Rain* amply demonstrates. Producer Willie Mitchell was best known for his work with Al Green, of which the beaty but graceful 'Sha-La-La (Makes Me Happy)', a hit on both sides of the Atlantic in November, was a prime example. Here he creates a typically relaxed but sharp sound, placing drums in the foreground and deftly integrating horns and strings at key moments. The playing from the studio musicians is faultless and the material (mainly written by Peebles and her husband, Donald Bryant), exceptional.

As for Peebles, her poise and understated emotion serve only to intensify her impact. John Lennon called 'I Can't Stand The

Rain' itself 'the greatest record ever' and it is hard to disagree with his assessment; it starts with the eerie sound of timbales simulating raindrops, whereupon Peebles, unaccompanied, mournfully intones the title phrase before the track advances at a measured but inexorable pace. But the rest of the album is of commensurate quality, especially 'I'm Gonna Tear Your Playhouse Down', a song of revenge rendered devastating by Peebles's iron control.

Betty Wright's punchy 'Shoo-Rah! Shoo-Rah!' was written by Allen Toussaint but recorded in Miami, now a favoured venue for African-American music of all types, from the moody, authoritative 'Let's Straighten It Out' by Latimore to George McCrae's infectious 'Rock Your Baby' which spent three weeks at the top of the UK singles chart during the summer. Chicago, on the other hand, was declining in importance though The Chi-Lites continued to fly the flag with the bouncy 'Too Good To Be Forgotten', the B-side of which, 'There Will Never Be Any Peace (Until God Is At The Conference Table)' berates politicians and their worthless plans.

'Everlasting Love' had been a 1967 hit for Robert Knight and seven years later Carl Carlton's spirited revival was also recorded in Nashville, the hometown of its composers, Buzz Cason and Mac Gayden. Yet despite the success of both records there was no influx of African-American singers to the Athens of the South. They were much more likely to gravitate to LA, undisputed home of commercial pop. As well as the number ones already mentioned by The Love Unlimited Orchestra, Barry White, Stevie Wonder and Billy Preston, it was also where chart-toppers by Al Wilson ('Show And Tell') and The Hues Corporation ('Rock The Boat') were recorded – not to mention those by white artists.

One band who found fame and fortune there were the Chicago outfit Rufus. Though their debut album drew a blank, their two 1974 releases, *Rags To Rufus* and *Rufusized* both made the US Top Ten; the former also yielded two hit singles, the Stevie Wonder composition 'Tell Me Something Good' and 'You Got The Love', written by Ray

Parker Jr and the group's singer, Chaka Khan. Their mix of rock, funk and reggae was entirely contemporary but as such was of absolutely no interest to a horde of soul music fanatics in the distant north-west of England.

CHAPTER 4

Avante, Camarada!

Of the right-wing dictators to emerge in Western Europe during the 1920s and 1930s, António de Oliveira Salazar is the least discussed. Yet he ruled his country, Portugal, for 36 years, far longer than Franco (26), Mussolini (22) and Hitler (a mere twelve) did theirs. Unlike the latter two, he did not meet a violent and premature death, nor did he promote a supremacist ideology; indeed he found Hitler's notions of racial purity repugnant. But perhaps the main reason for his relative neglect is that he did not engage in empire-building but focussed his attention on his own country, and its existing colonies. Although he supported Franco and the Nationalists in their struggle against the Republicans, no Portuguese troops were involved in the Spanish Civil War. During World War II Portugal remained neutral.

Yet within the country, he brooked no opposition. In 1933 he set up the Polícia de Vigilância e de Defesa do Estado (PVDE), a secret police agency modelled on the Gestapo; they were succeeded in 1945 by the even more notorious PIDE (Polícia Internacional e de Defesa do Estado), who indulged in summary arrest, torture and murder. But Salazar was not a stereotypical tyrant. He admired, for example, the work of the Brazilian writer Gilberto Freyre, whose *Casa-Grande E Senzala* (translated into English as *The Masters And The Slaves*) was published in the year the PVDE was formed. Freyre celebrated the racial mix in Brazilian society resulting from the slave trade and extolled the virtues of the Portuguese colonisers in a doctrine known as lusotropicalism.

Salazar was attracted to lusotropicalism and took the view that Portugal, as the oldest and in his eyes the most humane European colonising power, was indivisible from its overseas dependencies. When, in the late 1950s, Britain, France and Belgium began the process of granting independence to their African colonies, the Portuguese were unyielding. Their intransigence was perhaps unsurprising; in 1415 they had been the very first European country to get a foothold in Africa and had spent the next five hundred years seizing huge swathes of land in the east and west of the continent. They had also made conquests in South America, the Indian subcontinent and the Far East; although Brazil had been lost more than a century before, at the turn of decade they still ruled East Timor and the enclaves of Goa (India) and Macau (China).

But in 1961 Portugal's status as a world power was severely threatened. Trouble had been brewing in Goa since the early 1950s, when Salazar had refused to cede the territories of Dadra and Nagar Haveli, Daman and Diu and Goa (the latter three known collectively as Goa) to newly-independent India. In 1954 a local uprising ejected the Portuguese from Dadra and Nagar Haveli and in November 1961 President Nehru ordered the army into the much more prestigious Goa which was annexed by India shortly afterwards. Such humiliations were keenly felt by Salazar who regarded the colonies as part of Portugal itself and made him doubly determined to hang on to the African dependencies of Angola, Portuguese Guinea and Mozambique.

There were already serious problems in Angola. In January 1961 a group of peasants from the Bakongo tribe working in the northern part of the country refused to continue the cotton harvest, burned the crop and attacked Portuguese traders. Salazar's response was swift and uncompromising: in the bombing raids that followed over 7,000 Africans were killed. On 4 February there was an invasion by rebels from neighbouring Congo, many of whom were Bakongo tribesmen (the nineteenth century European land grab had arbitrarily cut across tribal boundaries so the frontiers between countries had little meaning for the indigenous population). Attacks were made on the prison at São João and on white settlements in the coffee-growing Carmona Province which was as big as Portugal itself. That there was unrest in Angola came as no surprise to Salazar – despite his protestations of beneficence, the African citizens of the Portuguese colonies were oppressed and heavily discriminated against. But what did take him aback was the strength of the revolt – replicated the following year in Portuguese Guinea and, in 1964, in Mozambique. The Portuguese armed forces spent the next ten years attempting to quell the rebellions in all three countries; taken together, these conflicts are known as the Portuguese Colonial War.

On the face of it there were many similarities between this War and that being waged by the USA over 5,000 miles away in Vietnam. In both cases the invading army contained a large percentage of conscripts – often young people from an inner city urban environment far removed both geographically and culturally from the theatre of war to which they were now transplanted. Unsurprisingly, cynicism ran deep and many wondered what they, and their country, were doing there at all. Given such circumstances, it was hugely to their credit that they fought as courageously as they did. As for the insurgents, they too often included men who had been press-ganged into service by threats of violence to themselves or their families.

Environmentally, the two conflicts had a great deal in common. Both were guerrilla wars in which the locals exploited their familiarity with the terrain to attack, and hide from, the enemy. There were even physical resemblances: northern Angola, for instance, was like many regions of Vietnam, with its dense forests, streams and backwaters used by the insurgents for transport and concealment. One of the key factors in both wars was the need to get the support of the local population; indeed, for the guerrillas this was of greater importance than gaining territory. The winning combination was military *and* political success. In both cases the reasons for the war, and the chances of a positive outcome, were seriously questioned at home with the strong impression, at least among the better educated, that their governments had bitten off much more than they could chew.

Of course there were differences, chief of which was the relative amount of media attention. In contrast to Vietnam, which attracted a monumental amount of coverage, the Portuguese Colonial War barely made the news at all – essentially because the USA had no direct involvement. The Portuguese public were astonished when, in 1974, they finally discovered what had been going on for the previous decade. Unlike the American campaign the Portuguese effort was, in addition, poorly planned and under-resourced, with few helicopters – essential for pursuing guerrillas into the bush – and outdated equipment. Some of the rifles in use dated back to the nineteenth century. Conscripts served for a two-year period, double that of their American counterparts. Portuguese forces also faced enormous logistical problems. Angola is twice the size of France, Mozambique twice the size of California and the distance between Lisbon and the Angolan capital, Luanda, is the same as from Washington to Berlin.

The Portuguese Army, however, were by no means all sent from Lisbon. There were, for example, a substantial number of local recruits, some from families who had not been in Africa long; during the 1950s Salazar had positively encouraged emigration to the colonies. The remainder were indigenous Africans who, owing to their bravery and local knowledge, comprised some of the best soldiers in the Army. They were also fiercely patriotic (indeed, even the rebels retained some ties to the 'home' country, following, for example, the fortunes of Portugal's football team during the 1974 World Cup). The Portuguese were also boosted by the support of other European nations, NATO and the USA. For their part, the rebels were assisted by China, Cuba, North Vietnam and in particular the Eastern Bloc: in Portuguese Guinea, Russia provided everything that was required by the PAIGC (Partido Africano de Independência de Guiné e Cabo Verde).

By far the smallest of the three colonies, Portuguese Guinea (renamed Guinea-Bissau in 1974 to distinguish it from Guinea, its neighbour to the south and east), was also the most difficult for Portugal to subdue. Not only were conditions unfavourable – a combination of jungle and swamp covered almost the whole country – but hostile forces from Senegal and Guinea made frequent and effective cross-border raids. Fearful of the international opprobrium that would accompany any attempt to pursue them, the Portuguese had to stay and fight it out and for a time their star general, António de Spínola, had rolled back the PAIGC. However the difficulties involved in sustaining any kind of ascendancy convinced him that the Portuguese Colonial War could not be won. As a result he wrote *Portugal E O Futuro (Portugal And The Future)*, published in early 1974 and hugely influential – on the Army, on the population as a whole, and on Marcello Caetano, who had taken over from Salazar six years earlier.

Spínola's vision was for gradual change, whereby all three countries would receive their independence in a managed process and perhaps maintain friendly relations with Portugal. His junior officers, on the other hand, had something much more radical in mind.

★★★★★

Disillusion with the Portuguese government was not confined to the Army. It was becoming evident to everyone that the War was unsustainable: in 1971 some 40% of the entire national budget was spent on hostilities in Africa, and this in the second poorest nation in Europe. Their forces numbered seven times those of the USA in Vietnam and although that War remained uppermost in the consciousness of the world's major powers, those who bothered to keep abreast with events in Portugal's African colonies were growing increasingly concerned.

Within Portugal itself, *canções de intervenção* – political songs –

had been an important means of protest for the civilian population since 1933, when Salazar created the *estado novo* (new state) and a constitution prohibiting all opposition. In some respects they may seem to complement the traditional Portuguese song-form, *fado* (fate), a mournful, emotional idiom specialising in tales of lost love and betrayal. Indeed *fado* – along with the urban pop music of Brazil and France – was a major influence on *canções de intervenção.* Yet it became increasingly associated with the totalitarian regime: during the *estado novo,* Portugal became known as the country of *fado, futebol* and Fátima – the location of the miraculous apparition of the Virgin Mary in 1917 (though Salazar apparently detested the first two). According to musicologist Raul Viera Nery, Amalia Rodrigues, the superstar of *fado*, was suspected of working for the PIDE (*blitz.sapo.pt/25-abril-e-o-fado-sobreviveu-a-revoluca).*

Nevertheless many singers were conversant with both genres. One such was Adriano Maria Correia Gomes de Oliveira (known simply as Adriano) who was born on 9 April 1942 and died of a stroke 40 years later. Adriano was an adherent of *fado de Coimbra*, a genre created by the students of that city, but he also composed numerous *canções de intervenção*, resulting in persecution by the PIDE. As member of the Communist Party, he wrote lyrics to the poems of Manuel Alegre, a prominent political activist. Alegre had served as a conscript in Angola where he had been jailed for participating in a mutiny; after a period of exile in Algiers, he returned to Portugal and was elected to Parliament. He subsequently stood in the Presidential elections of 2006 and 2011.

Other notable exponents of *canções de intervenção* included Luís Cília, Francisco Fanhais, Sérgio Godhino and José Mário Branco. The latter was pursued into France by the PIDE as early as 1963; Fanhais, a former priest, was banned from both teaching and singing in 1970, while Godhino's album, *Os Sobreviventes* (*The Survivors*), was suppressed immediately following its release in 1971. Cília, who was born in Angola, was the composer of 'Avante, Camarada!' ('Forward,

Comrade!'), the unofficial anthem of the Portuguese Communist Party first recorded by Luísa Basto in Moscow in 1967. To coincide with the revolutionary mood sweeping Portugal, Basto made another version in 1974 and recorded it for a third time seven years later. None of these artists played a direct part in the revolution of April 1974 – they were all abroad. But Adriano was involved, as was the most eminent singer of *canções de intervenção*, José (sometimes known as Zeca) Afonso.

As a child Afonso lived in both Angola and Mozambique and like Adriano studied at the University of Coimbra: his first record, *Fados De Coimbra*, was released in 1959. For the next fifteen years his political message grew louder and he was constantly harassed by the authorities, culminating in a spell in prison in spring 1973. A year later he was sharing the stage at the Lisbon Colosseum with other notable left-wing singers, musicians and activists. The event ended with a mass rendition of 'Grândola, Vila Morena', an Afonso song about brotherhood between workers. A few weeks later, on 25 April 1974, the same song was broadcast on the national radio station, Rádio Renascença, the signal that the Portuguese Revolution – the Carnation Revolution – had begun.

The idea for the signal came from military personnel who had attended the Colosseum concert; now, to celebrate what had been a bloodless coup, soldiers walked through Lisbon with red carnations in their gun barrels – an image that was relayed across the world and gave the revolution its name. Thus despite the sterling efforts of Afonso and his confreres, it was the military who had brought about the downfall of the Caetano regime and a dictatorship that had lasted for over 40 years. As we have seen, Spínola's book *Portugal E O Futuro* was the catalyst; in his memoirs Caetano recalled,

> On 18 February [1974], I received a copy of *Portugal And The Future* with a kind dedication from the author… when I closed the book I had understood that the military coup, which I could sense had been

> coming, was now inevitable. (Quoted in *Revolutionary Rehearsals*, edited by Colin Barker, p. 87)

Caetano resolved to deal with Spínola only, believing him to be the driving force behind the coup and on 25 April itself passed the responsibility for governing the country to him, as the representative of the MFA (Movimento das Forças Armadas: the Armed Forces Movement). But this was something of a misconception. The MFA was headed by two majors, Vitor Alves and Otela Saraivo de Carvalho, and two captains, Vasco Lourenço and Salgueiro Maia (it was Maia who instructed the government to resign and Caetano to surrender) – a clear indication that the coup was engineered not by the Army's top brass but by its junior officers.

Their militancy resulted from a number of interrelated factors. Due to their proximity to the rank and file, they saw first-hand the conscripts' disillusionment with the poor pay, long tours of duty, shoddy equipment and hostile conditions. They were also more sensitive to antipathy to the war back in Portugal – the Army was constantly getting blamed for its failure in an unwinnable war and in the last call-up before the coup only half of the conscripts had even turned up. During their own visits home on leave, the junior officers felt ashamed to wear their uniforms in public.

There were further humiliations within the Army itself. In order to remedy a shortage of trained officers, the Army Minister approved Decree 353/73 which enabled conscripted officers to gain promotion alongside regulars; the negative reaction to this measure provoked a partial reversal which guaranteed the status of officers but above the rank of captain only. This was a botched response that had the effect of alienating just about everybody. As Al J Venter has written in his comprehensive survey of the Portuguese Colonial War,

> The latent resentment which gradually built up to scalding point in the officer corps was a combination of bruised national pride and

> wounded professional vanity, an explosive mixture of sentiments which the Portuguese military establishment shared with revolutionary soldiers in Egypt and other Third World Countries. (*Portugal's Guerrilla Wars In Africa*, p. 219)

But perhaps the overriding factor behind the coup was the political orientation of the MFA. Alves had held left-wing convictions even as a cadet and Carvalho was, according to Venter (*ibid*., p. 45), 'both an insurrectionist and an anarchist' and wanted a full Communist takeover in Portugal; he was later imprisoned for plotting against the government he had helped establish. Both had served their country with distinction, Alves in south-east Angola and Carvalho in Portuguese Guinea, as had other members of the MFA; indeed patriotism was what drove them towards revolution.

Reaction to the coup was initially muted; there were fears that basics such as food and petrol would run short. But the slogan 'The MFA are with the people and the people are with the MFA' had a galvanising effect and before long mass celebrations were under way. Civilians mingled with soldiers in the crowds which flowed towards the Lisbon Flower Market, one of the key meeting places and source of the red carnation emblem. Government agents were pursued, the names of streets and bridges were changed, and Caetano fled to Brazil. Before long, however, the question arose: what next?

As the MFA had planned, the National Salvation Junta was formed on 26 April following an announcement by the new President, António de Spínola. Given the conflicting positions of the participants, this could only be a temporary fix. On 15 May the first Provisional Government was assembled with Spínola's choice, the moderate Adelino da Palma Carlos, as Prime Minister. In July, however, Carlos was replaced by the more radical Colonel Vasco Gonçalves, a Communist sympathiser who within a year had nationalised the country's banks and insurance companies. By the end of September Spínola himself had gone, unhappy that the independence of the colonies remained unresolved and worried at the governmental drift to the left. Yet in fact, as in the aftermath of all revolutions, there were those who felt that the new regime was too moderate. For example, the Communist Party, now well represented in government, found itself in opposition to both the striking shipyard workers' union and the Maoist MRPP (Movement to Reorganise the Party of the Proletariat). When Spínola departed the Junta collapsed and a third Provisional Government was formed with Francisco da Costa Gomes as President.

Meanwhile the revolutionary fervour felt by Portugal's composers and singers was beginning to cool, though many wished to comment on the momentous events of April 1974. Now, of course, there was no need to conceal the real meaning of their lyrics in a cloak of clandestine references. Yet by tradition Portuguese music is poetic, crammed with metaphors to the point of surrealism and so in many respects this new phase in its history was a continuation of the last. José Afonso's album *Coro Dos Tribunais (The Chorus Of The Courts)* – recorded in London on 30 November and 8 December and released later that month – exemplifies the transition.

Understandably the mood is predominantly positive: the extensive use of African percussion gives an animated, lively feel and the lyrics, though often opaque, suggest that good times are on the way. The cheery 'O Homem Voltou' ('The Man Returned'), for instance, hails the restoration of civilisation to Portugal and 'A Presença Das Formigas' ('The Presence Of The Ants') celebrates the triumph of the workers. The catchy 'O Que Faz Falta' ('What Makes Failure') provides an oblique definition of success while 'Eu Marchava De Dia E De Noite' ('I Marched Day And Night') demonstrates that it is invariably hard won. The latter has words by Bertolt Brecht translated into Portuguese by Luís Francisco Rebello, as does the title piece which bookends the album. Here the theme – the *in*justice of the justice system – is more sombre, a reminder that Afonso has not entirely lost his bite. Similarly 'Lá No Xepangara' ('There In Xepangara'), though superficially jolly with its bright tempo and Mozambican backing singers, is an ironic account of the joys of living in the bush. The album was greeted with hostility by some critics who yearned for the zeal of Afonso's pre-revolutionary output, but for everyone else it is an attractive, balanced showcase for his talents – rhythmically rich, lyrically clever and beautifully rendered in his delicate, quivering vocal style. Unfortunately, however, the immediate future for Portugal was not quite as untroubled as he had hoped.

★★★★★

Angola, Portuguese Guinea (now called Guinea-Bissau, after its capital) and Mozambique were, and are, very different countries in terms of size, terrain and culture. They are also geographically distant: Bissau is almost as far west as it is possible to be in Africa and some 2,500 miles north-west of Angola's capital, Luanda. Maputo (formerly Lourenço Marques) lies 1,800 miles south-east of Luanda. Yet following the end of the Portuguese Colonial War, Marxist governments came to power in all three.

This was no surprise in Mozambique and Portuguese Guinea. FRELIMO (Frente Libertaçã de Moçambique) had been the principal guerrilla group in the former and received substantial help from Tanzania to the north – indeed most of FRELIMO's supplies, predominantly from the Soviet Union and China, came in via Tanzania's largest city, Dar Es Salaam. After the War, FRELIMO faced an armed insurrection from rebels supported by Rhodesia and South Africa and hostilities continued for seventeen years; FRELIMO, however, was triumphant and has continued in power up to the present day.

In Portuguese Guinea, there was a pact of mutual support between the PAIGC and the more moderate FLING (Front de Lutte de l'Indépendance Nationale de Guinée), based in Senegal (hence the French name) and backed by the USA. As we have seen, the PAIGC armoury was fully stocked by the Soviet Union and its forces were well trained and highly effective, according to Venter 'streets ahead of anything in Africa' (*ibid.*, p.308). So when the War was over it had little trouble in casting the FLING aside. Apart from a period out of office in the early 21st century, it has dominated the country's politics ever since.

In Angola, on the other hand, no fewer than three guerrilla groups were vying for supremacy:

- The **MPLA** (Movimento Popular de Libertação de Angola), one of the most established guerrilla organisations in Africa. Founded in 1956 following a crack-down by the PIDE, it moved its headquarters to Conakry, then Paris and finally to nearby Congo-Brazzaville. Its military wing, the FAPLA, was much feared both by local civilians and the Portuguese Army.
- The **FNLA** (Frente Nacional de Libertação de Angola) – formerly the UPA – a centre-right group championed by a range of (mainly Western) organisations.
- **UNITA** (União Nacional Para a Independência Total de Angola), supported by South Africa and the US, though it co-operated with far-left groups during the War, including the MPLA.

Following the Carnation Revolution and the consequent cessation of hostilities, these three groups were supposed to get together to form a transitional government. The MPLA, however, decided to go it alone and seized Luanda in August 1975. Although the FNLA took over the north and UNITA the central and southern areas of the country, control of the capital was crucial and Agostinho Neto, the leader of the MPLA, declared the independence of Angola on 11 November 1975, becoming the country's first President in the process. But this was by no means the end of the country's troubles and conflict continued between the MPLA and the other groups. Neto also faced opposition from within his own ranks. Despite introducing a Marxist one-party state Neto was not considered sufficiently radical by some of his colleagues, including, in particular, the Interior Minister, Nito Alves. On 21 May 1977 Alves was expelled from the MPLA and six days later, with the support of the Angolan Communist Party, attempted a coup which was ruthlessly put down; over the following two years some 20,000 of his supporters, or alleged supporters, were massacred.

*****

Throughout the whole period of the Portuguese Colonial War, Angolan music flourished. Indeed some writers, notably Marissa Moorman, Professor of African History at the University of Indiana, view it as a golden era. In her notes to the CD *Angola Soundtrack* (Analog Africa AACD 069) Moorman explains how, during this time, the country's music became less reliant on that of Portugal and more open to external influences, especially from the USA and Cuba; so it was not uncommon to find in the same band traditional instruments alongside those from the West. In addition, Portugal's (belated) programme of educational and social reforms aimed at fostering loyalty to the 'home country' had the opposite effect of reinforcing indigenous Angolan culture. With the country on the brink of revolution, this process came to a head in 1974, a year of plenty for Angolan music in terms of quality, quantity and variety.

The leading bands at the time included Os Jovens do Prenda ('The Youth of Prenda'), Os Kiezos ('The Brooms') and Os Bongos, who also acted as a backing group for various singers. All three made outstanding records during the year. Os Jovens' 'Lamento De Mãe', for instance, incorporates clever changes of tempo and features the fluent guitar of Zé Keno. 'Ilha Virgem' is even better, an elegant instrumental composed by Keno's replacement, Baião. Fresh from the Portuguese Army, Baião had written the piece while sitting alone atop a mountain surrounded by beautiful scenery and intended its gentle cadences to contrast with the horrors of the War. The spirited 'Princeza Rita' by Os Keizos was one of the Angolan hits of the year and it is not hard to see why: the lively arrangement unfolds to reveal Marito's irrepressible guitar and a percussion interlude featuring Vaté Costa on maracas and chanting. Costa again leads the way on the galloping 'Comboio' in which the *samba* rhythm is hammered home by a repetitive riff and a long, animated guitar solo.

Os Bongos, as their name suggests, specialised in frantic instrumentals: 'Kazucuta' benefits from shimmering guitar and an exciting percussion break while 'Pachanga Maria', written by guitarist Boto Trindade, combines Portuguese and Cuban elements to powerful effect. They also feature on Gimba's 'Otjikenlu Ya Yndunduma', recorded live in front of an enthusiastic audience on 31 August 1974: anthem-like in structure, it is a direct appeal to General Spínola to show compassion for Angola.

The changing face of Angolan music is reflected in two contrasting releases. The slow-paced 'Pala Ku Nu Abesa Ô Muxima' by Carlos Lamartine, with its incisive trumpet obbligatos by Nando Tambarino, encourages Angolans to promote their own culture, while Santos Júnior's 'N'Gui Banza Mama' combines melodic influences from Western pop with the rhythm section sound of James Brown. It was recorded in 1971-72, just after Júnior's stint in the Portuguese Army. Both Lamartine and Júnior became members of the band Kissanguela, (sometimes spelt Kisangela), founded in 1974 by José Agostinho as part of the MPLA's youth movement. They were joined by the accomplished guitarist Nito who had played with the band Africa Ritmos before serving in the Army.

Another veteran to go over to the rebels was Mamukueno (real name: José Matias). His 'Rei Do Palhetinho' is a thinly-veiled piece of political comment which contrasts the excellence of the local wine with the inferior Portuguese product. Musically, it is equally compelling with an irresistible Latin rhythm, urgent percussion and sinuous guitar by Mamukeuno's nephew, Baião, who – alongside his colleagues from Os Jovens do Prenda – also appears on 'Kamaka' by Taborda Guedes. This stately, soulful song describes the sorrow experienced by the family of the eponymous freedom fighter who died in prison in 1943; again, however, it is a transparent comment on the present.

A paean to female beauty, Sofia Rosa's ballad 'Kalumba' may also have a double meaning: certainly the passion in his vocal delivery suggests he could be referring to Angola. Whatever the case, Rosa was killed by UNITA when they captured his home town of Lobito in 1975. Sadly he was not the only musician to perish in the aftermath of the Portuguese Colonial War. Many, such as David Zé, Urbano de Castro and Artur Nunes were dedicated members of the MPLA and specialised in songs of freedom and independence. However they made the fatal mistake of supporting Nito Alves and were all murdered in the massacre of 27 May 1977.

As for Kissanguela, they accompanied the FAPLA in its advance to victory and in 1976 were rewarded with a trip to Conakry alongside President Neto. Conscious of the international success of African performers such as Manu Dibango and Osibisa, they also began to develop alternatives to the prevalent *samba* form. But in 1977 Kissanguela also fell under suspicion; the group was disbanded and Agostinho imprisoned, never to sing again.

★★★★★

The conclusion of the Portuguese Colonial War in April 1974 signalled not only the collapse of Europe's oldest dictatorship, nor the decline of a once great world power. It was the beginning of the end of white rule in Africa, a process completed with the release of Nelson Mandela sixteen years later. Their newly-found liberation did not, however, immediately improve the lot of the citizens of Guinea-Bissau, Angola and Mozambique, particularly in the latter two cases where bloody conflict between factions continued for some time. Yet the situation was often no better when an African ruler was toppled by his own countrymen, as occurred on the other side of the continent some five months later.

Few outside Ethiopia could have predicted the downfall of Emperor Haile Selassie. In terms of both longevity and reputation he had no equals in Africa and few, if any, internationally. By 1974 he had presided over his country for some 58 years, first as regent and then, from 1930, as Emperor. During that time Ethiopia had made huge strides forward with the abolition of slavery, improvements to its infrastructure and the establishment of a well-equipped and professional army. But it was Haile Selassie the man who had attracted so much admiration – indeed, as far as Rastafarians were concerned, he was Haile Selassie the God, whose pre-regnal name Ras Tafari gave the Jamaican cult its name. Within Ethiopia, too, he was deified as the direct descendant of Solomon and Sheba and his divine right to rule was enshrined both within the Orthodox Church and the country's constitution. To the outside, secular world he was the hero who had stood up against Mussolini's invasion of his country in 1935 and the statesman who had hosted, and chaired, the first meeting of the Organisation of African Unity in 1963.

But his exalted status brought with it absolute power that bordered on despotism. He ruled his country in an imperious and autocratic manner and summarily dismissed any resistance to his decrees. His annexation of Eritrea in 1962, for example, was accompanied by the brutal suppression of all opposition, including the bombing of villages and reprisals against individuals. It may be argued that Haile Selassie's attitudes and actions stemmed from an extreme form of patriotism, but it was his very remoteness from those whose interests he professed to serve that would bring about his demise.

In the late 1960s the young people of Ethiopia had got wind of the cultural changes sweeping the USA and Europe. Student unrest, fuelled by the left-wing intelligentsia, became a regular occurrence while Western fashions engulfed the streets of Addis Ababa to the extent that it became known as 'Swinging Addis', a city celebrating all the symbols of the era: beehive and Afro hairdos, flares, miniskirts, the Pill. Central to it all was an outpouring of musical creativity that saw an unprecedented 500 singles and 30 albums released in less than ten years. Over 20% of these were issued on just one label, Amha Records, between 1969 and 1975. Its founder, Amha Eshèté, was a pioneer who openly defied an imperial decree dating back to 1948 which gave a monopoly to the national Aghèr Feqer Mahbèr (The Love of Country Association) in matters of recording, releasing and distributing music. The result was the eradication of pop and jazz in favour of an unadulterated diet of officially-sanctioned offerings from the bands of the Imperial Body Guard, the army, the police, or other such institutions.

It is probable that most of the musicians comprising these outfits chafed against the stultifying effect such restrictions had on their creativity; certainly many of them seized the opportunities for emancipation offered by Amha Eshèté. Formerly known as the 'Ethiopian Elvis', Eshèté had picked up on the public demand for more varied sounds when running a record shop in Addis; he swiftly saw the absurdity of being able to sell all manner of imports but no local contemporary product. He told *Tadias* magazine (25 May 2012 issue),

> During the 1960s and '70s modern Ethiopian music was emerging at an incredible pace even though there was extensive government control and censorship every step of the way. It was the first time that new and modern night clubs were being opened, record players were being installed in cars, and enjoying music was the spirit of the time… After many sleepless nights I was determined to take a risk of probable imprisonment and decided to ignore the decree to start producing modern Ethiopian music.

By no means all of the Amha releases, however, were in the pop idiom; many present traditional melodies and rhythms in new settings or blend the ancient and the modern in original ways. These methods bring renewed energy to music that was already passionate and powerful. One common structure is to begin with an unaccompanied instrumental interlude (often by, or involving, a *washent*, the Ethiopian bamboo flute) followed, in turn, by thumping percussion, lead vocalist and backing singers. In the case of Haylé Wèrqu's 'Tsegérèda Abèba' (1971) and 'Yèbèrèha Lomi' by Abaynèh Dèdjèné (1972), for instance, *washent* and viola provide the introduction; for Abbèbè Haylè-Michael's 'Qondjityé' it comes from *washent* alone. The latter is a prime example of how the combination of influences results in a sophisticated and compelling outcome: the dark, impenetrable vocal appears to operate independently of the hypnotic rhythm but is subtly entwined around it, keeping pace as the tempo doubles almost imperceptibly, while the presence of piano gives a jazzy feel.

At the more contemporary end of the spectrum, Alèmayèhu Eshèté 's 'Enkoy Nat Yabay Dar' from 1973 starts off like a soul number with a beefy horn arrangement, before taking a more orthodox turn; indeed this piece was conceived as a tribute to Ethiopia's musical past. Eshèté had courted danger by being the first artist to record for his namesake Amha, but Abbèbè Tèssèma went one step further by openly attacking Haile Selassie in his gritty 'Gèbrè Guratch Guté' (1972). Here Tèssèma makes reference to the Emperor's suppression of the Oromo culture in favour of that of the dominant Amhara Region, part of his conscious policy to centralise power.

By 1974, the Ethiopian music scene had matured in several key respects. Firstly, the country had its first national superstar, Tlahoun Gèssèssè. Tlahoun had been employed by the ultra-traditional Aghèr Feqer Mahbèr during which time he had been advised by the Emperor himself not to waste his talent on pop music. But his beautiful tenor voice endeared him to a legion of fans and he made a series of fine recordings of which 1974's 'Sèlam Lèhulatchen' is a highlight; its rolling rhythm, punctuated by accordion and mandolin, provides a gentle backdrop for a vocal performance of authenticity and authority.

Tlahoun was also involved in the local and distinctive brand of jazz being created by Mulatu Astatke, a vibraphone player/percussionist who had spent his musical apprenticeship in London and New York. He provided, for example, the hypnotic vocal for The All Star Band's 1970 release 'Lanchi Biye' ('Just For You'), which was written and arranged by Mulatu. Like the native pop music this new genre combined internal and external influences and reached its peak in 1974 with Mulatu's *Yèkatit: Ethio Jazz*, the first Ethiopian LP of any kind to be conceived as a unified album and not just a collection of singles. Here traditional melodies are transformed by replacing conventional instrumentation with riffing horns, guitar, bass, drums and the then fashionable electric piano and setting it all to a steady 4/4 time signature. Though to some this may have seemed like sacrilege, the resultant music is sparse yet intense, proficient but unflashy.

'Ené Alantchie Alnorem' ('I Can't Live Without You'), for instance, opens with quiet solo piano and wind effects and becomes a romantic ballad, led by flute. As the tempo picks up electric piano and guitar take over with an elegance totally devoid of pyrotechnics, before the piece ends as it began. But the key tracks are 'Yèkatit' and 'Nètsanèt'. The name of the former denotes the month, February, when anti-government riots occurred in Addis Ababa and its gloomy, brooding atmosphere suggests further trouble ahead. The latter is even more sombre, its title, 'Freedom', an indication of what was now at risk. Both compositions proved prophetic.

★★★★★

That Haile Selassie had lost touch with Ethiopian cultural developments was understandable. He was not the first, nor by any means the last, octogenarian leader to be out of step with their country's youth. But in the early 1970s he seemed oblivious to or, worse, purposely avoiding, the pressing issues facing the population as a whole.

First there was the two-year famine which started in 1972 and spread throughout the Wollo region of north east Ethiopia. Accurate figures are hard to come by but the ITV documentary *The Unknown Dead* estimated that 200,000 had perished by the time the programme was made in 1973. The Emperor did little to alleviate the crisis and was too proud to seek aid from abroad, preferring to regard the famine as an inevitable natural disaster. In fact he was planning land reforms at the time of the famine but these were being resisted by both the government and the Ethiopian Orthodox Church, adding to the growing impression both at home and abroad that he was losing control of the country. The oil crisis of 1973 also dealt Ethiopia a severe blow, since it led to a huge hike in the prices of basic commodities just when the famine was at its worst.

The beginning of 1974 saw the first stirrings of what was to become an avalanche of protest. On 12 January there was a mutiny in an army outpost at Neghelle, southern Ethiopia, when officers refused to share their water supply with their men following the breakdown of a pump. A month later, officers were held hostage at an airbase near Addis Ababa, an action motivated by poor pay and conditions. Soon the anger spread to the civilian population with four days of rioting in the capital leaving five dead. Among the demonstrators' grievances were inflation, the suppression of trade union rights and the government's proposed education reforms; on 23 February, Haile Selassie responded by promising a price freeze on essential goods, a reduction of the price of petrol and the postponement of the reforms. He also announced a 33% wage increase for the military, but this did not prevent an incident two days later in which a group of soldiers in Asmara, Eritrea, commandeered a radio station to broadcast their demands.

At this stage the protestors' wrath was directed at the government rather than the Emperor himself (though, of course, he controlled that government and was quite content to tolerate and even encourage a tangled web of patronage and corruption, providing it reinforced his power). Haile Selassie even showed them a degree of sympathy by dismissing the prime minister, Aklilou Habte-Wold and changing the Ethiopian constitution to make that office accountable to parliament. But it made no difference. As Martin Meredith reports:

> In March a chaotic profusion of strikes and demonstrations burst out in the towns and cities of Ethiopia. One group after another – civil servants, teachers, students, journalists, even priests and prostitutes – took to the streets. A massive demonstration was held in protest against official discrimination against Islam and calling for the separation of Church and state. The most persistent demand was for the arrest and trial of former ministers and palace officials on charges of negligence and corruption. The outbursts were unplanned and uncoordinated, but insistent on the need for widespread reform. (*The State Of Africa*, p. 214)

Even when a group of army officers formed a military committee (or 'Derg') to provide exactly this type of coordination, they remained loyal to the Emperor. In a striking parallel with the overthrow of the Portuguese government, it was the junior ranks who led the way, deeming their superiors incapable of supporting the revolution they believed was necessary. Originally a clandestine organisation, the Derg had acquired sufficient confidence by the summer of 1974 to invite a long list of members of the Ethiopian Establishment to surrender or be relieved of all their assets. Hundreds came forward, leaving the Emperor with precious few defenders and so the thoughts of the Derg turned to his removal.

On 11 September, nine princesses from the Imperial court were imprisoned and Haile Selassie himself interrogated about his personal fortune. He was then shown the film *The Unknown Dead*, intercut with footage of the Emperor eating caviar and drinking champagne. The following day a proclamation of dethronement was read to him; he was then taken to the barracks of the Fourth Division of the Ethiopian

Army in a green Volkswagen beetle. So ended the Solomonic Dynasty which had lasted for almost three millennia. Less than a year later, Haile Selassie died in captivity and was buried under a bathroom in the Imperial Grand Palace.

*****

The takeover of Ethiopia by the Derg did not bring peace and prosperity to the country. The curfew they had imposed at the time of the coup went on for seventeen years, a period of civil war in which 1.4 million people were killed. Yet despite the turmoil, the Ethiopian recording industry somehow kept going, at least for a while: Tlahoun Gèssèssè, for example, made some excellent records in 1975. One is reminded how, ten years earlier, Congolese musicians like Franco and Tabu Ley had played on during the revolution that led to the victory of Joseph-Désiré Mobutu. A few years later, as part of his 'Authenticity Campaign', Mobutu had renamed himself Mobutu Sese Seko Kuku Ngbendu Wa Za Banga – Mobutu Sese Seko for short – and his country Zaïre.

In September 1974, though separated at their closest borders by a mere 300 miles, the fortunes of Ethiopia and Zaïre could not have been more different. (The same may be said of Angola and Zaïre, alphabetically but not, as next-door neighbours, geographically disparate.) Just as Haile Selassie was being led away by the Derg, Mobutu was basking in the anticipation of two hugely prestigious events, one of which was – and still is – termed the greatest sporting event of the 20th century.

Zaïre had already reached a sporting landmark three months earlier when the country's football team appeared for the first time (including as the Congo) at the finals of the World Cup – no small achievement at a time when the presence of African teams at the tournament was still something of a novelty (none at all took part between 1938 and 1966). Granted their effort in West Germany could have gone better (played three, lost three, goals for – none, goals against – fourteen), but the fact that they were there at all was an eye-catching feather in Mobutu's cap. And there were more feathers to come.

In the early 1970s the quality of heavyweight boxing was at a pinnacle, with no fewer than three fighters who could be counted among the all-time greats. Muhammad Ali, the most illustrious of all, had not been back in the sport for long, having been banned for three years in 1967 for refusing to be drafted into the US Army. But his comeback was curtailed on 8 March 1971 when he lost on points to the WBA World Champion Joe Frazier, a boxer of devastating power and stamina. Two years later, Frazier himself fell to George Foreman, his superior in both height and reach and who had never lost a professional bout. When Ali got the better of Frazier on 28 January 1974, the stage was set for a first, and explosive, meeting between Foreman and Ali.

The fight was promoted by relative newcomer Don King who, though he had promised the winner $5 million, did not actually have the cash and so had to cast around for a venue and a sponsor; fortunately, he managed to secure both. Mobutu, seeking the undoubted international profile the event would bring, offered to hold the fight in the capital of Zaïre, Kinshasa, and the money was put up by a consortium including the Hemdale Film Corporation, co-founded by the British actor, David Hemmings. The date of the bout was set for 25 September 1974.

Meanwhile, the American record producer Stewart Levine and the South African musician Hugh Masekela conceived the idea of staging a music festival in Kinshasa to coincide with the fight: an event that would bring together African and African-American musicians in celebration of their joint ancestry, and heritage. It was a stroke of inspiration, although once again money was an issue. Mobutu gave the event his blessing but refused to provide any financial backing – in the end, this was secured from a Liberian investment company who, understandably, kept a close eye on the proceedings. But disaster struck at the eleventh hour: having made all the arrangements, Levine was informed that Foreman had cut his eye in training and the fight would have to be postponed for at least a month. By then it was too late to go back and so the organising team, which included the avuncular former rock and roll star Lloyd Price, pressed on with the project.

The choice of acts for the festival could hardly have been more propitious. Top of the bill was James Brown, the man who had, through his taut, rhythm-based brand of soul – now dubbed funk – re-introduced Africa to its own musical roots; he was, in addition, a well-known advocate of African-American self-reliance and racial pride. Blues giant BB King represented the more traditional aspects of African-American music; jazz-fusion band The Crusaders, singer/songwriter Bill Withers and vocal groups The Spinners, Sister Sledge and The Pointer Sisters, its present. Alongside the US acts were the international superstars Celia Cruz, from Cuba, and the South African, Miriam Makeba, together with big names from Zaïre itself – Abeti Masikini and the aforementioned Franco, with his band OK Jazz, and Tabu Ley, accompanied by Afrisa International.

Thanks to director Jeffrey Levy-Hinte, we are able to view the highlights of what must be considered one of the great music festivals of the 20th century. Levy-Hinte had worked as an editor on *When We Were Kings*, Leon Gast's 1996 documentary of the Ali/Foreman fight, and in the process discovered extensive, and unused, footage of the musicians – in conversation, at rehearsals and on stage. He was able to convert this into his own film, *Soul Power*, released in 2008. Some of the most arresting material comes from the informal interviews conducted with the participants. Ali himself launches into a spontaneous rap on the subject of 'The Rumble in the Jungle', the popular name for his match-up with Foreman; noting the preconceptions and prejudices held in the West about Africa, he holds forth about what he now sees as the *real* jungle – New York City. At the very end of the film James

Brown, whose sincerity and modesty is apparent throughout, adds a spoken message. Coming immediately after the closing credits during which his ode to self-respect, 'Same Beat' with its refrain of 'I *am* somebody', is heard in the background, he tells us:

> Let me say another thing – I hope that it can be put on the tail end of this. When you walk out of this movie, if you walk away from your television set, there's one thing you walk out with in your mind. When you get up and walk out and look down the street, you say to yourself, "Damn *right* I'm somebody".

Brown, in closing out the festival on its third day, also gives a memorable musical performance. Moustachioed and slightly plump, he opens his set with a dazzling dance routine that includes doing the splits twice. Tough, tight renditions of 'The Payback' and 'Cold Sweat' follow and we also see him play 'Soul Power' which fittingly begins the film. But Cruz is equally dynamic, both on 'Quimbara' from Day Two of the festival, and 'Guantanamera', sung as part of her soundcheck but surely one of the most vibrant versions ever of this hackneyed number. The Zaïrean bands acquit themselves superbly and both BB King and The Crusaders give exceptional renditions of their respective signature pieces, 'The Thrill Is Gone' and 'Put It Where You Want It'. A welcome contrast to all the excitement comes with Makeba's relaxed but irresistible 'Click Song' and the heartrending 'Hope She'll Be Happier' by Bill Withers.

The Rumble in the Jungle finally took place at 4 am, local time, on Wednesday 30 October. After such a brilliantly successful music festival, it might have come as an anticlimax. Most boxing experts, however, consider it to be of the great fights in the history of the sport, a classic confrontation between Ali's mobility and tactical acumen and Foreman's colossal power. In the end, the former won the day when Foreman was counted out in the eighth round. But this glittering occasion did not end there: it led to a book by Norman Mailer, several songs, a TV movie and a full-length feature film. It also provided the closing scene for the biopic *Ali.*

The two men later became close friends – in 1997 it was Foreman who helped Ali, then suffering from Parkinson's disease, to the stage at the 69th Academy Awards after the Oscar for Best Documentary went to *When We Were Kings*. They therefore fulfilled to the letter the slogan emblazoned on placards before the fight itself:

> The Foreman-Ali fight is not a war between enemies but a sport between two brothers.

In a year of horrendous internecine conflict across the continent of Africa, however, its message of fraternity had little resonance.

CHAPTER 5

You Ain't Seen Nothing Yet

The worldwide recession that began in autumn 1973 naturally affected the UK, perhaps disproportionately so, since, with a predominantly manufacturing economy, it was seriously damaged by the embargo on oil. A separate but related problem was that constant preoccupation of British governments of the 1970s (and many since), inflation. But despite the ever-increasing gloom of the international scene the Conservative administration of Edward Heath seemed to be achieving a modicum of success in controlling prices and incomes – and the relationship between them. This was a difficult task at a time when the trade unions wielded much greater power than they do today and were perpetually demanding wage rises for their members. At the same time most union leaders were principled, and sensible, enough to realise that compromises were required in order to serve the country's best interests. Some of them – Tom Jackson of the postal workers' union and miners' leader Joe Gormley, for example – even met Heath in secret, with no other ministers present, to discuss mutual concerns.

Publicly, however, the TUC were opposed to the government's policies and, in particular, the Industrial Relations Act of 1971 which placed restrictions on union activity including legal intervention to prevent disputes. The Act triggered mass protests and worse was to come when the National Union of Mineworkers (NUM) went on strike in January 1972. Like all the unions, the NUM abhorred the Act, but the main grievances were the lack of investment in their industry and, more immediately, declining pay levels. Terrified that the dispute would bring British industry to a standstill, the government set up an inquiry which vindicated the miners by awarding them a wage rise of 20% and, after the addition of other concessions, the strike ended on 25 February.

Anxious to avoid a repetition in other industries Heath began to consider an incomes policy, a measure that, provided it was linked to prices, the TUC were unlikely to oppose outright. Such manifestations of governmental interference in the economy were anathema to diehard Tories but unrest among railway workers and dockers during the summer of 1972 provided Heath with the impetus to announce a 90-day pay and prices freeze, effective from 6 November; by January he had introduced a commission to monitor and, if necessary, veto price rises. For much of 1973, there was a truce between government and unions with neither side wanting to appear unreasonable, but towards the end of the year the equilibrium was tested to the limit.

The steep rise in the cost of imported goods made the Price Commission's task difficult and, when the oil crisis began to bite, impossible. There was also pressure from the NUM for another substantial pay increase for their members. After his experience the previous year, this caused Heath understandable disquiet: another defeat would have dealt a mortal blow both to his price and incomes policy and to his personal credibility. Yet the unions offered Heath two escape routes, neither of which he took.

First, Gormley gave him to understand that the award of payments for unsocial hours might meet the miners' demands while at the same time avoiding a breach in the policy. But though Heath did build this into the provisions of the policy, he made it applicable to all unions, thus neutralising any advantage that would have accrued to the miners. It could be argued that a generous pay award to the miners would have been incongruous when the country was starting to suffer the privations of the oil crisis, let alone the recession that accompanied it, yet at the same time the embargo meant that oil could not replace coal as an energy source in the event of a protracted miners' strike.

Heath, however, had a solution to these apparently irreconcilable alternatives. On 13 December 1973, he announced that in the New Year the country would be put on a three-day week, thus cutting the industrial consumption of energy, especially electricity, by 40%. By taking such drastic action, he also believed that the miners would have to back down: any strike action in these circumstances would be seen as irresponsible and attract universal condemnation. A week later, however, the TUC made Heath a proposal which, had he accepted it, would have maintained the supply of coal, and with it his administration.

If Heath were willing to treat the miners as a special case – that is, outside the prices and incomes policy – they would not demand parity for other workers. In the context of the time this amounted to an olive branch but Heath spurned it, convinced that giving the miners what they wanted would set off a stampede. In short, he did not trust the word of the TUC. On 4 February 1974 the miners voted to go on strike and on the same day Heath sent a telegram to the Queen (who was in New Zealand) requesting the dissolution of Parliament: a General Election would be held on 28 February.

Traditionally the February 1974 election has been viewed as a stand-off between Heath and the miners to determine 'who governs Britain'. Yet Heath had agonised over whether to call an election at all. His characteristic decisiveness was shaken by the crisis and by the conflicting advice of his colleagues. Heath's biographer Philip Ziegler describes a meeting of the Inner Cabinet at which a debate took place on the desirability and timing of the election:

> It was Heath's practice to listen to what people had to say and then to pronounce his inflexible decision. This time he listened but failed to decide. (*Edward Heath*, p. 426)

It even got to the stage where those in favour of calling an election felt the need to shield the Prime Minister from coming into contact with those who considered it a mistake, just in case he changed his mind at the last minute.

But once the date had been set, Heath campaigned with renewed vigour and took charge of the associated PR to the extent that other ministers seemed almost irrelevant. Given that he was not especially popular with in his own party, never mind the country as a whole, this was something of a gamble, but Heath believed that whatever people felt about his personality they would acknowledge the justice, and logic, of his implacable attitude to the miners.

Unfortunately, the electorate were far more divided on the issue than Heath, and indeed almost all the opinion polls, had anticipated. When all the votes had been counted, the Conservatives had won 297 seats, Labour 301, the Liberals fourteen and the other parties 23 between them. Heath did not, however, intend to bow out gracefully. Immediately after the election he investigated the potential for forming a coalition, either with the Liberals or the Ulster Unionists, or both. The latter were thought to be too unpredictable but Heath – very much on the left of his party – was at least partially in tune with the Liberal leader, Jeremy Thorpe; both, for example, were enthusiastic Europhiles. But the price of Thorpe's co-operation was electoral reform, an impossible commitment for either major UK political party, then or now. At the end of a weekend in which the country's future had rested on a knife edge, it became clear that its next Prime Minister would be Harold Wilson.

★★★★★

During the late 1960s and early 1970s, British pop and rock musicians had not been slow to react to events around them, even if their observations were sometimes expressed via metaphor or allegory. It therefore seemed strange that so few chose to write about the political and economic turbulence of early 1974, or its consequences. Perhaps the relative affluence that many, if not most, now enjoyed meant that the privations suffered by the rest of the country did not apply to them. As we shall see, it was the next generation, especially those disadvantaged by unemployment, who would use these experiences to fuel a new style of music.

Among the exceptions to the rule were 10cc, whose second album, *Sheet Music*, was recorded at the height of the crisis and released in May. 'Oh Effendi', for instance, is a wry comment on the growing power of the Arab states and the concomitant compulsion to court them while in 'The Wall Street Shuffle' the crunching riff and caustic lyrics neatly evoke the cruel consequences of capitalism. The ingenious 'Clockwork Creep' features a bomb on a jumbo jet counting down to its own explosion. The cleverness extends to the rest of the record, though the flow of compositional and sonic ideas is sometimes so rapid as to compromise the overall coherence of individual tracks, and of the album as a whole.

Made at exactly the same time as *Sheet Music*, Alan Price's *Between Yesterday And Today* is a largely autobiographical account of his working-class roots and in 'Jarrow Song' he projects himself back to 1936 when the unemployed shipyard workers of the town marched from County Durham to London. Despite the piece's period orchestration, there is no escaping its contemporary allusions. Price's erstwhile partner, Georgie Fame, also commented on current affairs, though in his case the topic was rather less politically-charged: the lively, African-flavoured 'Ali Shuffle' (and its instrumental B-side, 'Round Two') celebrated the comeback of the world's most illustrious heavyweight boxer.

Otherwise, the mainstream pop scene was permeated by the same apolitical hedonism that characterised its major influence, glam rock (though the latter had a darker side which we will explore later in the chapter). Granted, thoughts were occasionally provoked by chart records such as Brian Protheroe's 'Pinball', a swaying, multilayered ballad about the vicissitudes of life, though The Hollies' attempt to follow up the cloying but hugely successful 'The Air That I Breathe' with a creditable version of Chip Taylor's far more interesting 'Son Of A Rotten Gambler' condemned them to chart oblivion for six years. The best of the rest included The Pearls' Motown-ish 'Guilty', the thumping 'I Got The Music In Me' by Kiki Dee, The Arrows' rock and roll pastiche, 'Touch Too Much', and the plaintive 'Emma', the biggest hit so far for Hot Chocolate – but not a patch on the funky, hard-hitting B-side, 'Making Music'.

Unlike prog, heavy metal and the various rock fusions, glam was, at least at the beginning, a form of music that everyone could enjoy – unpretentious, colourful and fun. But by 1974, glam had been intellectualised by the likes of David Bowie, Roxy Music and Cockney Rebel, thus leaving a gap at pop's lowest common denominator. Enter The Bay City Rollers, whose string of smash hits reached levels of vapidity not seen for a decade. Remarkably their success was unaffected by a dispute which took *Top Of The Pops* off the air for ten weeks towards the end of the year. As ever, the BBC's flagship pop programme showcased the latest trends in teenybop, including new DJs such as Dave Lee Travis and the African-American ex-PIR executive Greg Edwards who, regrettably, presented only two editions.

Anyone curious to know, had there been no strike, what records may have featured on the show could have done worse than purchase the 42nd volume of Pickwick's *Top Of The Pops* series. Despite the name, these compilations had no connection with the BBC but were budget-price albums on which uncredited studio performers simulated recent hits. This particular edition was released with Christmas in mind – nine of the twelve songs made the charts in November, the other three in December – so buyers had to put up with tracks like 'Wombling Merry Christmas', almost identical to the original (which was also by an anonymous bunch of session singers).

As with previous releases in the series, some of the renditions are passable, some of the material is good, but rarely do you get both at the same time. The versions of The Rubettes' 'Juke Box Jive' and

Alvin Stardust's 'Tell Me Why', for example, stand comparison with the originals but both songs were fairly lame in the first place; 'Oh Yes You're Beautiful', the last Top Five single Gary Glitter had (and is now ever likely to have) and 'Dance The Kung Fu', Carl Douglas's feeble follow-up to his autumn number one, 'Kung Fu Fighting,' receive far better treatment than they deserve. 'You're The First, The Last, My Everything' features a fine singer but his attempt, in unsuitably high-pitched tones, to recreate Barry White's spoken intro is unintentionally comic.

Suzi Quatro's 'The Wild One' is accurately copied, but the song is not one of her best (the pounding 'Devil Gate Drive' might have been a better choice); conversely the effervescent 'You Ain't Seen Nothing Yet' by Canadian band Bachman-Turner Overdrive becomes pallid in comparison. The nadir is reached with cover versions of hits which themselves were covers: 'Tell Him' derives from the Hello rendition but is miles away from the energy of Gil Hamilton (or even Billie Davis, who charted with it in 1963) and 'Lucy In The Sky With Diamonds', based on Elton John's already pointless version, is, to a Beatles fan's ears, unlistenable.

Proof that session musicians could come up with something more creative came from the USA and ad hoc studio group Reunion's 'Life Is A Rock (But The Radio Rolled Me)', one of the most unusual releases of 1974 in which sections of rapid-fire patter listing, among other things, DJs, songwriters, musicians and record labels of the previous 30 years are interspersed with an anthemic chorus. Though unquestionably unique, it was not without influence: in 1987, REM recorded the not dissimilar 'It's The End Of The World As We Know It (And I Feel Fine)' for their album *Document.*

'She's Gone' by Hall and Oates was, however, a genuine harbinger: produced by Arif Mardin, its tuneful take on blue-eyed soul proved to be a template not just for the duo themselves, who went on to have six US number ones, but for much of the soft rock of the late 1970s/ early 1980s. Mardin also rescued the career of The Bee Gees, going nowhere after a dispiriting tour of English variety clubs. The resultant album, *Mr Natural*, encompassed a range of styles from the glossy ballad 'Charade' to the harsh, bluesy 'Heavy Breathing' but Mardin slowly but surely steered them towards the Miami disco sound he, and they, were to perfect the following year with 'Jive Talkin''.

Back in the UK, the highlight of the year for mainstream pop was the Eurovision Song Contest, held on 6 April at the Brighton Dome. Originally the competition was exclusively about the song, but in recent times the performer's appearance had acquired equal – if not greater – importance. Of course, for women this equated to good looks, though just to retain a shred of credibility, it was useful to have one or two unprepossessing men around. These trends culminated at the 1974 event: glamorous women featured in all four of the entries receiving the most votes while unglamorous men appeared in two of them. But the Eurovision identikit also extended to hair and clothes, as the following table makes clear:

Position	Act	Glamorous female	Blonde hair	Blue outfit	Unglamorous bearded bloke
1	Abba (Sweden)	Yes (2)	Yes (2)	Yes (1)	Yes (1)
2	Gigliola Cinquetti (Italy)	Yes	No	Yes	No
3	Mouth and MacNeal (Netherlands)	Yes	Yes	Yes	Yes
4	Olivia Newton-John (UK)	Yes	Yes	Yes (plus five female backing singers also in blue)	No

It is tempting, therefore, to view the whole contest as a cynical marketing exercise.

Several eminent music critics have professed to like Abba, but 'Waterloo', other than the continual repetition of the title word, does not have much to commend it even though the group's performance on the night was, despite an anaemic drummer, livelier than most of their rivals. Certainly they were more animated than Olivia Newton-John whose movements to the perky, 'Puppet On A String'-like 'Long Live Love' were as stiff as the proverbial board. With its marching tempo and big build-up, Mouth and MacNeal's 'I See A Star' was standard Eurovision fare but Gigliola Cinquetti's 'Si' was anything but: a change of tempo and an instrumental interlude in which Cinquetti turned her back on the audience made it one of the more compelling entries that, or any other, year. Much to the disappointment of Eurovision statisticians, no country received nul points, though there was a spectacular four-way tie for last place involving Norway, West Germany, Switzerland and Portugal.

The contest spawned an array of records designed to cash in on the Eurovision sound. One of these was 'Born With A Smile On My Face', by Stephanie De Sykes with Rain – essentially singalong pop with an irritatingly catchy chorus. De Sykes went on to write two Eurovision entries for the UK but with her blonde hair and propensity for blue outfits she must have wished she had gone in for the 1974 event as a performer. The more established Europop acts, however, continued to go their own way: during the summer Frenchman Charles Aznavour spent four weeks at the top of the UK charts with the sentimental ballad, 'She', while his countryman Sacha Distel crooned his way inoffensively through the Tony Macaulay-Roger Cook-Roger Greenaway composition 'Oh My Joe'; however for the B-side, 'My First Guitar', he reverted to the gypsy jazz style in which he had begun his professional career. Meanwhile Belgian singer-songwriter Jacques Brel had the dubious pleasure of seeing his 'Seasons In The Sun' reach number one in both the US and UK – not his own rousing original but an insipid cover by Canada's Terry Jacks, formerly of The Poppy Family.

*****

The Eurovision Song Contest attracted its customary mass TV audience but for many viewers the highlight of the year was *The Pallisers*, the BBC's 26-part serial based on Anthony Trollope's eponymous series of novels. Simon Raven's dramatisation adroitly contrived to retain Trollope's in-depth characterisation and gentle humour without sacrificing any plot essentials and the performances were on a par with the corporation's universally acclaimed 1967 adaptation of John Galsworthy's *The Forsyte Saga* (Susan Hampshire was in both). *The Pallisers,* however, provided the more enthralling cliffhanger when the last two episodes, scheduled for June, had to be postponed until November owing to industrial action at the BBC.

The final edition of another British television classic was screened the following month. *Monty Python's Flying Circus* had been commissioned back in 1969 by the then controller of BBC2, David Attenborough, and had made the transition from what was essentially a cult sketch show to mainstream entertainment. Its passing was predictably mourned by its legions of adherents but by then tastes were changing. 1974 saw the appearance of two undemanding but enjoyable (and ultimately long-running) US comedy shows each of which, in their different ways, celebrated the antihero. *Happy Days* traded on nostalgia for the rock and roll era but its chief selling point was the charismatic drop-out Fonzie, played by Henry Winkler. *The Rockford Files* starred James Garner as the eponymous ex-con turned private investigator and featured an appropriately ebullient title theme by Mike Post, his first major TV commission.

In film, Mel Brooks was the man of the moment with two hugely popular releases, both of them spoofs of movie genres. *Blazing Saddles* satirised the Western and its enduring racial stereotypes though there was also plenty in the way of slapstick and visual gags. The follow-up, *Young Frankenstein*, was just as closely observed, if more subtle. Shot in black and white to give an authentically gothic atmosphere, it also – like the story it was based on – contained moments of genuine pathos. The fine cast included Gene Wilder, Marty Feldman, Peter Boyle, Teri Garr and Gene Hackman. Co-written, produced, scored and directed by John Carpenter, *Dark Star* was another excellent parody, this time of sci-fi films like *2001: A Space Odyssey.* A not very bright, dysfunctional crew have been in space for 20 years but now run into a series of mishaps, not helped by a mischievous pet alien and a bomb that knows its own mind.

Dark Star also took a swipe at disaster movies, the popularity of which remained undiminished in 1974. Not all of them were distinguished. *Earthquake* had good special effects but a weak plot and the part disaster film/part thriller *The Taking Of Pelham 123* was rich in clichés but lacking in suspense, despite a taut, edgy soundtrack by David Shire. Measured by the standards of the genre, John Guillermin's *The Towering Inferno* was, however, an unqualified success, largely due to the gripping action sequences directed by producer Irwin Allen. It also benefited from an all-star cast including Paul Newman as the distressed but courageous architect; Steve McQueen as the phlegmatic fire chief; William Holden as the builder of the world's tallest skyscraper, in the construction of which corners were cut to meet the budget; and Fred Astaire as the pathetic but ultimately good-hearted con-man.

Astaire was also prominent as one of the narrators of *That's Entertainment*, a self-congratulatory but absorbing documentary about the musicals made by MGM between the 1920s and the 1950s. He also appears, with Eleanor Powell, in some of the best clips, and there are also gems from Gene Kelly, Judy Garland, Ann Miller and Esther Williams. One of the maxims of the studio was that if you were in a musical you had to sing, even if you couldn't – a principle proved beyond question by the excerpts featuring Clark Gable, Jean Harlow, Elizabeth Taylor and James Stewart.

Over the previous ten years developments in popular culture had been so rapid that Hollywood film-makers must have felt it was time to look back. For alongside retrospective surveys like *That's Entertainment* came a resurgence of interest in the past, expressed, not in the costume dramas that had proved so popular in the sixties but in stories about early 20th century America. No fewer than three major films of 1974 came into that category.

Chinatown, directed by Roman Polanski and starring Jack Nicholson and Faye Dunaway, was about the California Water Wars of 1902-07 though several other plotlines operated simultaneously. The fundamental pessimism of the film was underlined by Jerry Goldsmith's bleak soundtrack, in which the lonely sound of solo trumpet recalled Miles Davis's score for *Lift To The Scaffold.* In total, *Chinatown* received eleven Academy Award nominations and won one – Best Screenplay (by Robert Towne).

F Scott Fitzgerald wrote *The Great Gatsby* in 1925 and in the subsequent 50 years it was adapted for film on no less than three occasions. The 1974 version was directed by Jack Clayton with a cast including Robert Redford, Mia Farrow, Bruce Dern, Sam Waterston and Karen Black, one of the outstanding actresses of the 1970s, whose portrayal of the callous, grasping Myrtle Wilson stole the show. Stunning both visually and aurally, it led to Oscars for Theoni V Aldredge (Best Costume Design) and Nelson Riddle (Best Original Song Score). Riddle's orchestrations were an object-lesson in the sophisticated yet sensitive use of standards and his use of Irving Berlin's melancholic 'What'll I Do' as a motif throughout the picture was a masterstroke.

Unfortunately there was no Academy Award for Francis Ford Coppola's screenplay but that may not have concerned him too much, since his own film, *The Godfather II*, scooped a total of six Oscars, three of which came to Coppola himself – Best Picture, Best Director and (with Mario Puzo) Best Adapted Screenplay. His father Carmine also received, with Nino Rota, the Oscar for Best Original

Dramatic Score, making the 47th Academy Award Ceremony, highly appropriately given the subject of the film, something of a family affair. *The Godfather II* cleverly contrives to be both a prequel and sequel to its predecessor. In the opening scene, set in Sicily in 1901, we meet nine-year-old Vito Corleone, about to escape a bloody feud to travel alone to New York. The action then switches to 1958 when Vito's son and successor Michael (played by Al Pacino) is struggling to deal with a variety of personal and business issues, and back to 1917 when the grown-up Vito (Robert De Niro) is establishing the family hegemony. For the rest of the film, these scenarios alternate, thus painting a vivid contrast between the auspicious start of the Corleone empire and what, by the end, is beginning to look like its decline.

Much of the foreboding atmosphere of *The Godfather II* is created by the gloomy, low-light photography, a speciality of the cinematographer Gordon Willis, who had also worked on its predecessor and Alan J Pakula's highly acclaimed *Klute*. In 1974 Willis and Pakula renewed their collaboration for *The Parallax View*, starring Warren Beatty. Pakula employs techniques made famous by Alfred Hitchcock: innocent objects become sinister and characters are enmeshed in a web of shadows to symbolise their powerlessness. The film was based on the 1970 novel by Loren Singer and its depiction of the cover-up following a political assassination clearly links to the murder of John F Kennedy – the film ends with a Warren Commission-like panel concluding there is 'no evidence of a conspiracy' – but its release on 14 June coincided with anxieties over Watergate and the dawning realisation that cover-ups were a matter of fact, not fantasy. The controversy over the White House tapes also did nothing to harm the success of *The Conversation,* another 1974 masterpiece directed by Francis Ford Coppola, in which a surveillance expert accidently discovers a murder plot and thus is himself spied upon. The claustrophobic atmosphere in which boredom and panic sit side by side was conveyed to perfection by Coppola, much assisted by an excellent performance by Gene Hackman and a fine supporting cast which included Cindy Williams and Harrison Ford (who had both appeared in the Coppola-produced *American Graffiti* the previous year), as well as Teri Garr, who had worked with Hackman in *Young Frankenstein.*

That films such as *The Godfather Part II*, *The Parallax View* and *The Conversation* represented the cutting edge of contemporary cinema was demonstrated most graphically by the shortcomings of the more traditional approaches. Ten years before, *Goldfinger* – pacy, stylish, and above all, vibrant – had seemed like the future, but the latest James Bond movie, *The Man With The Golden Gun,* now felt horribly outdated, in spite, or perhaps because, of its clumsy attempts at contemporary references ranging from the energy crisis to the martial arts craze. Furthermore Britt Ekland's portrayal of the hapless, hopeless female agent was, perhaps deliberately, an affront to women's liberation. On the plus side, Christopher Lee made an excellent villain and, as with all Bond pictures featuring Roger Moore, there was a welcome element of self-parody.

★★★★★

The British media had plenty to keep them busy during 1974. The three-day week, miners' strike and political comings and goings, both at home and in the USA, provided a perpetual source of headlines, editorial comment and in-depth analysis. But if all of that were not enough, there was a plethora of other news stories to interest the public.

One such was the reorganisation of council boundaries which took place on 1 April, a consequence of the Local Government Act 1972. One major and obvious effect was the restructuring of counties which had survived quite happily for centuries in favour of metropolitan areas (containing, naturally, metropolitan boroughs). This led to some odd and controversial results. The proud Yorkshire folk of Saddleworth, for example, now found they lived in Oldham, Greater Manchester;

and though it boasted one of the country's leading cricket teams (who played at the game's world headquarters, Lord's), Middlesex simply ceased to exist. Some proposed changes failed to make the final cut, including plans to merge Bury and Rochdale (dubbed 'Botchdale' by local MP Michael Fidler) but there were still lots of new names to grapple with including Cleveland, Cumbria and Avon. In typically British style, many people simply ignored the newly-created areas and stuck with their previous address. In 2016, the use of pre-1974 terminology remains widespread – and Middlesex County Cricket Club is still very much in business.

Unsurprisingly, given the economic situation, plans were shelved for large-scale infrastructure projects such as the Channel Tunnel and a new London Airport. A study investigating London's future transport needs proposed the construction of a railway line, which it dubbed 'Crossrail', to traverse the capital, but the go-ahead was not given for a further 34 years. Elsewhere in London, work was completed on the Heygate housing estate which provided homes for 3,000 families in the Elephant and Castle area. Its futuristic, neo-brutalist design allowed residents to access any part of the development via concrete bridges, but opinions were sharply divided as to the desirability of living in such an environment and conditions on the estate began to degenerate. £44 million was spent on vacating Heygate and a further £15 million on its demolition, which was completed in June 2014.

Alongside these weighty matters came the usual crop of scandals and sensations. To lose one member of the Establishment may be regarded as a misfortune, to lose two looks like carelessness, but this is what occurred in a remarkable twelve-day period in November. First, on the 8th, Richard John Bingham, 7th Earl of Lucan, vanished without trace. A former merchant banker who now made his living from gambling, Lord Lucan was estranged from his wife and had recently failed to regain custody of their three children. The day before Lucan's disappearance, the children's nanny, Sandra Rivett, was beaten to death in the basement of the family home in Belgravia;

Lady Lucan was also attacked and subsequently identified the assailant as her husband. At the inquest into Rivett's death, Lord Lucan was officially named as her murderer, the first Member of the House of Lords to be so indicted since 1760. Despite a massive international search operation, he was never found and in February 2016 was finally pronounced dead.

Then, on 20 November, the Labour Member of Parliament John Stonehouse went missing in Miami. Initially he was thought to have committed suicide, or drowned, since a pile of his clothes was found on a nearby beach. Stonehouse was already known as a larger-than-life figure. As Postmaster General he had introduced the UK's two-tier stamp system in 1968 and two years later organised the jamming of the pirate radio station, North Sea International. He had also been suspected (rightly, as it turned out) of spying for Czechoslovakia, but in 1969 successfully rebutted MI5 claims to that effect. Five years later, however, the Department of Trade and Industry were on his trail for financial irregularities and rather than risk exposure and arrest, Stonehouse decided to fake his own death and escape to Australia with his secretary, Sheila Buckley. Perhaps if Lord Lucan had not absconded he might have got away with it, but after a period of surveillance the Australian police apprehended Stonehouse on Christmas Eve, believing him to be the fugitive peer. When the truth emerged he was deported to Britain where he was sentenced to seven years in prison for fraud.

The inside pages also featured some interesting stories. Two of them emanated from the food and drink industry and reflected the increasingly polarised attitudes of consumers. In April CAMRA (the Campaign for Real Ale), founded in 1971 to combat the mass production and homogenisation of beer, issued its first *Good Beer Guide*; six months later McDonald's opened its first UK store in Woolwich, London (there are now 1,200). Meanwhile on 7 August (the day before Richard Nixon's resignation speech) Philippe Petit made his famous tightrope walk between the Twin Towers of New York's recently-built World Trade Center. Completely unauthorised, it was the culmination of six years' planning by the French high-wire artist and his team of assistants who, on the day, used fake IDs to pose as construction workers. The following month an equally sensational feat was achieved by lawyers representing Doris Day when they secured for their client the then largest-ever civil judgement (nearly $23 million) in Californian history. It was only when her husband Marty Melcher died in 1968 that Day had discovered that he and his business partner, Jerome Rosenthal, had squandered the huge fortune she had built up during her singing and acting career. The lawsuit against Rosenthal had dragged on from that day onwards, with Day reluctantly having to resort to television work to remain solvent. In contrast, the death in October of the Czech-born entrepreneur Oskar Schindler passed almost unnoticed. It was not until writer Thomas Keneally and, subsequently, film director Steven Spielberg told his story that the world came to appreciate his heroism: during the Holocaust he had employed over 1,000 Jews, thus saving them from almost certain extermination in the Nazi death camps.

In July, the magnificent Garman Ryan Collection was opened to the public for the first time at the New Art Gallery, Walsall. Assembled by Kathleen Garman and her friend Sally Ryan, the collection comprised over 350 works, many of them by Garman's family, including sculptures by her husband, Joseph Epstein, and paintings by their son Theodore and son-in-law Lucian Freud. Among the books issued during the year was *The Story Of The Albanian People*, a title which would perhaps have attracted little attention were it not for the fact that the author was William Ash, the war hero believed to have inspired the character of Virgil Hilts, played by Steve McQueen, in the film *The Great Escape*. Ash was a colourful character who during the Depression had train-hopped around America in search of work and subsequently joined the Royal Canadian Air Force; after the War, his exploits continued: he received the MBE, was posted to India by the BBC and helped found the Communist Party of Great Britain (Marxist-Leninist) in 1968.

In football, the highlight of the year was the World Cup, held in West Germany between 13 June and 7 July. The tournament was memorable for a number of factors, one of which was the trophy itself. Brazil's victory in 1970 had meant they were allowed to keep the original Jules Rimet Trophy, so now a new cup, The FIFA World Cup Trophy, was to be awarded to the winning team (and is still awarded today). There were also changes to the disciplinary system: though many players had been sent off in previous World Cups none had received a red card until Chile's Carlos Caszely was dismissed during their match against West Germany.

The tournament also marked the first appearance of East Germany who, as luck would have it, had been drawn in the same group as the hosts and were scheduled to play them in Hamburg on 22 June. I was living in Freiburg im Breisgau, West Germany, at the time and watched the match in a crowded bar. A television had been installed at each end, one for the West German supporters, mainly older customers, and one for the East German fans, pretty much all of whom were young people – not actually East Germans themselves but typical of the left-wing, anti-Establishment stance taken in those days by the majority of West German students. East Germany won the game 1-0, an eventuality that led to an angry confrontation between the two factions.

But this defeat did not impede West Germany's progress to the Final where they met a Netherlands side brimming with confidence. The Dutch star forward, Johan Cruyff, had terrorised opposition teams with a devastating move whereby, feinting to pass or cross, he would drag the ball behind his other foot, turn and race past the defender. Known as the Cruyff Turn, it was to become a widely-used technique and is still to be seen in the modern game. Yet despite taking the lead with a first-minute penalty, the Netherlands lost the match 2-1, and West Germany thus became world champions for the second time.

England had failed to qualify for the World Cup and as a result their manager Sir Alf Ramsey, who had led them to victory in 1966, was replaced in April by Don Revie of Leeds United. Revie's successor at Leeds, Brian Clough, had won the League with Derby County two seasons before but was dismissed after only 44 days in his new job. And Bill Shankly, who had taken Liverpool from Second Division mediocrity to three First Division Championships, retired on 12 July, two months after they had won their second FA Cup under his management. Giants fell, too, among the leading club sides. In the Cup, West Ham, Leeds and Everton were knocked out by lower league opposition and Manchester United were relegated to Division Two following a 1-0 home defeat by Manchester City: to make matters worse, City's winner came from a back-heel by a former United player, Denis Law.

*****

As we have seen, glam had started as a hedonistic form of music, a welcome alternative for ordinary young people to the increasingly ponderous, and old-fashioned, sound of mainstream rock. It was therefore ironic that David Bowie, who had done so much to inspire glam, helped to return it once more to the realm of intellectual respectability and critical analysis. The writing was already on the wall with 1972's *The Rise And Fall Of Ziggy Stardust And The Spiders From Mars*, an allegory of the life of a rock star, whose isolation from his followers is represented by the space-traveller trappings. *Diamond Dogs*, released on 24 May 1974, went one step further by grafting elements of George Orwell's novel *1984* on to his own pessimistic vision of mankind ten years hence.

Yet the record can also be read as an indictment of contemporary society – Bowie described it as 'my most political album... my protest' – and it is not difficult to recognise the deteriorating fabric of British society in its deliberately harsh, tinny sound and terrifying imagery: in the opening 'Future Legend', for instance, we hear about 'rats as big as cats' while on 'Sweet Thing' the protagonist describes himself as a 'portrait in flesh who trails on a leash'. As with *Ziggy Stardust*, Bowie uses pop music culture itself to reinforce his message: the only escape routes from this horrific world are the reckless abandon of glam ('Rebel, Rebel') or suicide, as on 'Candidate' where the lovers will first 'buy some drugs and watch a band'. There is even a (remarkably accurate) prophecy about the next musical trend with the vicious, iconoclastic diamond dogs of the title track seeming to prefigure punk rockers. This was to be Bowie's final glam album – during the year he moved to New York and then to Los Angeles to create a totally different kind of music – but he signed off in style with its chilling final track, 'Chant Of The Ever Circling Skeletal Family', in which the repetitive, discordant mantra intimates that the nightmare will never cease.

Despite its bleak subject-matter, *Diamond Dogs* was Bowie's third consecutive UK number one album (and his first Top Five entry in America), so it was hardly surprising that he had his imitators. His compositions tended to be too individual to cover; although Lulu did have a number three hit in January 1974 with 'The Man Who Sold The World', the song was four years old by then and was all the less effective for being removed from its original context. But any number of singers tried to replicate his vocal style. Two in particular sounded almost exactly like him. Mick Ronson had ample opportunity to study Bowie as a member of his backing band, The Spiders From Mars. His debut album, *Slaughter On Tenth Avenue*, contained two songs ('Growing Up And I'm Fine' and 'Hey Ma Get Papa') by his former employer, but it was on his own slightly camp 'Billy Porter' – released as a single in late 1974 in anticipation of the follow-up, *Play Don't Worry* – that he captured Bowie's intonation to perfection.

David Essex had hit the big time a year before with two Top Ten singles and the leading role in the film *That'll Be The Day*, the story of a would-be rock and roll singer called Jim MacLaine. Now in the follow-up, *Stardust*, he reaches the top but grows increasingly dissolute.

Though its title prompted some to suppose MacLaine was based on David Bowie, the screenplay does not fit his biography. But its title theme, written and sung by Essex, is an exact match, both vocally and lyrically – so much so that it is tantamount to a parody of Bowie's *Ziggy Stardust* persona. Heard over the film's closing credits, its use of pipe organ cleverly refers to its predecessor in which MacLaine was employed as a fairground worker.

Mott The Hoople vocalist Ian Hunter mimicked Dylan rather than Bowie but the band owed their continued existence to the latter's patronage: in response to rumours that they were on the verge of quitting he had written 'All The Young Dudes' for them, bringing them both chart success and a new image which merged mainstream rock with glam. Two years on, and the album *The Hoople* reveals a mixture of past, present and future – obsolescent and forward-looking at the same time. 'The Golden Age Of Rock 'N' Roll', for example, celebrates the continued strength of a music that many had written off, but the reference to governmental restrictions on decibel levels smacks of a strictly grown-up perspective. Recorded during the period of the three-day week, 'Pearl And Roy (England)' is a more relevant and better targeted dose of political vitriol: Britain is declining fast and young people are suffering from the policies of the 'big white chief' (presumably Heath), 'false teeth showing'.

In contrast, 'Crash Street Kids' anticipates punk with its rudimentary melody, stomping tempo and staccato riff. 'Born Late '58' is in similar vein but the frenetic guitar solo anchors it in blues-rock orthodoxy. Other tracks are more autobiographical. 'Marionette' is a compelling song about the struggle for sanity while in 'Through The Looking Glass' Hunter takes a wry look at what he sees in the mirror. At the end of 'Alice', he states, 'You didn't make the book' – an allusion perhaps to his *Diary Of A Rock 'N' Roll Star* – an account of the band's 1972 American tour – which was published in 1974.

Though *The Hoople* reached the UK Top Ten, Mott's cheery, unselfconscious blend of styles did not bring them sustained success;

a live recording, released later in the year, spent only two weeks in the charts and their final album, ironically entitled *Drive On*, just one, at number 45. The more precise fusion of prog and glam achieved by Queen, on the other hand, was unquestionably to the public taste; according to the website *list25.com*, they are the sixth biggest band of all time, with record sales exceeding 100 million – and this despite a debut album that failed to chart until the follow-up made the Top Five in spring 1974.

Though two writers are at work on *Queen II* – the first side is largely by Brian May, the second by Freddie Mercury – they have a lot in common, principally a predilection for Tolkienesque subject-matter and melodramatic, guitar-led arrangements. The results, nevertheless, are mixed. By now the stock prog stereotype of the idealised female figure was becoming unbearably hackneyed but that doesn't stop May using it for 'White Queen (As It Began)'; on the other hand Mercury's 'The Fairy Feller's Master-Stroke' works well, its range of bizarre vocal and instrumental effects complementing Richard Dadd's fantastical painting on which it is based. Changes of mood and tempo characterise 'The March Of The Black Queen' though it lacks the coherence of Mercury's subsequent, and not dissimilar, composition, 'Bohemian Rhapsody'. His 'Seven Seas Of Rhye', however, closes the record in exuberant style; as it fades out, the strains of 'I Do Like To Be Beside The Seaside' are heard, thus linking it to 'Brighton Rock', the first track on Queen's next album, *Sheer Heart Attack*.

This inspired device typified the approach of a band whose efforts to be inventive continually placed them on a knife-edge between ingenuity and pomposity. For example, on the following track, 'Killer Queen', the references to Marie Antoinette, Kennedy, Khrushchev, Moët and Chandon risk accusations of gratuitous name-dropping but successfully evoke the world of the high-class prostitute who is the subject of the song. The quote from Chuck Berry's 'Little Queenie' in 'Now I'm Here' is also a witty touch. 'Bring Back That Leroy Brown' is, however, a clumsy and anomalous pastiche and the lyrics to John

Deacon's aptly titled 'Misfire' are little short of abysmal. The album is perhaps most remarkable for three tracks that prefigure the future: 'Stone Cold Crazy' is the blueprint for speed metal while the two-part 'In The Lap Of The Gods' anticipates both 'Bohemian Rhapsody' and 'We Are The Champions'.

What might be termed 'progressive glam' acknowledged the theatricality and commercial appeal of Queen but followed the more consciously arty approach pioneered by David Bowie. Cockney Rebel, for example, demonstrated that it was possible to make pop music of substance without the bombast that pervaded mainstream rock. They hit the charts for the first time in May with the lively single 'Judy Teen' which integrates smart, punning lyrics and subtle instrumental touches with catchy melodies and a trendy subject, 'the queen of the scene'. Singer Steve Harley exaggerates Bowie's vocal mannerisms to the point of parody, somehow contriving to sound angst-ridden and insouciant at the same time; but although this was to make him an influence on how UK punk would sound, in 1974 it was his compositional abilities that marked him out as a rising star.

These came to full fruition on *The Psychomodo*, released on 2 June. It is undoubtedly difficult to divine the exact meaning of every song but at the very least, as in the dramatic ballad, 'Ritz', the imagery is impressive. Prior to becoming a full-time musician, Harley had worked as a journalist and his familiarity with the jargon and the clichés of, in particular, the rock press surfaces in the gently despairing 'Tumbling Down' ('look what they've done to the blues') and 'Singular Band' (possibly a play on 'singles band') which contrasts Cockney Rebel's earlier, carefree days with the constraints brought by success. 'Mr Soft' cleverly conflates the roles of muse and idol while 'Sling It!' makes the startling but apposite link between fear and euphoria. Musically, the album is equally compelling, with frequent variations in tone and texture: the opening of 'Sweet Dreams', for example, recalls the climax of The Beatles' 'A Day In The Life' before it transmutes into a brisk rocker with violin solo.

The outstanding Cockney Rebel track of the year was, however, not even included on *The Psychomodo*. 'Such A Dream' was in fact no more than the B-side of 'Mr Soft', issued as a single in July. But as the evocation of a dream turning to a nightmare, it may well be unsurpassed – at least in pop music terms. It begins with a simple, metronomic motif played on what sounds like a glockenspiel, thus creating a child-like, innocent ambience. But Harley's eerie vocal improvisations take it in a more sinister direction and after a series of disconcerting instrumental and sonic effects, the piece hurtles to a terrifying climax.

There was something scary, too, about another leading progressive glam band, Sparks. Part of this no doubt emanated from the persona created by pianist Ron Mael, a silent, mirthless Charlie Chaplin who provided a perfect foil for the animated gyrations and piercing falsetto of his brother Russell. Although Sparks broke through in Britain, they were US Maels, who, as Halfnelson, had failed to make it in their home country. But a spot on the BBC's rock show *The Old Grey Whistle Test* led to a contract with Island Records and a UK Top Five album, *Kimono My House*, released in May.

The title itself, a pun on Rosemary Clooney's 1951 hit, 'Come On-A My House', sets the tone for a record stuffed with wordplay and references to popular culture while the unusual, staccato melodies, dramatic tempo changes and clean, sharp production make for a shimmering new sound. That Sparks had found the dream combination of power, sophistication and originality seemed to be confirmed by the opening track, 'This Town Ain't Big Enough For Both Of Us' which, when released as a single, made number two on the British singles chart. Before I had heard it, it was described to me as a 'new kind of music' and that seemed – and still does – about right: a quirky take on an old story, it remains an exhilarating blend of delicacy and ferocity. 'In My Family' is similarly idiosyncratic – dissociating himself from such motley (and by implication undesirable) characters as Paul Getty, Nelson Rockefeller and Edward Teller, the inventor of the hydrogen bomb, the protagonist sees his family as clones of himself, but ends with the cryptic line 'Gonna hang myself from the family tree'. 'Equator' is another absorbing track in which a slow, pounding beat underpins the jig-like tune while the waltz 'Falling In Love With Myself Again', as the title suggests, is redolent of 1930s Berlin.

Despite their powers of creativity, Sparks' partiality for breakneck tempos and heavy metal guitar had the effect of homogenising their music. But *Propaganda*, released six months later, contained two outstanding tracks which were both issued as singles. The stop-start 'Something For The Girl With Everything' is the equivalent to 'This Town Ain't Big Enough For Both Of Us' but is perhaps even more astonishing – a radical, and riveting, version of the Nativity Story; 'Never Turn Your Back On Mother Earth' is slow, sombre and spiritual.

For both Cockney Rebel and Sparks the path to success was already smoothed by the groundbreaking efforts of the premier progressive glam band, Roxy Music, who had burst on to the scene two years before. Their original image was based around the tacky glitz of 1950s rock and roll but by 1974 their net was cast wider and Bryan Ferry's songs were exploring the lexicon of 20th century popular culture as a whole. His vocal style – located somewhere between Bob Dylan and a dance-band crooner – was well placed to interpret them and the band added the requisite instrumental colour with violin, tenor saxophone, oboe and harmonica supplementing the conventional rock sound. This was the musical landscape for *Country Life*, issued on 15 November.

The opener, 'The Thrill Of It All', encapsulates the methodology: the title comes from a 1963 film starring Doris Day (though it might equally have been a Noel Coward epigram) and the lyrics quote from 'Resume', a poem by Dorothy Parker. For all that, it is tense, hard-driving and hypnotic. 'Three And Nine' is lighter and takes us back to the world of Saturday morning cinema while 'All I Want Is You' is again reminiscent of Noel Coward ('Going out with other girls was always such a bore'), though it also includes a genuine quotation, 'L'amour, toujours l'amour', from Rudolf Friml's 1922 operetta, *Bibi Of the Boulevards*. 'Bitter-Sweet', set to an oom-pah rhythm and sung partly in German, is a tribute to the songs of Bertolt Brecht and Kurt Weill. But alongside the yearning for the excess and artifice of the past comes a celebration of the present. The exultant 'Prairie Rose' is about the model Jerry Hall, with whom Ferry had just begun a relationship, while 'Out Of The Blue' features a fashionably funky bass guitar break and a swathe of synthesisers.

*****

Unlike 1964, when they had swept to power with a coherent suite of policies, the Labour Government of March 1974 lacked a co-ordinated programme – partly because, just weeks before, the prospect of their imminent return to office was, to say the least, remote. It was also hard to envisage that such a programme could be devised, since in a hung parliament the Prime Minster normally attempts to form a coalition. Edward Heath had tried that immediately after the Election but the price required from the Liberals – progress on electoral reform – was too high. Not wanting a rerun of the same failed negotiations, the new Prime Minister, Harold Wilson, decided to go it alone.

In some ways, the lack of preparation and the precariousness of his position suited Wilson: he was able to use both as a reason for not introducing any radical and potentially controversial initiatives. Instead he set about getting relations with the trade unions back on an even keel. The mechanism for achieving that was the 'social contract': restraint on the part of the unions when it came to wage demands (including, for example, twelve-month gaps between settlements) in exchange for repeal of the Industrial Relations Act plus food and rent subsidies. Although doubts have been raised about the fine detail of the deal – to Wilson's biographer, Ben Pimlott, it had a 'soothing, if mysterious, quality' (*Harold Wilson*, p. 644) – it had the desired effect. Despite a number of unofficial strikes, a measure of equilibrium was restored and day-to-day life gradually got back to normal. Yet Wilson knew that in order to maintain any sort of stability he would need to go to the country; the only surprise was that it took him until October to do so.

For two General Elections to take place in the same year is a rare occurrence in Britain: it has happened just twice, in 1910 and in 1974. On the former occasion, the second poll failed to resolve the deadlock produced by the first; on the latter, Wilson was rewarded for steadying the ship with an overall majority of three seats. It was exactly ten years since his first election victory but euphoria of that era was entirely absent. Threats now seemed to outweigh opportunities. Industrial unrest was still lurking and there were fears that the return of a Labour Government would raise expectations among the trade unions. Rising inflation and plummeting share prices made for an unpleasant cocktail and the Party was split over European union.

But perhaps the most deep-seated problem was the conflict in Northern Ireland. 1974 had seen the violence spread to the mainland, with a coach bombing in West Yorkshire and pub bombings in Guildford and Birmingham leaving a total of 38 fatalities. There were bomb attacks, too, on the Houses of Parliament and – just prior to the announcement by the Provisional IRA of their Christmas ceasefire – on Edward Heath's home.

These shocking events were the culmination of five years' worth of mayhem during which the British Army had been deployed to support the Royal Ulster Constabulary, a move which, far from bringing peace, had further inflamed passions among many in the Catholic community and, in particular, the Provisional IRA. These passions were rooted, certainly, in political strife but encompassed a whole range of cultural factors among which were religion, social class and – as we shall see shortly – music.

CHAPTER 6

Aspirations

On 14 August 1974 the 79-year-old British soprano Isobel Baillie entered Abbey Road Studios to record 'I Will Walk With Thee'. She had made her very first recording, 'One Morning Very Early', on 19 February 1924 at EMI's headquarters at Hayes, Middlesex, and, despite the lo-fi technology of the period, it is possible to discern the poise and gracefulness that was to make her one of the world's great oratorio singers – and which was still in evidence 50 years later. But her longevity as a creative artist was matched by another major musician of the 20th century. Three days after Baillie's recording debut, the weekly entertainment newspaper *The New York Clipper* made two announcements:

> The first says, "The Washingtonians, under Elmer Snowden's direction, have renewed their contract at the Hollywood, NY, for six months more"... The second notice is an advertisement paid for the band that quotes an earlier review by the *Clipper*'s band reporter, Abel Green: "This colored band is plenty torrid... Duke Ellington leads from the piano." (James Lincoln Collier, *Duke Ellington*, p. 51)

This apparent contradiction is explained by the fact that, unbeknownst to the Hollywood nightclub, Elmer Snowden had left the band – possibly in a dispute over money – and The Washingtonians now wanted to make it clear who their new leader was. In November 1924, Ellington and his group made two records, 'Choo Choo' and 'Rainy Nights', the first in a discography – most of which was under the name of Duke Ellington and his Orchestra – that ran to several thousand titles culminating on 20 March 1974 with a live (and as yet unissued) recording of 'Take The "A" Train' at the Northern Illinois University Center.

Two months later, on 24 May, Edward Kennedy 'Duke' Ellington, the greatest bandleader jazz has ever known, and possibly will ever know, died of pneumonia brought on by lung cancer, aged 75. Paul Gonsalves, who had been with Ellington for nearly 25 years, had passed away nine days earlier; he had helped revive the band's fortunes with his epic tenor saxophone solo at the 1956 Newport Jazz Festival and was so devoted to Ellington that he gave him as his next of kin on his passport application. October saw the death of Harry Carney; during his 48 years with the band, Carney had become the top baritone saxophonist in jazz. When Ellington died, he reportedly said that 'Without Duke, I have nothing to live for'.

Gonsalves, Carney and other recently-deceased Ellingtonians such as Johnny Hodges and Ben Webster had made indelible contributions to the orchestra's output but Duke (thus nicknamed for his suave, refined manner and sartorial elegance) was the genius who wove it all together, contriving to bring out each musician's individuality while retaining, and developing, the distinctive sound of the whole band. This sound was much copied, especially by the white swing bands of the late 1930s, yet never emulated, and he produced superior music throughout his career, including the final years: 1970's *New Orleans Suite*, for example, stands comparison with his very best work.

Ellington was conscious of his status as a high-profile African-American but he felt it was beneath his dignity to confront racists and bigots directly; his racial pride was expressed through his music. In 1943, for example, he wrote the suite *Black, Brown And Beige* in which he portrays the various influences on African-American culture while at the same time stressing the centrality of family life and education. 20 years later an exhibition entitled *A Century Of Negro Progress* was held in Chicago to mark the 100th anniversary of the Emancipation

Proclamation. Ellington contributed *My People*, a multidimensional stage show which traced the history of African-Americans from slavery to the contemporary struggle for civil rights. However, he showed no political affiliation and was a frequent guest at the White House, no matter who the occupant was: he visited Lyndon Johnson on no fewer than seven occasions and Richard Nixon hosted his 70th birthday party, taking to the piano himself to lead a chorus of 'Happy Birthday To You'.

Naturally Ellington's death gave rise to a host of tributes. Perhaps none was stranger, nor more poignant, than 'He Loved Him Madly' by fellow jazz giant Miles Davis, whom Duke had once compared to Picasso. Its title paraphrases Ellington's jovial salutation to his audience, 'We love you madly', but there is nothing cheery about this 32-minute requiem. Commencing with some eerie organ chords played by Davis, it proceeds at a funereal tempo, with rumbling percussion and sparse, bluesy guitar. Dave Liebman's alto flute is given a touch of reverb by producer Teo Macero and Davis plays amplified trumpet using a wah-wah pedal; although these electronic effects were foreign to Ellington's music they are a fitting way to commemorate such a forward-thinking musician.

'He Loved Him Madly' was made within a month of Ellington's death, yet the double album on which it appears, *Get Up With It*, contained only two other tracks from 1974, both from a session on 7 October. The latter produced the extraordinary 'Maiysha', ostensibly a bright, up-tempo number with a Latin feel but which is nevertheless suffused with melancholy; half-way through it solidifies into rock with a funky bass line and stratospheric guitar. Davis's anguished, stabbing solo in the headlong 'Mtume' is perhaps indicative of the excruciating hip pain he was suffering at this time. While he continued to play live for several months, these were the last two studio tracks he would record until his remarkable post-op renaissance seven years later.

★★★★★

Coming so soon after the death of Duke Ellington, Miles Davis's decline meant that an already gaping hole in the jazz scene just got a whole lot bigger. Fortunately, some other leading performers were still at the top of their game, in particular Ella Fitzgerald, whose *Fine And Mellow* found her in the sympathetic company of an all-star band including trumpeters Clark Terry and Harry Edison, saxophonists Zoot Sims and Eddie 'Lockjaw' Davis and a dream rhythm section of Joe Pass, Tommy Flanagan, Ray Brown and Louie Bellson. The title track is absolutely outstanding, a powerhouse version of Billie Holiday's rueful twelve-bar blues featuring an uncharacteristically roaring Fitzgerald vocal and some stinging guitar fills by Pass. Whereas Fitzgerald drew on the jazz tradition, Peggy Lee's *Let's Love* was more contemporary in feel with material by Thom Bell and Linda Creed, James Taylor and Melissa Manchester alongside a title track written and produced by Paul McCartney.

However the mode of the moment was fusion and 1974 was the *annus mirabilis* for one of its leading exponents, Billy Cobham. Miles Davis had begun to incorporate rock into jazz as early as 1965 and indeed had employed Cobham on the sessions that led to his 1970 classic *Bitches Brew*. At that stage the music was a volatile amalgam of the two genres but it slowly became streamlined, seamless and grounded. This transition – from jazz-rock to fusion – can be traced in the work of Cobham himself. A drummer of phenomenal dexterity, speed and accuracy, he was given his head in The Mahavishnu Orchestra, a group led by the equally virtuosic guitarist, John McLaughlin. Cobham played a prominent part in their intense, exhilarating music, although for *Spectrum*, his first album as leader, he opted for a less frenetic approach. The opener, 'Quadrant 4', is in the Mahavishnu vein, but by the closing track, the deliciously cool and funky 'Red Baron', new textures have appeared and the rhythm has stabilised to a steady 4/4.

Spectrum entered the American album chart on 12 January 1974, reaching number 26; the follow-up, *Crosswinds*, went three places higher in June. Once more, all the tracks were by Cobham, but this was a more ambitious project, inspired by the splendour of nature. The opening track, for instance, is a seventeen-minute suite named 'Spanish Moss' after the spectacular flowering plant that hangs from trees throughout the south-east United States. Cobham calls it a 'sound portrait' and the four sections, each preceded by a howling wind effect, depicts a different natural phenomenon, from the moss itself, flowing and funky, to 'Savannah The Serene' with its slow, smooth trombone and the simulation 'Storm' featuring the leader's heavily phased drums; the piece concludes with the surging 'Flash Flood', in which guitarist John Abercrombie contrives to be introspective and expansive at the same time. 'The Pleasant Pheasant' boasts a tricky, intricate theme and a juggernaut of a tenor saxophone solo by Michael Brecker while 'Heather', written immediately after a visit to the Atomic Dome, Hiroshima, is appropriately sombre and haunting.

Next, and perhaps best of all, was the self-explanatory *Total Eclipse*. Again it begins with a suite, 'Solarization', in which moods swing from the desolation of 'Second Phase', intensified by Milcho Leviev's free-form piano, to the elation of 'Voyage' with its ferocious Abercrombie solo. The tight yet buoyant 'Lunarputians' contains some superlative drumming and the rock-flavoured 'Moon Germs' contrasts the bluesy guitar of Cornell Dupree with Abercrombie's death-defying pyrotechnics. The centrepiece, however, is the title track, its constantly shifting colours, textures and rhythms confirming that Cobham, already renowned as an exceptional musician, could now be counted an accomplished jazz composer.

Detractors of fusion, however, failed to acknowledge it, just as they failed to understand the heterogeneity that the music had to offer. Another variation came from the Brazilian Eumir Deodato who specialised in funked-up versions of well-known themes such as 'Also Sprach Zarathustra' and 'Rhapsody In Blue'. The hallmark of Deodato's style was a solid, immutable groove, over which he would intersperse lush string arrangements with pared-down electric piano and guitar interludes. This formula was at work again on 1974's *Whirlwinds* (related to *Crosswinds* only through Billy Cobham's presence on both). This time 'Moonlight Serenade' and 'Ave Maria' are given the treatment, but although the latter gets an unneeded dose of additional orchestral sugar, Glenn Miller's classic is unsweetened and thus leaves a better taste in the mouth. Elsewhere, the percussive 'West 42nd Street' features a wailing, McLaughlinesque solo by John Tropea and on the title track layers of sonic effects serve to pile on the excitement.

Any attempt to amalgamate jazz and rock (or any other idioms, come to that) naturally runs the risk of forfeiting the characteristics distinctive to each, but no such accusation could be levelled at Lonnie Liston Smith, at least in his early career. *Cosmic Funk* was his second album and there is no doubting its credibility in jazz terms. For example, the three tracks by current or former Miles Davis sidemen are accorded respect, if not reverence. The complex, shifting 'Footprints' was originally a vehicle for the restless tenor saxophone of its composer, Wayne Shorter, but here it features the leader's cascading piano; the version of John Coltrane's meditative 'Naima' is, unusually, largely sung – by Smith's brother, Donald. The spirit of Coltrane also permeates the James Mtume piece 'Sais (Egypt)' in which a thicket of percussion and electronic effects are superimposed on a repetitive bass drone.

External influences are more apparent on the tracks written by Smith. 'Beautiful Woman' has a disco feel and on the title track a heavy bass groove provides the backcloth to wild vocal and instrumental improvisations. The aptly serene 'Peaceful Ones' with its naive sentiments – 'We'll all live in harmony' – is, at least lyrically, more akin to contemporary soul or, indeed, the brand of fusion purveyed by Santana. *Borboletta*, issued in October, was the band's sixth album and the culmination of their transition towards what Bob Palmer (*Rolling Stone*, 20 December 1978) has called 'sincere but simplistic cosmic drivel'. Nevertheless, musically the album was stylish and sophisticated, influenced in particular by contemporary Brazilian music.

1974 was a landmark year for Brazil since it marked the collaboration between two national superstars, singer Elis Regina and composer Antônio Carlos Jobim. The result, *Elis And Tom,* is rated one of the finest Brazilian albums of all time. Moreover it contains what is considered the definitive version of 'Águas De Março' ('Waters Of March') which, according to a poll conducted by the newspaper *Folha de São Paulo*, is the greatest-ever Brazilian song: the duo's relaxed yet sensitive rendition certainly reflects the bittersweet theme of summer's end, a metaphor for fading love. The wistful 'Corcovado' is another justly praised Jobim composition, though Regina's emotive interpretations of the lesser-known ballads 'Modinha' and 'O Que Tinha De Ser' are equally memorable.

For *Borboletta*, however, Santana did not look to Regina and Jobim for inspiration but to their compatriots Dorival Caymmi and, in particular, the husband-and-wife partnership of percussionist Airto Moreira and singer Flora Purim. In 1973 Purim had released her second album *Butterfly Dreams* and both its cover design and title – the Portuguese for 'butterfly' is 'borboleta' – directly influenced the Santana album. In addition both Purim and Moreira appear on *Borboletta* and contribute its opening and closing tracks, though these are little more than sound effects plus percussion. Sadly Purim was imprisoned for possession of cocaine just a few weeks before the record was released.

Caymmi, who in contrast celebrated his 60th birthday while the album was being recorded, wrote 'Promise Of A Fisherman', part of the four-part suite that concludes the album; its stately melody, underpinned by lively Brazilian rhythms, is the springboard for a soaring solo from Carlos Santana himself. Tracks like 'Canto De Los Flores', 'Aspirations' and 'Flor De Canela' exude musicianship and finesse but, as Bob Palmer suggests, the album is at its weakest when peddling empty platitudes – 'Practice What You Preach', 'Give And Take' – or transcendental banalities as in 'Life Is Anew' and 'One With The Sun'.

The rock-jazz fusion process was not always so complicated, especially when lyrics were jettisoned altogether. The Average White Band's visceral 'Pick Up The Pieces' was so funky that many people assumed they were an African-American outfit; in fact they were from Dundee. And Joni Mitchell's backing group, Tom Scott and The LA Express, developed a form of fusion which was never less than immensely listenable. Rather than a band photograph, their eponymous debut album had a cover design depicting the front and rear views of a bejeaned female from waist to thigh – probably a wise choice because all five members were by then seasoned session musicians well beyond the first flush of youth (bassist Max Bennett was in his mid-forties). But, as might be expected, their playing is immaculate and the music, given its potential limitations, surprisingly varied. 'Easy Life' features Scott's serene soprano saxophone, 'Nunya' is all hustle and bustle and the sultry 'Sneakin' In The Back' features a suitably sensuous solo by guitarist Larry Carlton. 'Bless My Soul' and 'Strut Your Stuff' are pure funk while Carlton and keyboard player Joe Sample – then members of another fusion combo, The Crusaders – cut loose on the oriental-oriented 'King Cobra'.

★★★★★

At the same time as the jazz-rock-funk fusion was reaching its zenith, attempts to blend rock with other styles were beginning to falter. Blues-rock, for example, had become sterile. True, there were occasional exceptions such as Bad Company's exultant 'Can't Get Enough' and the pleasingly rustic 'Slip And Slide' by Medicine Head, but in the main it was monotonous, repetitive, and fatally shackled to the marathon guitar solo – tedious in the extreme unless executed by one of the very few virtuosi left in the idiom. As we have seen,

Eric Clapton, who arguably had started it all in the first place, had long since moved on and his former colleague, Jack Bruce – despite a recent unproductive collaboration with Cream substitutes Leslie West and Corky Laing – was wandering into more interesting territory.

Released in November, *Out Of The Storm* was in fact Bruce's fourth solo album. Its original title, *Into The Storm*, would perhaps have been more appropriate since it was made at the height of his addiction to heroin. This could have been a recipe for chaos but, paradoxically, Bruce is on top of things; apart from guitarist Steve Hunter and drummers Jim Keltner and Jim Gordon (both ubiquitous in 1974), he plays all the instruments himself and keeps his anguished, highly-wrought vocal style in complete control. Furthermore the music is far from simple: 'Pieces Of Mind', for instance, begins like a hymn but switches to full-blooded jazz-rock and the intricate melody of 'Timeslip' is matched by the agility of the playing, particularly by Bruce himself on bass. Yet what is memorable about the album is not so much the excellence of the musicianship but its underlying theme – the yearning for escape from the torments that surround him.

Though no doubt indicative of his personal circumstances, Bruce's feelings of despair were evident more widely, especially in the world of British folk-rock. Ralph McTell's single, 'Streets Of London', was at the more commercial end of the idiom. Originally written in 1969, its blend of sentimentality and social comment was more in tune with a country reeling from recession and it consequently leapt to number two at Christmas 1974. And Richard and Linda Thompson's debut album, *I Want To See The Bright Lights Tonight*, belied its upbeat title: only four of the ten tracks (all written by Richard) offer any optimism. Three of these hark back to the rambunctious days of Fairport Convention in their pomp: a jig, 'Little Beggar Girl'; an anthem, 'We Sing Hallelujah'; and the thumping 'When I Get To The Border' – guitar-fuelled, yet with some charming traditional touches.

The CWS Silver Band give the title piece a jovial, period feel, but double tracking robs Linda's voice of its customary expressiveness, as a comparison with the live version (included on the 2004 CD reissue) and indeed the rest of the album will reveal. On 'Down Where The Drunkards Roll', for example, it is rich and resonant, on 'Has He Got A Friend For Me', quietly desperate. She can, however, do nothing about the nihilism of 'Withered And Died' ('this cruel country has driven me down'), a harbinger for the even more depressing 'End Of The Rainbow' in which Richard warns a newborn baby, 'there's nothing to grow up for any more'.

Some of the gloom emanating from the folk-rock scene was perhaps indirectly related to the deteriorating mental health of Nick Drake, label-mate of the Thompsons, John Martyn and The Incredible String Band. Though (then) lacking a massive following, Drake was considered by the cognoscenti to be one of the best singer/songwriters in the country, yet by February 1974 he had not had an album out for two years. Some recordings were actually made around this time but they led nowhere and by autumn Drake was living as a recluse at his parents' home in Warwickshire and it was there that he was found dead from an overdose of antidepressants on 25 November, aged 26. Drake was a unique talent and thus irreplaceable, but various candidates were advanced to help fill the void left by his death. One was Steve Ashley, whose debut album, *Stroll On*, issued in April, includes string arrangements by Robert Kirby, who had contributed so memorably to Drake's *Five Leaves Left.* Ashley was, however, a more traditionally-oriented artist, as demonstrated by the plainsong intro to 'Fire And Wine' and the epic 'Lord Bateman', one of the many songs in the folk repertoire collected by Francis Child in the nineteenth century.

Among the folk-rock bands, String Driven Thing continued to make interesting music. 'I'll Sing One For You' backed by 'To See You', made for a strong single release, even though the B-side label was erroneously imprinted on both sides. Each is reminiscent of Dylan: the former is a dynamic number with full orchestration, the latter a narrative ballad. Founder-member Chris Adams wrote them both, but later in the year he quit the band owing to ill health. That no dip in quality ensued is clear from releases such as the engaging 'Mrs O'Reilly'; at a time when the electric guitar still dominated most bands, this up-beat piece features outstanding tenor saxophone, fiddle and, especially, piano.

★★★★★

Instrumental excellence had now become the norm in all forms of rock – indeed some rock musicians seemed exclusively concerned with pursuing technique for its own sake. This was a marked contrast to ten years before when standards were, to say the least, variable and keyboard players, bassists and drummers tended to be obscure and – compared with guitarists (and, of course, lead singers) – unloved. Technical proficiency led inexorably to longer, more complex compositions and ultimately to extended works on the classical music model. Where some of these pieces dispensed with lyrics altogether, most attempted to tell some sort of story – normally of a fantastical kind but occasionally experiential or at least rooted in reality.

Released in September 1974, Supertramp's *Crime Of The Century* falls into the latter category. Though the songs tend to be written in the second person, the album has the feel of an autobiographical journey through the insecurities of adolescence. 'School', for example, offers nothing positive – the teachers are 'old and white' and 'the schooling is phony'; instead you 'Hide In Your Shell' and become a 'Dreamer'. The answer is to 'gain control' but mankind is, in any case, destroying the universe in the 'Crime Of The Century'. Put like that, the plot seems juvenile yet that scarcely impaired its appeal; in fact it was Supertramp's breakthrough album, marking their chart debut on both sides of the Atlantic. Despite the occasional lyrical infelicity the production, by Ken Scott, is razor-sharp and the arrangements dramatic, varied and powerful.

While not dissimilar in theme, The Electric Light Orchestra's *Eldorado* was more sophisticated on every level. The protagonist this time is a daydreamer who pictures himself in a variety of roles but, contrary to what that may suggest, the all-conquering hero is not one of them. On the contrary his imaginary adventures bring with them nothing other than self-doubt. In 'Boy Blue', he is a warrior returning from the Crusades but the experience has left him empty and disillusioned; 'Mister Kingdom' finds him searching for answers but never finding them; and in 'Illusions In G Major' he is a rock star consulting his shrink. Salvation finally arrives with the title track but there is the sense that this, too, is only a phantom.

Writer Jeff Lynne thus cleverly avoids the clichés of the concept album format yet at the same time exploits its potential flexibility to the full. Following 'Eldorado Overture', which sports a narration by Peter Ford-Robertson and a quote from Edvard Grieg's *Piano Concerto*, each track represents a different daydream so Lynne is able to deploy a wide range of sounds and styles. 'Mister Kingdom' recalls The Beatles' 'Across The Universe'; 'Illusions In G Major' is straight-ahead rock; 'Poor Boy (The Greenwood)' is Dylanesque. 'Boy Blue' opens with a baroque trumpet fanfare and 'Can't Get It Out Of My Head', a US Top Ten hit in January 1975, sets driving cellos against ethereal violins. Additional colour is provided by the brief instrumental interludes that link the tracks, a device that also gives unity to the work as a whole. With *Eldorado* Lynne solved the problem of mixing classical music with rock: use the former sparingly and when you do, make sure it fits the mood and structure of the piece.

Such subtlety was not, however, a feature of the most successful rock-classical fusion album of the year, Rick Wakeman's *Journey To The Centre Of The Earth.* Based on Jules Verne's novel of the same name, it was recorded live at the Royal Festival Hall, London, on 18 January 1974, and featured the London Symphony Orchestra, the English Chamber Choir conducted by David Measham, narration by the actor David Hemmings, two vocalists, a rock band and Wakeman himself on a variety of keyboard instruments including mellotron, moog synthesiser, organ, grand piano, electric piano and clavinet.

Regrettably, the quality of the result was in inverse proportion to the conglomeration of instrumentation and talent on display.

True, there are some inspired moments. The piece begins in dramatic fashion with a stirring introduction and the resplendent main theme in its wake. However things soon go downhill. Orchestra and choir give way to the vocalists who get the story started with a scene-setting song, but the lyrics are horribly gauche – 'Two men incensed with one man's journey from the past', 'In Iceland where the mountain stood with pride, they set off with their guide to reach the mountain side'. The spoken narrative, though portentous in tone, is also curiously bathetic. We are told, for example, that 'the Eastern route they had taken had come to a dead end' and shortly afterwards that Axel chose a path 'only to reach a dead end'. Scientific detail – 'mosses from the Silurian epoch', 'vegetation of the Tertiary period' – is designed to impress but only succeeds in courting ridicule.

As might be expected, the battle between sea monsters and the subsequent storm provide the opportunity for some spectacular choral and instrumental effects with Wakeman's keyboard arsenal in the vanguard but we are soon back to lyrical banality: 'Burial ground of ancient man – I wonder where he's been?' The party's escape from the earth's core is followed by a synth solo, a quote from Grieg's 'In The Hall Of The Mountain King' (shouldn't that have come earlier?), a reprise of the main theme and a big finish to tumultuous applause. Little did the audience, or anyone else, realise that this pinnacle of symphonic rock (US: number three, UK: number one) signalled the start of its rapid decline; like Wakeman's intrepid travellers, it had reached a dead end.

It was supplanted by new-age music, a hybrid of rock, classical, jazz and folk which dispensed with jagged edges and awkward conjunctions in favour of a smoother, ambient sound. It was also largely lyric-free and therefore avoided the solecisms that had bedevilled symphonic rock and prog in general. New-age music was intended to induce relaxation and feelings of optimism and well-being and so one of its hallmarks was the sort of hypnotic repetition derived from minimalist composers such as Terry Riley, Philip Glass and Steve Reich.

Mike Oldfield had employed this technique on his 1973 debut release *Tubular Bells*, but the follow-up, *Hergest Ridge* can more genuinely claim to be one of the first new-age albums. Recorded in spring 1974 and issued on 28 August, it consists of just one track of 40 minutes and fourteen seconds' duration on which multi-instrumentalist Oldfield is assisted by a choir and string section conducted by David Bedford and a small team of backing musicians. Though not announced as such, it is clear from the outset that his intention is to depict a rural idyll, the eponymous moorland that marks the border between Herefordshire and Powys. The introduction, with its sustained drone and distant oboes, portrays the wide open countryside that characterises the area while the austere beauty of the landscape is encapsulated by the simple trumpet figure that follows. Medieval melodies convey the timelessness of the topography. A violent thunderstorm is evoked by the ensuing heavy metal interlude but tranquillity is restored as acoustic guitar and organ quietly lead the way to the finale.

Here is a fusion of rock and classical music in which – unlike the work of Deep Purple, The Nice and Rick Wakeman, for example – it is impossible to see the join, partly because it sacrifices instrumental pyrotechnics for changes in mood and ensemble texture. *Hergest Ridge* is as unified and integrated a composition as anything by, say, Ralph Vaughan Williams, but was not considered 'serious' music. It entered the UK album chart at number one on 14 September and remained there for three weeks: perhaps that is why.

★★★★★

Meanwhile, over in the world of legitimate classical music, things were changing rapidly; indeed from this period onwards, its modern incarnation would be known simply as 'contemporary music'. In time this would come to embrace a variety of sub-styles including postmodern and neoromantic. But in 1974 the overriding force was the minimalism of composers such as Steve Reich.

Reich had visited Africa in 1970 and drew inspiration from the way in which the combination of acoustic instruments, voice and – especially – percussion produced music of a variety and depth comparable with anything produced synthetically. The following year he wrote *Drumming* but did not make a studio recording of it until 1974, possibly because he was still working on his phasing methodology in which two or more instruments playing the same melodic pattern gradually move out of synchronisation. Whatever the case, he considered the session to be 'the final refinement of the phasing technique' (sleeve note to Deutsche Grammophon issue of *Drumming*). Yet there are other innovations here, too, one of which is to change timbre gradually while rhythm and pitch remain constant; indeed these changes are the means by which the piece achieves both its structure and its length, as opposed to the changes of key which perform the same function in more conventional extended compositions. Reich also uses the human voice to simulate instrumental sounds.

These technical matters do not in any way prevent the natural flow of the piece – on the contrary, they serve to enhance it. It begins with a single stroke of a drumstick on a bongo drum and as these multiply the rhythmic pattern is set for the whole composition. Cross rhythms weave in and out without disturbing momentum though at various junctures different groups of percussion instruments assume the leading role. Some of these transitions are ingenious: at the end of the second section, for example, the marimbas give way to the glockenspiels by moving to their highest range, the glockenspiels' lowest – for a time, the two groups of instruments are indistinguishable. The fourth and final section repeats the opening and then builds incrementally as bongo drum, glockenspiel and marimba repeat their previous parts and mesh together for an exciting climax.

Reich allows the musicians to select particular patterns but is careful to stress that this is not improvisation (as is to be found in jazz, for instance):

> There's a certain idea that's been in the air, particularly since the 1960s, and I think it is an extremely misleading idea. It is that the only pleasure a performer can get while performing is to improvise, or in some way be free to express his or her momentary state of mind. If a composer gives them a fixed musical score, or specific instructions to work with this is equated with political control and it means the performer is going to be unhappy about it. But if you work with musicians you see that what gives them joy is playing music they love, and whether that music is improvised or completely worked out is really not the main issue. (*Ibid.*)

However it has to be said that the distinction between selecting patterns and improvisation is, to the naked ear, a fine one. This is particularly true of *Music For Mallet Instruments, Voices And Organ*, the gentle alternative to the more aggressive *Drumming*. Its lilting, floating quality is created, at least in part, by the use of augmentation, a process by which the duration of notes previously played in shorter values is lengthened to create a slowing-down effect. The presence of two female vocalists, whose wordless chanting replicates the higher notes of the organ and marimba, provides an additional impression of spontaneity.

In contrast, *Six Pianos* – the third of Reich's compositions to be recorded in 1974 – is controlled and uncompromising. It was conceived to show what would result if all the grand pianos in a music shop were played simultaneously. In the event, the sound was too dense and overpowering so Reich settled for just(!) six. What emerges is a graphic demonstration of phasing. Three pianists play the same eight-beat rhythmic pattern; when the other three come in, they put the notes of the existing first beat on to their third, and so on, lending the composition both tension and cohesion.

Alongside Reich's forays into the future came radical reworkings of past masterpieces. Inspired by Walter Carlos's moog synthesiser stylings of Johann Sebastian Bach, the Japanese film and TV composer Isao Tomita released an album called *Snowflakes Are Dancing: The Newest Sound Of Debussy* with the additional subtitle *Virtuoso electronic performances of Debussy's beautiful tone paintings.* It was a well-chosen source since these compositions, mainly from piano suites written in the early years of the 20th century, were by definition impressionistic in character, thus allowing for further layers of imaginative interpretation. Two – 'Snowflakes Are Dancing' and 'Golliwog's Cakewalk' – come from *Children's Corner*, a work dedicated by Debussy to his young daughter, Claude-Emma, and Tomita imbues them with just the right amount of gentle playfulness, using the synthesiser to create new sounds rather than imitate existing instruments.

That he is able to do that is at least partly attributable to his formidable amount of hardware: there are no fewer than 37 attachments to the moog, plus four mixers and six accessories including a mellotron. Yet Tomita seldom uses this vast resource gratuitously: on the contrary, he selects his sounds with precision and taste. The wind effect on the otherwise unadorned 'Girl With The Flaxen Hair' adds mystery, romance and pathos. 'Arabesque No 1', on the other hand, features the comic juxtaposition of a church organ sound with vocalised noises reminiscent of Donald Duck. Perhaps the best illustration of Tomita's talents is, however, to be found in 'Gardens In The Rain', written by Debussy to simulate a thunderstorm in the Normandy town of Orbec. Here the effects are varied, at times startling, but always sympathetic to the composer's intentions.

The same cannot be said of the music made by The Portsmouth Sinfonia, whose first two albums were both released during the year. The orchestra comprised a combination of musicians playing their usual instruments, musicians playing unfamiliar instruments and non-musicians, all of whom tended to play from memory rather than using the written score. The result was invariably an out-of-tune cacophony which, conducted and executed in mock seriousness, debunked the conventions of classical music. On *Portsmouth Sinfonia Plays The Popular Classics*, much-loved compositions by the likes of Grieg, Tchaikovsky, Bach and Beethoven get the treatment and while the joke starts to wear thin fairly early on, somehow the orchestra contrive to create an overall sound that is not as arbitrary as their methodology might suggest.

Rather than listen to their music repeatedly on a record, it was probably preferable to see The Portsmouth Sinfonia in concert, and thus enjoy – if that is the right word – them as a one-off experience. But although they did release a live album of their concert at the Albert Hall on 28 May, the full range of their iconoclasm is perhaps better appreciated by viewing footage of the event (available at the time of writing on *www.youtube.com*). It is quite clear that many members of the audience queuing to get in had no idea what they were letting themselves in for. On *The 1812 Overture*, the brass section are two full bars behind the rest of the orchestra; 'In The Hall Of The Mountain King' is played on the jew's harp; Sally Binder performs Tchaikovsky's 'Piano Concerto No. 1' in the wrong key; and the climax to the concert is a chaotic version of Handel's 'Hallelujah Chorus', sung by a 350-piece choir. Throughout it all John Farley conducts the orchestra, and himself, as if nothing untoward was happening.

The Portsmouth Sinfonia was associated with some the biggest names in contemporary music: playing cello at the Albert Hall was Gavin Bryars, who had helped found the orchestra in the first place, while Michael Nyman was on euphonium. But it was a member of the clarinet section who was to have most impact on the music of 1974.

★★★★★

Disenchanted with life on the road and with singer Bryan Ferry's increasing dominance of the band, keyboardist Brian Eno left Roxy

Music in July 1973. Two months later he recorded his first solo album, *Here Come The Warm Jets.* Though essentially a rock album – it hit the charts in March 1974, reaching number 26 – it crossed over with contemporary music, or at least the aspects of it that preoccupied Eno. In 1971 he had participated in the first recording of Cornelius Cardew's *The Great Learning*, which used graphics and written instructions alongside traditional notation and mixed musicians with non-musicians playing both orthodox and unconventional instruments. Like The Portsmouth Sinfonia, however, this did not produce anarchy and suggested to Eno that something musically coherent – and, of course, stimulating – could stem from the permutation of random elements.

Some of this is at work in *Here Come The Warm Jets.* For one thing, the lyrics were, in the main, written spontaneously without any preparation or preconceived meaning. This gives them a dreamlike or, more often, nightmarish quality – as in 'Baby's On Fire', underscored in this case by sneering vocals and a crazed heavy metal guitar solo by Robert Fripp. For another, Eno was given to dancing in the studio and asking the musicians to play what came into their mind as they watched. But the record was also a product of the environment in which he had worked for the previous two years. In effect it is a distillation of what was interesting about glam rock – the energy, the theatricality and the sense of abandon. And unlike prog, where the material tended to be dictated by the instrumental proficiency of the musicians, here the potentially huge array of sounds was put to the service of the effect desired by Eno – from the relentless 'Driving Backwards' to the minimalist 'On Some Far Away Beach'. Furthermore macabre humour is never far away and it is impossible not to smile at the parody of Bryan Ferry's vocal mannerisms in 'Dead Finks Don't Talk'.

For the follow-up, *Taking Tiger Mountain (By Strategy)*, Eno introduced a new way of fostering creativity among his accompanists: instead of dancing for them, he used 'oblique strategies', a set of 55 cards he had developed with Peter Schmidt. Each one contained an instruction to encourage lateral thinking – 'Use an old idea', 'Work at a different speed,' 'Ask your body', and so on. Again, lyrics were written on the spur of the moment, although two tracks in particular suggest premeditation. 'Burning Airlines Give You So Much More' is a caustic comment on the Turkish Airlines plane crash in March, while the waltz 'Put A Straw Under Baby' – 'your good deed for the day' – with its fairground organ and wheezing strings (courtesy of The Portsmouth Sinfonia), harks back to Eno's Catholic upbringing and the precept that every time you commit a sin you remove a piece of straw from the crib in which Jesus was born. Other tracks, however, point to the future: the pulsating 'Third Uncle' prefigures punk; 'The True Wheel' ('we are the 801, we are the central shaft looking for a certain ratio') was the source of at least two band names; and the closing ballad 'Taking Tiger Mountain' points to his subsequent immersion in ambience.

April 1974 had seen the publication of David Toop's book *New/Rediscovered Instruments*, in which he celebrated the invention of such oddities as the bathosphere and the centriphone – the type of instruments, in fact, that Cardew had employed on *The Great Learning.* Eno made the ensuing album, by Toop and Max Eastley, one of the first releases on his own label, Obscure Records, and played on it himself as one of 'The Cetaceans'. This pioneering record is considered seminal in the development of improvised/ambient music, but another ambitious project in which Eno was involved proved to be an aesthetic cul-de-sac. Robert Calvert's *Captain Lockheed And The Starfighters* was a satire on the purchase by the German Air Ministry of the Lockheed F-104 Starfighter, known as the 'widow-maker' due to its poor safety record. What might have been an amusing if idiosyncratic record is ruined in the event by the clumsy ve-haf-vays-of-making-you-talk caricatures.

In the meantime real Germans were getting on with the job of making music at the cutting-edge of rock. Tangerine Dream, for instance, were taking the synthesiser in new directions and while their work bore some resemblance to the interstellar improvisations of early Pink Floyd it was more abstract, with no guitars, drums or vocals. *Phaedra* was their breakthrough album: with scarcely any airplay it entered the UK chart on 20 April 1974, reaching number fifteen. It was also their most influential, since it marked their first use of the moog sequencer – in effect, acting as a surrogate bass but with a fatter, fuller resonance. Before long this became one of the defining sounds of ambient music.

The epic title track, especially when listened to with headphones in a darkened room, conjures up visions of the cosmos, the soundtrack to an imaginary documentary on distant solar systems. Its sweeping, surging synthesiser sounds surface sporadically throughout the rest of the album, though 'Mysterious Semblance At The Strand Of Nightmares' is more static and 'Movements Of A Visionary' more diverse. Its freeform opening features a series of hissing and gurgling effects, before hitting a metronomic tempo; simulated marimbas give an exotic feel to the coda. The record closes with the brief 'Sequent C'', a stately flute solo with tape echo.

Tangerine Dream, along with their former drummer, Klaus Schulze, typified the West Berlin style of electronic music that in many ways was the counterpart to Eno's work in the UK; indeed it was, arguably, more significant since it led directly to trance and its 1990s sub-styles. It was also quite different from what has been termed the Düsseldorf School, the foundations for which were laid by Can, formed in 1968 in Cologne, some 27 miles away.

Can's innovative, atmospheric music had come increasingly to rely on a steady rhythmic pulse, sustained by Jaki Liebezeit's fluent yet rock-steady drumming. *Soon Over Babaluma,* recorded in August 1974 and released three months later, epitomises this blend of relentless experimentalism and dance-floor potential. 'Quantum Physics' is an amorphous journey into sound and 'Splash' a breathtaking high-velocity thrash; the thumping beats that drive 'Chain Reaction', however, are harbingers of house music. 'Dizzy Dizzy' is little short of hypnotic. Liebezeit sets the pace with a snare (switched off) and tom-tom combination redolent of African drumming, supported by Holger Czukay's throbbing bass and a jabbing, nagging violin riff by Michael Karoli; 'Come Sta, La Luna' is in the same vein, but this time Karoli's elegant guitar is to the fore, along with keyboardist Irmin Schmidt's incomprehensible yet strangely affecting vocals.

Though more edgy and unpredictable, Can were at times tantalisingly close to the form of music pioneered by the other major band of the Düsseldorf School, Kraftwerk. Yet there was one fundamental and crucial difference. What Kraftwerk achieved was not just the creation of a musical idiom but of a distinct, and distinctive, image which, while novel at the time, has endured well into the 21st century. Short hair and smart suits replaced the hirsuite, scruffy norm and gradually morphed into an automaton-like appearance that matched the exactitude of their music. Most rock bands to that point looked to the US or UK for their inspiration, but Kraftwerk oriented to the industrial environment of their native Rhineland. They dispensed, too, with conventional rock instrumentation in favour of synthesisers, a step so apparently radical that they were invited on to the BBC's technology programme *Tomorrow's World* to discuss their album *Autobahn.*

Released on 1 November 1974, it included some pieces that recalled their prog origins. 'Kometenmelodie 1' ('Comet Melody 1'), for example, is a leaf out of Pink Floyd's book; 'Mitternacht' ('Midnight') is an impressionistic composition with sudden bursts of sound and scary background noises; and 'Morgenspaziergang' ('Morning Walk') is accompanied by chirruping birds and a babbling brook. But this was not the stuff that earned the album its immortality.

'Autobahn' was inspired by the motorway drive between Düsseldorf and Bonn – a seemingly prosaic subject. Yet the regulated monotony of the experience is in fact the whole point. After a quiet introduction, the inexorable synthesised beat begins, rolling along in steady 4/4 time for the full 22 minutes' duration of the track. The repeated phrase 'Wir fahren, fahren, fahren auf der Autobahn' ('We drive, drive, drive on the motorway') and the deadpan observations – 'Fahrbahn ist ein graues Band, weisse Streifen, grüner Rand' ('Road is a grey band, white stripes, green edge') – are so banal as to reinforce the impression of uniformity, relieved only by gentle acceleration, the occasional flash of a passing vehicle and, as twilight approaches, the sonic simulation of the distant city lights.

After a tumultuous era when rock seemed to be growing ever more distant from reality, the clear, precise music of Kraftwerk represented a refreshing and grounded alternative. Why not write music about a car journey? It made more sense to many than the narcissistic musings of bloated rock stars or the fantastical visions of the prog bands. But it was the *sound* of 'Autobahn' that was its key selling-point. Synthesisers were played with a restraint that bordered on minimalism, vocals were processed through a vocoder and electronic percussion laid down a metronomic but propulsive beat. It was arty but accessible and its influence would spread beyond dance styles like synthpop and techno into almost every genre of music. This was not just an autobahn but an expressway to the future.

CHAPTER 7

Hang My Country

There were times in the late 20th century when it seemed like the sectarian conflict in Northern Ireland would never end. Day after day there were reports of bombings, murders and atrocities scarcely credible in a civilised society. The British Army were brought in to restore law and order but became embroiled in an inexorable cycle of violence. Politicians and community leaders searched for solutions but were reluctant to give ground and if anything became more entrenched; some even seemed to delight in bringing the emotions of both supporters and opponents to boiling point.

It was all a long way from the Belfast of 1791 where the Dublin Protestant lawyer Wolfe Tone founded the Society of United Irishmen. His aim was to 'unite Protestant, Catholic and Dissenter' and his vision of a country independent of British rule did indeed appeal to all sections of the population – apart from the aristocratic elite whose families had come from the mainland to appropriate vast tracts of land in the seventeenth century. They feared a repetition of the recent French Revolution, as indeed did the British Government. The 1798 rebellion led by Tone was duly crushed and three years later an Act of Union passed which abolished the kingdom of Ireland as a separate entity.

The campaign for Home Rule for Ireland, however, did not go away, and after more than a century of struggle, there were signs that it would achieve its aim. But in 1912 it became clear that the Army, should Home Rule become a reality, would refuse to enforce it on the nine counties of Ulster, where the country's Protestant minority were centred. At the same time antipathy to Home Rule in the Conservative Party was hardening to the extent that on 9 April their Leader, Andrew Bonar Law, personally reviewed a march by 100,000 Ulster Volunteers, a paramilitary group formed by Edward Carson and James Craig with the wholehearted support of the Protestant fraternal organisation, the Orange Order. It was in response to such pressure that the idea arose of a partition between Ulster and the rest of Ireland.

Republican groups continued, nevertheless, to push for a United Ireland. 1913 saw the formation of the Irish Volunteers who, like their counterparts in Ulster, pursued their aims by using physical force. Following their refusal to enlist in the British Army in 1917, they began to style themselves the Irish Republican Army, or IRA. Two other groups, the Irish Citizen Army and the Irish Republican Brotherhood, planned and executed the 1916 Easter Rising in Dublin which, though a failure, drew sympathy to the cause owing to the severity of the government's response. At the end of World War I these organisations participated in a Republican guerrilla campaign against British rule. Known as the Irish War of Independence (1919-1921), it culminated in negotiations between the British Government and Sinn Féin, the political voice of Republicanism. The result was the Anglo-Irish Treaty and the formation of an Irish Free State. In theory this comprised the whole of Ireland, but the six Ulster counties with the highest Protestant populations immediately exercised their right to secede and formed Northern Ireland.

What on the surface seemed a reasonable compromise soon erupted into violent conflict. Northern Ireland became a sectarian bloodbath and the Free State descended into a year-long civil war between those who saw it as a stepping-stone to full independence and those who were vehemently opposed to the compromises it contained, including an oath of allegiance to the King. Following the civil war the Irish Free State continued as a British Dominion until, in 1937, it adopted its own Constitution and the name Eire (though in more recent times it has become more widely known by the English translation, Ireland). From that point on, it tended to concentrate on internal issues: it remained neutral during World War II and, by the end of the 1950s, was achieving economic growth.

The IRA, however, still harboured dreams of a United Ireland and between 1956 and 1962 conducted a campaign of guerrilla warfare on the border between the Republic and Northern Ireland. At this time the IRA were opposed to both the British and Irish Governments, who – thanks largely to their common policy of interning suspected terrorists without trial – were able to defeat the operation with minimal casualties. The reaction of the IRA leader, Cathal Goulding, was to move to a less militaristic, more political approach. But this caused considerable dissension and in 1969 there was a split. The 'Official' IRA continued to follow the Goulding line while the more action-oriented 'Provisional' IRA resolved to take up arms against what they saw as the British occupation of the Six Counties, a campaign that was to last nearly 30 years.

One of the main priorities for the Provisionals, sometimes nicknamed 'Provos' or 'Provies', was to help Catholics in the North combat the discrimination they were encountering in employment, education and housing. The Northern Ireland Civil Rights Association (NICRA) was already protesting these issues – though peacefully, in the manner of contemporary civil rights marches in the USA. On 5 October 1968 NICRA planned a demonstration in Londonderry. (The title of the city is disputed; most Nationalists, disliking the allusion to the British capital, prefer 'Derry', and to this day one can see road-signs with the prefix painted out. The author has no affiliation with either side but will from this point on use 'Derry', on the basis that it is the city's original name.) The Belfast administration, fearing trouble in a city in which anti-Catholic feeling was especially rife, imposed a ban on the march; when it went ahead the protestors were attacked with batons by the Royal Ulster Constabulary.

In effect this marked the beginning of what has come to be called the

'Troubles'. Although the reader may question the need for such a lengthy preamble, it is important to understand the context of the events which took place in 1974. And indeed a preoccupation – at times, an obsession – with the past was an essential part of the culture of Northern Ireland in the period under discussion. These days, all communities continue to celebrate the people and events that shaped their history, but thankfully the emphasis is now on the present and, in particular, the future.

★★★★★

From 1968 to 1974, the picture in Northern Ireland deteriorated rapidly, with several tragic landmarks. On 12 August 1969, the Apprentice Boys' Parade – a march commemorating the thirteen Protestant apprentices who precipitated the 1688 Siege of Derry by locking out forces loyal to James II – inflamed tensions when it passed through the Catholic Bogside area of the city and a two-day riot ensued. The British Army arrived to quell the disturbances on a temporary assignment that was to last 38 years, the longest continuous campaign in their history. Though initially welcomed, they tended to lack the requisite people skills and their relatively heavy-handed methods alienated them from, in particular, the Nationalists, who believed they were agents of Unionism. 8 March 1971 saw the murder of three Royal Highland Fusiliers, including two teenage brothers, sparking off a crisis that culminated in the resignation of the Northern Ireland Prime Minister, James Chichester-Clark.

His replacement was Brian Faulkner, who as Minister of Home Affairs during the IRA's Border Campaign had found internment such an effective strategy. But now the circumstances were very different. British intelligence was not good enough to ensure the correct individuals were targeted, a fact of which the Provisionals were well aware: indeed they positively welcomed internment, knowing it would turn into the PR disaster it swiftly became – in effect a recruiting sergeant for their ranks.

1972 was a horrendous year. On 30 January (subsequently known as 'Bloody Sunday'), thirteen Catholics were killed by soldiers from the Parachute Regiment during another NICRA March in Derry – an incident that provoked widespread outrage. When the British Home Secretary, Reginald Maudling, told the House of Commons the following day that they had fired in self-defence, he was punched by the MP for Mid-Ulster, Bernadette Devlin, who had witnessed the shootings in person. Two months later Prime Minister Edward Heath suspended the Northern Ireland Parliament at Stormont for one year pending a political settlement, but the prospects for that looked bleak. On 21 July – 'Bloody Friday' – the Provisionals detonated 20 car bombs, killing nine civilians and injuring 130.

Individuals from the music community, both famous and obscure, began to react to these events. Wings' 'Give Ireland Back To The Irish' was released in the aftermath of Bloody Sunday, while Derry teacher Tony Johnston set up two labels with the express intention of releasing rebel music. Blackthorn's 'Lid Of Me Granny's Bin' was recorded live at the Bogside Inn, Derry; written by Joe Mulhearn, it is the humorous story of the attempt by the British soldiers to confiscate the eponymous bin-lids, which were banged together by women in Nationalist areas to warn of Army patrols.

Further evidence that laughter was an effective way of lifting the spirits in the face of such an appalling situation is provided by a compilation album issued by Johnston on Derry Records in 1974, of which 'Lid Of Me Granny's Bin' is the title track. A revival, also by Blackthorn, of the 1920s satire 'The Man From The Daily Mail' and The Wolfhound's cover of the mocking 'Helicopter Song' are to be found alongside less light-hearted fare such as Owen McDonagh's mordant 'Free Belfast' and Declan Hunt's version of the Dominic Behan composition 'Come Out Ye Black And Tans' which alludes to the hated auxiliary police force formed during the Irish War of Independence.

1973 brought some welcome relief to the British Government,

not least in the propaganda war. The first loyalist internments were, for example, offered as proof of their impartiality, while most Nationalists were now voting for the moderate Social, Democratic and Labour Party (SDLP): Dr Raymond McClean was elected Mayor of Derry, the first Nationalist to hold the office for 50 years. On 18 July the Northern Ireland Constitution Bill became law, effectively keeping Northern Ireland in the UK unless its citizens vote otherwise. Internments were falling and convictions were rising, largely due to the high quality intelligence being passed to the Army by informers such as Eamon Molloy. Furthermore, according to Ed Moloney, Nationalist leaders like Gerry Adams became convinced that

> the British were using [Molloy's] information to shape and mould the composition of the [IRA's] Belfast Brigade to their liking. This was done... to boost elements in favour of a cease-fire by releasing more pragmatic figures from internment while simultaneously rounding up the IRA's so-called Young Turks, those identified as hard line associates of Adams, [IRA commanders] [Ivor] Bell and [Brendan] Hughes. (*A Secret History Of The IRA*, p.138-9)

It was in this atmosphere of relative optimism that the British and Irish Governments, together with the main political parties in Northern Ireland, signed an agreement on 9 December at Sunningdale, Berkshire, for a Council of Ireland and a devolved, power-sharing administration in the North, with Prime Minister Faulkner as chief executive. It was what even as stern a critic of the peace process as Tim Pat Coogan has described as 'the only really significant attempt to resolve the Irish issue for most of the Troubles' (*Ireland In The Twentieth Century*, p. 577).

On 1 January 1974 the new executive of the Northern Ireland Assembly took office. It was composed of eleven members of the Unionist, SDLP and Alliance parties, there being no question at this stage of involving Sinn Féin, who were seen as too closely associated with the IRA. But any form of power-sharing was anathema to hard-line Unionists and after only three days the Ulster Unionist Council voted to reject it. Faulkner was thus forced to resign as Unionist Party leader and set up an alternative body, the Unionist Party of Northern Ireland. This new organisation was in no position to contest the General Election the following month and the seven candidates who stood as Pro-Assembly Unionists were all defeated, leaving the Unionist vote in the hands of the anti-assembly coalition of the Democratic Unionist, Ulster Unionist and Vanguard Unionist Progressive Parties. There was no better news for the Assembly from the Nationalist side: the SDLP went down to one MP (their leader and Deputy Assembly chief executive, Gerry Fitt), while the non-sectarian Alliance Party won no seats at all.

In April the United Ulster Unionist Council – who despite their name was comprised solely of organisations hostile to the Assembly including the Ulster Workers Council (UWC) and the paramilitary Ulster Defence Association (UDA) – held a conference at Portrush, County Antrim. The speakers included the right-wing politician Enoch Powell, who was to win South Down for the Ulster Unionists at the October General Election. Unsurprisingly, the conference called for the Assembly to be scrapped, a demand followed up at Stormont itself by the anti-Assembly Unionists. When this failed, the UWC organised a general strike which as well as suspending essential services became a focus for sectarian violence, leading to over 40 deaths. 17 May proved to be the worst day of the Troubles so far: the Ulster Volunteer Force (descendants of the Ulster Volunteers formed to defend Protestant Ulster) detonated four car bombs without warning in Dublin and in Monaghan, killing 33 people, mainly young women.

By now the Labour Government was in office and on 25 May Prime Minister Harold Wilson denounced those who 'viciously defy Westminster, purporting to act as though they were an elected government' (quoted in Coogan, *ibid.)* but in truth his Secretary of State, Merlyn Rees, did little to prevent either the strike or the violence. He did, however, refuse to negotiate with the UWC, an act which led to the resignation of Faulkner and his Pro-Assembly Unionists thus, after an existence of just under five months, bringing to an end the Northern Ireland Assembly.

★★★★★

Music was of prime importance to both Unionists and Nationalists: traditional songs told of historic struggles and heroic exploits, contemporary compositions of harsh realities. Orange Order parades, the quintessential manifestation of loyalist sentiment, were (and still are) invariably accompanied by marching bands while Nationalists drew on the rich Irish folk music heritage. In all cases, music transcended mere entertainment to become a source of inspiration and an outlet for the emotions.

In 1974, the recording of loyalist songs was sporadic and almost exclusively confined to small labels; very few of the artists concerned had been, or became, well known outside Northern Ireland. Almost all of them owed a debt to Richard Hayward (1892-1964), the actor, writer, musician and Orangeman who championed the traditional culture of Ireland as a whole and, particularly, that of the Six Counties. Though session and release dates are often difficult to identify with any certainty, it is clear that the year yielded music which traversed the whole history of Unionism.

At one end is Sally Young's account of the traditional song 'Aghalee Heroes'. Set to a jaunty accordion accompaniment, it commemorates the victory in 1798 of troops from Aghalee, County Antrim, over a group of rebels in Lurgan, only five miles away but located in County Armagh – and hence now in the Irish Republic. At the other, 'The Ballad Of Andy Tyrie' by Sadie Myers brings the story right up to date. Tyrie had taken over the leadership of the UDA in 1973 and, as a former shop steward, played a leading role in the UWC strike which brought down the Northern Ireland Assembly. His achievements are celebrated in this primal power ballad in which walloping drums vie for supremacy with Myers's trenchant vocal:

> There's a man just down our street whose name's a legend
> For he has led his army all alone
> In case you do not know he's Andy Tyrie
> And we will back him up through right or wrong
> For the UDA is stronger now than ever
> At his command we'll rally to the fore

In comparison, Nationalist music – more commonly known as Irish rebel music – was on a more established footing. It was to be found, for example, in the work of the big-name traditional folk bands from the Irish Republic, though often as just one element in an otherwise mixed repertoire. The Dublin City Ramblers' *End It Someday*, for example, contains a version of 'Come Out Ye Black And Tans' while the opening track on Planxty's *Cold Blow And The Rainy Night* is the Jacobite ballad 'Johnny Cope'.

The Wolfe Tones, as befits their name, featured a higher percentage of rebel music. 'Broad Black Brimmer' was written by the band's Noel Nagle and is set just after the Irish civil war in which the protagonist's father has been killed fighting against the Treaty; his son must now don the IRA uniform his father wore, including the eponymous hat. 'Bodenstown Churchyard' is a composition by Thomas Davis (1814-1845), leader of the militant Young Irelanders, and refers to the site of Wolfe Tone's grave – a place of pilgrimage for subsequent generations of Nationalists. Paddy McGuigan's 'The Boys Of The Old Brigade' looks back fondly to the Easter Rising; 'Must Ireland Be Divided' and 'Ireland Over All' are self-explanatory. The Wolfe Tones' 1974 album *'Till Ireland a Nation* contains all five tracks.

However, Nationalist music from north of the border naturally has additional bite. The Wolfhound were formed in Belfast in 1970.

Founder member Danny Burns (1946-2002) later recalled, 'The Troubles were in full swing and all being from Republican families, we said we were going to play our part through our music'. As noted above, their version of the Wolfe Tones' hit, 'Helicopter Song' appeared on the 1974 compilation *Lid Of Me Granny's Bin* but they are perhaps most famous for two singles they released during the year. 'Provie Lullaby' is an original composition in which the IRA man of the title is assured that when he goes to heaven, 'there'll be no peelers there'; despite – or probably because of – its underlying sentimentality, it became one of their biggest hits. 'Take Me Home To Mayo' was written by Seamus Robinson in response to the death on 3 June of the hunger striker Michael Gaughan, a volunteer with the Provisionals. Though set, somewhat incongruously, to waltz time, its direct message and instantly memorable chorus led to numerous covers, but The Wolfhound's version is considered definitive.

The other major Belfast band specialising in rebel music were The Barleycorn. Formed in 1971, they included Paddy McGuigan, who wrote the band's debut single, 'The Men Behind The Wire', in the aftermath of internment. It became another widely-recorded contemporary rebel song and was even appropriated by the loyalists, but it was The Barleycorn original that hit the top of the Irish singles chart on 22 January 1972. As noted above, McGuigan also composed 'The Boys Of The Old Brigade' which The Barleycorn included on their 1974 album, *The Winds Are Singing Freedom,* a well-programmed blend of originals, covers and traditional material, made at Trend Studios, Dublin.

McGuigan picks up the theme of 'The Men Behind The Wire' with the stirring, anthemic 'Bring Them Home' while band-mate Liam Tiernan chips in with the up-tempo 'This Little Place Called Ireland' – 'the sorrow that I speak of is the history you all know'. 'Our Lads In Crumlin Jail' alludes to the IRA officer and anti-Treaty militant Joe McKelvey, who was executed in 1922 but who 'did not die in vain'. Other songs also honour Republican heroes: 'Henry Joy'

(McCracken) of the Society of United Irishmen who was martyred in the Irish rebellion; 'John Mitchell', the Young Irelander and elected MP deported to Van Dieman's Land for political activism; 'Tom Williams', the IRA soldier hanged in 1942 for killing an RUC officer; and 'Billy Reid', the Provo responsible for the first death of a British soldier during the Troubles. The lachrymose 'Irish Soldier Boy' and Phil Coulter's much-covered but maudlin 'The Town I Loved So Well' are balanced by two lively instrumentals and the rousing title track, a Tommy Makem composition which, fifteen years later, was sung across Eastern Europe during the break-up of the Soviet Union (and, fifteen years after that, was parodied by Christopher Guest in his satire of the folk revival, *A Mighty Wind*).

Also recorded at Trend was the remarkable *Hang My Country (The Story Of A Tragedy)* by Tony Kearney and Geraldine. Kearney was a civil rights activist, who had recorded the singles 'Bloody Sunday' and '100,000 Guns' for Tony Johnston's Cúchulainn label. Geraldine (McKeever) was a Derry folksinger, managed by Johnston, whose debut album had included covers of material by Gordon Lightfoot, Joni Mitchell and Randy Newman. Her single 'She Wept For The Fighting Of Orange And Green'/'Danny Boy' was on one of Johnston's other labels, Flame.

The first album to be issued on Cúchulainn, *Hang My Country* is, compared with releases by the likes of The Barleycorn, The Wolfe Tones and The Dublin City Ramblers, stark and unvarnished. Even the cover design, depicting a noose (the border between North and South) around the neck of the island of Ireland, is forbidding. But this merely adds to its intensity, and authenticity. The second side is relatively conventional, comprising Johnston's brisk 'Clan Of The Brave'; the rebellion ballad 'The Croppy Boy'; and four tributes to Republican martyrs – two United Irishmen ('Henry Joy' and 'Roddy McCorley') and two leaders of the Easter Rising: Patrick Henry Pearse ('Pearse To Ireland') and 'James Connolly'.

Side One, however, is startlingly original in conception. Each of the six tracks represents what, from a Nationalist viewpoint, has been a tragedy for Northern Ireland and consists of a spoken introduction by Kearney followed by a song on the same theme. Thus 'The Tragedy Of Partition (Four Green Fields)' begins with the words

This is an island
This is my country
This is one country...
But divided by a few...
This is the tragedy of Ireland

before segueing into Tommy Makem's 'Four Green Fields' ('one of them in bondage'), sung by McKeever. 'The Tragedy Of Guns (100,000 Guns)' reprises Kearney's Cúchulainn single which was written by the album's producer, Flan Mac A'Bhaird: 'We'll haul down the barricades and call in our sons when 100,000 loyalists hand in their guns'. Next comes Johnston's 'The Tragedy Of Derry (Speak, My Beloved City)'. Here the spoken intro is underpinned by a chorus of 'We Shall Overcome' before McKeever serenely hums 'Danny Boy' (aka 'The Londonderry Air'); in a manner reminiscent of the chilling juxtaposition of grim news bulletin and Christmas Carol in Simon and Garfunkel's '7 O'Clock News/Silent Night', Kearney continues his rant in the background.

'The Tragedy Of Repression (The Men Behind The Wire)' has Kearney's lively version of Paddy McGuigan's classic prefaced by his assertion that 'The difference between Long Kesh and Belsen was only a matter of degrees'. 'The Tragedy Written In Blood (Bloody Sunday)' includes the sound of rioting and gunfire while 'The Tragedy Of Hate (She Wept For The Fighting Of Orange And Green)' opens with battle noises; but Kearney brings the side to a peaceful conclusion. His solemn version of Johnston's gentle ballad follows the affirmation that 'true Irishmen mourn for the fighting of the orange and the green'.

That was as far as Kearney was prepared to go in the spirit of reconciliation and very few Northern Irish singers went further than that. But Tommy Sands, born in the Catholic Ryan Road district of Mayobridge, County Down, was an exception. Not only did his music (and actions) promote peace but, uniquely, he even attempted to see the other side's point of view. 'You Sold Us Down The River', for example, sums up the way that many working-class Unionists felt about successive British governments. But the song for which he is best known is 'There Were Roses', written in response to the murder of two friends in 1974. The first (called 'Allan Bell' in the song) was a Protestant killed by Republicans, the second, 'Sean O'Malley' – a Catholic – killed by loyalists in revenge:

> I don't know where the moral is or where this song should end
> But I wondered just how many wars are fought between good friends
> And those who give the orders are not the ones to die
> It's Bell and O'Malley and the likes of you and I

★★★★★

Many more innocent people were victims of the Troubles as the conflict spread to mainland Britain. Throughout 1974 the Provisional IRA carried out a series of bombings which, though in theory aimed at military or political targets, had an equal impact on civilians. On 4 February 1974, a coach travelling on the M62 motorway in West Yorkshire was bombed, killing twelve people – nine off-duty British soldiers and the wife and two children of one of the soldiers, Clifford Haughton. The National Defence College (NDC), Buckinghamshire, was bombed on the 12th. On 17 June a bomb exploded in the Houses of Parliament and, exactly one month later, in the Tower of London, causing one fatality. In October, bombs were detonated in two pubs in Guildford, killing five, including four soldiers; at Brooks's Club, of which the Home Secretary, Roy Jenkins, was a member; and in the car belonging to the Sports Minister, Denis Howell. And on 7

November, one soldier and one civilian were killed when a bomb was thrown into the bar at the King's Arms, Woolwich.

All of these incidents were greeted with horror but by far the greatest outrage was caused by the bombings in Birmingham. On 14 November a Provisional IRA man, James McDade, had been killed when a bomb he was planting in a Coventry telephone box went off prematurely. Republicans wanted McDade buried with full paramilitary honours. But permission was refused, both by Jenkins and the local authorities through whose areas the funeral procession would march. McDade's body was therefore driven to Birmingham Airport and flown to Ireland on the afternoon of the 21st. At 8.11pm a call was made to the *Birmingham Post and Mail* with the following brief message:

> There is a bomb planted in the Rotunda. There is a bomb planted in New Street at the tax office. This is Double-X.

Six minutes later a bomb went off in the Mulberry Bush, a pub located on the lower two floors of the Rotunda office block, and ten minutes after that another bomb exploded in the Tavern In The Town, above the New Street Tax Office 50 yards away. The blasts killed 21 people and injured 182, none of whom were military personnel. In the resultant mayhem, pubs were evacuated, bus services stopped and rooms in the City Centre Hotel commandeered for first-aid posts. The need for emergency treatment was so great that medical students from the University of Birmingham were drafted in to assist; these included the President of the Guild of Students, Andrew Vallance-Owen, who later became Group Medical Director of the private healthcare company, BUPA.

The atrocity provoked a furious reaction across the West Midlands. Irish businesses, clubs and community centres were attacked and many shops refused to serve anyone with an Irish accent – this included Bridget Reilly whose sons Desmond and Eugene were killed in the bombing of the Tavern In The Town. The government, too, were quick to respond: on 25 November, Jenkins announced an official ban on the IRA and two days later he signed the Prevention of Terrorism Act 1974 which permitted the detention of suspects for up to seven days. But the police response was the quickest of all.

Any act of terrorism leads to public demand for the immediate capture and conviction of those responsible and given such pressures, there is always the risk of a miscarriage of justice. Such was the case with Judith Ward, who was apprehended just two days after the bombing at the NDC, to which she subsequently confessed. She also admitted responsibility for a bomb attack at Euston Station the previous year and for the M62 coach bombing. On 4 November Ward was sentenced to life imprisonment, though it later emerged that not only had she been mentally ill and prone to attention-seeking behaviour during this time but that the forensic evidence against her was also unsafe. She was released from prison in May 1992.

After Birmingham, the police acted even more swiftly. Within three hours of the bombings, five suspects had been arrested at Heysham, Lancashire, where they were about to board a ferry to Belfast; another was picked up the following day. These men became known as the Birmingham Six and their case became a *cause célèbre* over the ensuing sixteen years. On the basis of the suppression and fabrication of evidence and of the unreliability of forensic reports given at their original trial, they were released in March 1991.

As to who *was* responsible for the Birmingham pub bombings, this remained unclear for 40 years. At the time, the IRA vehemently denied any involvement but in December 2014 the Dublin lawyer Kieran Conway, a former senior member of the organisation, stated that not only did the IRA carry out the bombings but, horrified by the outrage they provoked, began to consider a ceasefire. At the same time, the number of weapons being supplied to the IRA had been reduced to a trickle due to the intelligence provided by informers who, as we have seen, were also able to identify those IRA officers who favoured a suspension of hostilities.

For what was probably a combination of all these reasons, an IRA ceasefire did indeed commence on 22 December 1974. Like the Northern Ireland Assembly, it would not last very long but at least it provided a ray of hope for all of those in Northern Ireland, the Republic of Ireland and mainland Britain seeking a peaceful settlement. It also proved to be a glimpse of the future.

*****

Very few individuals, or organisations, derived any satisfaction from the Birmingham pub bombings. But – as in so many areas of politics, religion, or simply civilised, human behaviour – the National Front swam against the tide. Immediately after the carnage, NF members patrolled the city stirring up trouble and fomenting still further the anti-Irish sentiment that was already in the air. Such actions were, in fact, part of their overall strategy of exploiting any incident which had the potential to provide them with a platform for publicising their policies. As far as Northern Ireland was concerned, the NF had been keen to link up with the UWC strike in May, partly due to their support for the loyalist cause but also because they believed in the power of the working man to overthrow governments.

On this occasion, they were rebuffed. Suspicious of their motives and perceiving that they knew nothing of the complexities of Northern Irish history and politics, Andy Tyrie declined to co-operate. Undeterred, they created the NF Trade Unionists Association in July. Of course, the NF were antipathetic to traditional left-wing union beliefs but thought that they could turn to their advantage what they saw as the undercurrent of racism among the working class – a policy not unlike that pursued by the United Kingdom Independence Party 40 years later. And, as in the case of UKIP, it brought results – 1974 was, without a doubt, their most successful year to date.

Founded in February 1967, the National Front were essentially a reaction against the two major political parties and their apparent consensus on immigration. Both Labour and the Conservatives had leaders (Harold Wilson and Edward Heath) on the left of their respective parties and openly encouraged good relations with the country's ethnic minority communities – the focus of the NF's fear and loathing. No-one took much notice until 1972 when Heath, by then Prime Minister, agreed to accept into the UK about half of the 60,000 Asians expelled from Uganda by the President, Idi Amin.

The Front orchestrated a series of protests, including a picket of Downing Street, a march to Uganda House and noisy demonstrations to greet the refugees when they arrived at Heathrow and Manchester airports. Such activities led to a huge growth in NF membership and at the May 1973 West Bromwich by-election their candidate, Martin Webster, received 4,789 votes, only 3,000 fewer than the Conservative, David Bell. (The seat was won by the future Speaker of the House of Commons, Betty Boothroyd.) At the local elections in June, over 18,000 people voted for the NF in Leicester, while they took over 20% of the vote in each of the five wards they contested in Blackburn.

By this time the oil crisis was looming and the NF managed to capitalise on the resultant gloom by blaming the immigration population for all of the country's ills. As Martin Walker has written,

> The NF tried, during 1974, to develop a wider base than simple racial appeals, by linking race and immigration to other political themes. Unemployment was explained as black workers taking British jobs; bad housing as blacks jumping the council house queue; clogged health and social services were the fault of diseased immigrants taking the place of deserving Britons; bad schools were caused by illiterate black kids, and crime was their fault too. (*The National Front*, p. 271)

This approach proved extremely effective. At the February General Election, the NF won a total of 76,000 votes; by October, this mushroomed to 113,000. During the course of the year NF membership went from 12,000 to 20,000. They had made the transition from the lunatic fringe to redoubtable minority party. But at the same time there were signs that their new-found success may not last.

On 15 June the NF held a rally in London to protest at the government's amnesty for illegal immigrants; members of the International Marxist Group and the London Area Council for Liberation held a counter-demonstration. Unaccountably, the police allowed both marches to coincide at Red Lion Square, on the boundary of Bloomsbury and Holborn. Their belated efforts to keep the two sides apart merely exacerbated the violence and in the resultant chaos Kevin Gately, a student at the University of Warwick, was killed by a blow to the head. It was the first fatality at a demonstration in the UK for 55 years and though no culprit was ever found the incident was of concern to many casual NF supporters. Then, in September, ITV broadcast a documentary about the National Front on its *This Week* programme in which former party chairman John O'Brien exposed the Nazi connections of both Webster and the current chairman, John Tyndall. Within a month, Tyndall was voted out of office.

Though the NF subsequently went into decline, their electoral success had brought right-wing extremism into the realm of legitimate democratic politics, a position which it has continued to occupy ever since.

★★★★★

Though the National Front's racism appealed to a small but significant minority, most white Britons were tolerant of their immigrant neighbours. By 1974 the term 'immigrant' was in any case becoming outdated. Levels of immigration had fallen sharply and a large percentage of the country's ethnic minorities, as they came to be known, were born in the UK – their parents, or grandparents, having settled here in the 1950s and 1960s. Yet the pull of their country of origin remained strong, especially in aspects of culture such as religion, dress, food and music. In some cases, these were taken up by the country as a whole – the widespread popularity of Asian cuisine, for example, led the then Foreign Secretary, Robin Cook, to proclaim chicken tikka masala a British national dish in 2001.

The adoption of reggae was, in musical terms, equally significant. Earlier Caribbean styles such ska and rocksteady had found an audience among British young people, especially in the working-class areas in which West Indian families tended to settle. But despite the occasional hit, they had failed to cross over to a wider record-buying public. Reggae, on the other hand, became accepted as a major idiom, a process accelerated by the developments that took place in the music during 1974.

As we saw in Chapter 1, Eric Clapton included a version of Bob Marley's 'I Shot The Sheriff' on his album *461 Ocean Boulevard*; released as a single, it made number nine in the UK and number one in the US, reaching the top spot on 14 September. At that time Marley, though prominent in Jamaica, was not well known elsewhere. But Clapton's status was such that any material he covered generated enormous interest; the versions by his former band Cream of compositions by the likes of Robert Johnson, Skip James, Muddy Waters, Blind Joe Reynolds and Howlin' Wolf had brought their music to mass attention, thus igniting the second British blues boom.

For Marley, the timing was perfect. Exactly six weeks after 'I Shot The Sheriff' hit the top of the American charts came the release of his album *Natty Dread*. Credited to Bob Marley and The Wailers, it was his first since the break-up of the original Wailers (including Peter Tosh and Bunny Wailer) earlier in the year. The dry, tight production was quite a departure from the looser, more experimental sound of dub, then fashionable in reggae, but made it instantly accessible to an audience raised on rock. Yet there was no compromise when it came to political content: '(Them Belly Full) But We Hungry' and 'Revolution' articulate the mixture of anger and frustration felt by impoverished Jamaicans and, by extension, oppressed peoples around the world, while 'Rebel Music (3 O'clock Road Block)' is a plea for personal freedom but also hints at the potential of reggae to bring about change.

Conventional religion, in Marley's eyes, had failed – the destitute protagonist of 'Talkin' Blues' tells us that 'I feel like bombing a church'. Rastafari, in contrast, offered hope: 'Not one of my seeds shall sit in the sidewalk and beg your bread' ('So Jah Seh') and 'I and I couldn't never go astray' ('Natty Dread'). But the album is far from being an unrelieved political and religious diatribe. The elegiac 'No Woman, No Cry' became perhaps his best-known number and 'Lively Up Yourself' and 'Bend Down Low' evoke the easy, playful sensuality that was the flipside of Marley's musical personality.

Natty Dread was recorded at Harry J Studios, Kingston, Jamaica which thereafter became the studio of choice not only for reggae artists but major rock bands such as The Who and The Rolling Stones. Harry J (real name: Harry Johnson) was an entrepreneur and producer who had had a hit under his own name in 1969 with 'The Liquidator'. In addition to his own studio he also ran his own Harry J label, a subdivision of Trojan Records. Among its many outstanding 1974 releases was Turnell McCormack and The Cordells' celebratory 'Irie Festival'– not to be confused with the similarly-titled 'Ire Feelings (Skanga)' (both 'irie' and 'ire' are Jamaican slang for 'good') by Rupie Edwards, a floating, bewitching sliver of dub that entered the UK singles chart on 23 November.

Another reggae singer to peak in 1974 was Ernie Smith, whose relaxed yet elegant 'Duppy Gun-Man' was a throwback to rocksteady. Smith also specialised in cover versions of songs like 'Everything I Own' by David Gates and Kris Kristofferson's 'Help Me Make It Through The Night'. It was these very songs that helped establish lovers rock, a softer, more romantic style of reggae that offered a seductive option for those alienated by the experimentalism of dub or the politically-charged output of Bob Marley. Both were hits for other artists. Ken Boothe's 'Everything I Own' featured the irresistible combination of a strong song, plaintive vocals, a gentle, tugging beat and quiet instrumental accompaniment with organ, glockenspiel and guitar; it bounded to the top of the UK singles chart on 26 October, remaining there for three weeks. The follow-up, 'Crying Over You', made number eleven and had as its B-side 'Now You Can See Me Again', an answer-song to The Three Degrees' 'When Will I See You Again', employing the same melody. 'Help Me Make It Through The Night' was a number six hit for John Holt in December, its lively tempo counterbalanced by his smooth vocal delivery.

During 1974 the commercial success of lovers rock gave reggae a place in the mainstream of British pop music, a process much assisted by the simultaneous purchase by Saga of Trojan Records and the subsequent release of numerous budget-price compilation albums. Never had black music sold so well in the UK before: lovers rock and contemporary soul between them accounted for over a quarter of the year's number one singles. Yet there was also a strong, at times fanatical, interest in the black music of earlier eras.

★★★★★

Quite when northern soul began is a moot point, though the consensus of opinion among the cognoscenti is that it reached a peak in 1974. But northern soul is not really a musical idiom at all in the sense that the term is applied to jazz, rock and roll, blues and so on. It did not grow organically, nurtured by a series of major artists and influencing, and influenced by, other forms of music. Essentially, northern soul was about *records*. Records made in the USA by a group of artists – mainly African-American, but some white – with a sound and a beat that inspired a musical cult, centred on dance, espoused by a generation of working-class British teenagers. Very few of the artists were well-known (and those who were, such as Edwin Starr, Frankie Valli and Paul Anka, found their fame doing something else), but that was the whole point: the more obscure the singer, the better it was for the quasi-clandestine milieu in which northern soul fans moved. In any case, the artist was of passing interest – what mattered was the record.

So what did the records sound like? The first point is that they were not reflective of the contemporary soul scene as discussed in Chapter 3: indeed many of the singers discussed there were anathema to northern soul fans. Though the 'northern' in northern soul refers to the geographical area of England (especially the north-west) in which the scene was centred, it could equally well refer to where many of the records were made – northern US cities like Chicago and, especially, Detroit.

Les Hare runs Manchester's Kingbee Records, one the UK's leading independent record shops; he is also an authority on northern soul. Rather disarmingly, he says, 'Some people have said it's failed Motown!' But there was clearly more to it than that. Les adds,

> From '66 onwards Tamla Motown really began to take off and groups all over America tried to emulate that sound. Most of them weren't successful, but they were probably just as good as the ones who were. They were trying to make hit records that sounded like the Motown stuff and it developed from there.

Indeed for the nascent northern soul fans of the late 1960s, the successful Motown records were both too commercial and too familiar:

> Obviously you couldn't keep playing the same old 50 popular Motown records, so other records that sounded similar came into the equation and the kids at the time wanted that fast beat, and the

> beat went even faster. They were just club records at the time – they weren't described as northern soul.

But, though crucial, the urgency of the beat was not the sole attraction. Northern soul DJ Kev Nolan recalls,

> Once you'd heard northern soul everything else was watered down… you had wailers, you had lamenters, you had people that pined for love, people that glorified love, and people that longed for love and those were the things that appealed to me.

The origins of the northern soul scene lay in the youth clubs of north-west England where legendary DJs like Stevie James (catchphrase: 'The super soul sound of Stevie James') captivated their adolescent audience with records like 'Soul Time' by Shirley Ellis and Frankie Valli's 'You're Ready Now', a particular favourite for its relentless, metronomic rhythm. Older/bolder teens gravitated to Manchester's Twisted Wheel to hear Roger Eagle spin the cutting-edge discs they craved.

Early northern soul fans were former mods who had grown disillusioned when the music had become too commercial and drifted away from the hardcore R&B that had characterised it at the start. This cycle was to repeat itself in northern soul. Like the mods, northern soul fans were fixated with the right clothes (for boys – Oxford bags, jaytex shirts, checked Banner shirts with a button-down collar, brogues, a crombie with a Lancashire Rose on it, for girls – knitted tank tops, slim-fit shirts, ankle-length skirts and platform shoes); the right dance moves (break-dancing, rolling in and rolling out from a circle); and the right behaviour (cool, but on the dancefloor – wild).

By 1974 the scene was flourishing. The Twisted Wheel had closed in 1971 but the clubs were, in any case, becoming too small to cater for the burgeoning demand. The favoured venues were now former ballrooms like Wigan Casino, which held its first all-niter on 23

September 1973, and the Highland Room of the Blackpool Mecca where DJs Colin Curtis and Ian Levine were the tastemakers. So many records were classified as northern soul that it would be impossible to list them all; the following is a tiny sample:

- Eddie Parker – 'I'm Gone' (1966), written by Ermastine Lewis and Jack Ashford; produced by Ashford and Joseph E Hunter, former leader of Motown house band The Funk Brothers. Roaring vocals and a pulsating beat with stop-time breaks to rack up the tension.
- Roy Handy – 'Baby That's A Groove' (1966), probably the only song to be written by the team of Brian Holland, Lamont Dozier and George Clinton. Produced by R&B Renaissance Man Gene Redd, it bears a resemblance to The Four Tops' 'I Can't Help Myself'.
- R Dean Taylor – 'There's A Ghost In My House' (1967), a breathless, almost frantic number by Motown's only white Canadian.
- The Gospel Classics – 'More Love, That's What We Need' (1968), written by Sonny Thompson and Matthew Parker in the aftermath of Martin Luther King's assassination and appropriately impassioned. Produced by another veteran, Ralph Bass.
- Mel Britt – 'She'll Come Running Back' (1969), more laid-back, with floating vocal and cool vibes within a busy arrangement. Slightly slower but eminently danceable.

It will be noted that none of these releases are from 1974, or even from the 1970s, but they are all northern soul classics of the period.

One of the remarkable aspects of northern soul is that it appealed almost exclusively to a single socio-economic-geographic group: white, working-class teenagers living in the northern half of Britain, often (probably as a consequence) rebellious by nature. Most were in jobs – they had to be, in order to support their addiction to music and, often, to alcohol and/or amphetamines – but these were frequently menial and dead-end. Elaine Constantine's 2014 film *Northern Soul*, set in 1974, is considered by the experts to be an accurate depiction of both the lifestyle and the music.

But as northern soul began to attract wider attention, including from the media, it lost its unique selling proposition, exclusivity. In order to cater for this new and bigger audience the music at Wigan Casino became more pop-oriented, a trend which culminated in the release of 'Footsee' by Wigan's Chosen Few (from Canada!) and 'Skiing In The Snow', 'Per-so-nal-ly' and 'Super Love' by Wigan's Ovation, all of which were UK hit singles in 1975. This was the point at which many of the most devout northern soul fans quit the scene – in both senses. Just like the mods before them, they felt a sense of betrayal. But their devotion to the music remained, and remains, undiminished. Original copies of key singles now change hands for enormous prices. Les Hare monitors the market closely: 'Mel Britt's "She'll Come Running Back" sells for about £1,000, and "I'm Gone" by Eddie Parker – someone's just bought that for £9,000'.

American blues had, in the early 1960s, provoked a fervour not unlike that aroused by northern soul. Seminal records were sought out, information eagerly exchanged, and visiting singers lionised. And any whiff of commercialism – the pop charts, the teen idols, Beatlemania – was to be avoided. But there were important differences. Blues fans tended to come from the white middle classes and were not restricted to any particular location: indeed blues was popular throughout the whole of Western Europe. A decade later, and the fans still turned out for the touring troupes of African-American blues artists that had been crossing the Atlantic ever since the German impresarios Horst Lippmann and Fritz Rau had organised the first American Folk Blues Festival in 1962.

By 1974 the mantle of Lippmann and Rau had been assumed by British music entrepreneur Jim Simpson who entitled his packages the American Blues Legends and recorded the artists during their visits for his Big Bear label. That the tours were fun for the participants, as well as the audiences, is borne out by the closing track on *American Blues Legends 74*, 'From Birmingham To Rotterdam', in which New Orleans pianist Cousin Joe tells the story of their escapades.

The rest of the record is a pleasing mixture of styles. Mississippi bluesman Doctor Ross ('the harmonica boss') contributes two country-flavoured numbers, the bouncy 'It Seems Like A Dream' and the mournful 'On My Way To School', a peculiar piece, perhaps, for a 48-year-old to be taking on. Eddie 'Playboy' Taylor's stinging guitar is featured to good effect on the slow, crunching blues 'I Know My Baby' and the medium-tempo shuffle 'I Used To Have Some Friends', the most exciting number on the record. He also plays guitar on the two Big John Wrencher pieces, 'Big John's Boogie' and 'I'm A Root Man', both of them characteristically gruff, gutsy performances. Surprisingly, given his relative obscurity, GP Jackson is allocated three tracks. Jackson was once known as 'the Kansas City Bo Diddley' but on this evidence it is hard to see why; there is, however, something endearing about his elemental guitar work and approximate vocal delivery. Cousin Joe completes the proceedings with the wry 'Problems' ('I got problems with my woman and I got problems with my wife') and the suitably swaying 'I Can't Lose With The Stuff I Use'.

Appealing though packages like the American Blues Legends were to dyed-in-the-wool aficionados, they failed to recapture the exhilaration of the early 1960s and the first British blues boom. In those days, not only was the music fresh, it also presented a radical alternative to a sterile pop scene dominated by has-beens or never-weres. In 1974, music had come full circle. Prog – which had actually originated with the British blues bands – had grown bloated and overbearing, glam was becoming ever more elaborate, singer/songwriters seemed self-indulgent and the superstars of the sixties were sticking around to no purpose. Yet there were glimmers of hope. Rumours were crossing the Atlantic of a new, stripped-down form of rock while at home it was back to blues basics in the pubs and clubs of London.

CHAPTER 8

New Favourites

'I saw rock and roll future and its name is Bruce Springsteen'. Thus wrote Jon Landau for Boston's *The Real Paper* following Springsteen's appearance at the Harvard Square Theater, Cambridge, Massachusetts, on 9 May 1974. At that point Springsteen had two albums out, but six months had elapsed since the last one and it would be sixteen before the next. So Landau's prediction seemed tantamount to a shot in the dark. But then in 1974 no-one was quite sure where rock was going. The first edition of *The New Musical Express Book Of Rock*, published in 1975, was largely derived from content that had appeared in the weekly pop journal the previous year. Understandably, therefore, the entry entitled Punk Rock referred only to the artfully amateurish garage band scene of the mid-1960s. The second edition, issued in 1977, reprinted the piece but added a postscript:

> Punk revived as a popular term in the seventies, though in a much more loosely defined context, to refer to US acts like Bruce Springsteen, Patti Smith and particularly, Nils Lofgren; in UK, London bands like Eddie and The Hot Rods helped initiate the new punk rock vogue. (p. 405)

Again, this text is likely to come from a year earlier – indeed it must do, because by November 1976 The Sex Pistols had released their debut single, 'Anarchy In The UK', and it was clear that a rock revolution was underway. Soon afterwards the *NME* itself espoused the new trend to the virtual exclusion of anything else.

Whatever the case, the terminology used in *The NME Book Of Rock 2* looks, in retrospect, horribly wrong. Lofgren was a well-known musician, having played guitar on Neil Young's 1970 album *After The Goldrush* at the age of seventeen. His band Grin broke up in 1974 and his eponymous debut album, released the following year, was best known for 'Keith Don't Go', a paean to Rolling Stones guitarist Keith Richards – hardly the sort of stuff to inspire would-be musical iconoclasts. As for Grin, they were a competent MOR rock band with blues and country influences but their final album, *Gone Crazy*, included two dreary ballads and another tribute, this time to guitarist Danny Whitten who had preceded Lofgren in Young's band, Crazy Horse. Quite why the *NME* was classifying Lofgren as punk is thus a mystery – unless they found his habit of doing back flips on stage somehow suggestive of the zeitgeist.

Springsteen, whose E Street Band Lofgren joined in 1984, was another anomalous inclusion. His music at this stage was more redolent of Bob Dylan, while 1975's *Born To Run* looked back to Phil Spector rather than forward to any coming craze. What may well have seduced the *NME* writers, and indeed Jon Landau, into their claims for Springsteen was the irrepressible energy and drive of his live performances plus a series of highly-wrought compositions that painted a vivid picture of life on the streets. This will have come as a refreshing departure from the torpid, self-obsessed drivel characteristic of so many old-school rock bands. But Springsteen, whatever his virtues, was not punk – rather the native superstar that America had been searching for ever since the British Invasion.

It was also misleading to say that Eddie and the Hot Rods 'helped initiate the new punk rock vogue'; certainly they were one of the bands whose direct, vigorous brand of rock and roll was permeating the London pub circuit but, though change was clearly in the wind, the new genre was yet to crystallise – in Britain at any rate. The US version of punk, however, *had* taken root, nurtured, not by Springsteen or Lofgren, but by Patti Smith.

★★★★★

The seemingly interminable Vietnam War; the energy crisis; inflation; Watergate; bussing and the concomitant race riots; the collapse of the Franklin National Bank; the Patty Hearst affair with its cataclysmic conclusion; the brutal murder of fourteen young women by the as yet unidentified serial killer, Ted Bundy; the assassination in church of Martin Luther King's mother, Alberta Williams King; the on-screen suicide of the talented TV presenter, Christine Chubbuck; revelations of domestic spying by the CIA. America was a depressing place to be in 1974. As is often the case, it was the nation's young people who felt its trials and tribulations most deeply. But their response was very different from that of their older brothers and sisters who had vented their feelings in street and campus demonstrations. In fact their reaction was to have no reaction.

Paradoxically, however, negativity produced creativity. Disenchantment, disaffection and disengagement became core characteristics of an artistic movement that turned its back, not just on contemporary political, economic and social degeneration but on what had preceded it, the much-vaunted swinging sixties. The fruits of that unprecedented era of innovation were now starting to taste sour, and nowhere was that more evident than in the central leisure pursuit of American young people, rock music.

In 1974 this new wave was little more than a ripple. But it was beginning to pick up momentum, due largely to the impetus provided by the writer, singer and bass player Richard Hell. Born Richard Meyers, he attended the Sanford School, Delaware, where he met Tom Miller, later known as Tom Verlaine. The two friends reunited in New York where they formed The Neon Boys and then, in 1974, added guitarist Richard Lloyd and changed their name to Television.

Though Verlaine eventually became the band's frontman, it was Hell who attracted the attention, not least for his striking appearance: with his spiky hair and torn T-shirts, written/drawn on and held together with safety pins, he created the template for punk fashions on both sides of the Atlantic. He was also setting the pace musically, as evidenced by Television's live recording in March of his song 'Blank Generation'. Its driving rhythm, elemental melody and sneering vocals were, again, much imitated in punk, but it was the punch-line that encapsulated what the new wave was about: 'I belong to the blank generation but I can take it or leave it each time'.

This first recorded version of 'Blank Generation' was made at CBGB, the recently-opened New York club that was to be the focus of the new movement. Television were fundamental to CBGB's success in more ways than one – they actually built the club's stage; they also persuaded the owner, Hilly Kristal, to book rock bands on a regular basis. Its original title was CBGB-OMFUG, which stood for 'country, bluegrass, blues and other music for uplifting gourmandisers' but thanks to Television and their manager Terry Ork it wasn't long before the 'other music' took over. It was Ork who, for six months up to autumn 1974, recommended bands for CBGB's Sunday shows. He was, in addition, connected to the world of film, theatre and poetry and brought friends from those fields to the club to see the bands he managed such as The Ramones, The Stilettos and, of course, Television who released their first single, 'Little Johnny Jewel', on his Ork record label in 1975.

Richard Hell left the band the same year, allegedly because his onstage antics were distracting audiences from Verlaine's songs, but Television went from strength to strength. In September 1976 they recorded *Marquee Moon*, now widely considered to be one the best albums of the period; in 2005 it was placed number 129 in *Rolling Stone*'s *500 Greatest Albums Of All Time.* One of the reasons for such posthumous acclaim is that it is now clear that it resolved one of the issues that preoccupied contemporary observers of punk, namely, how could an idiom predicated on denying, and decrying, all accepted musical standards possibly survive?

For many, however, it was this very lack of expertise that gave the music its energy. Hilly Kristal himself recalls,

> When I think of that as the beginning of new wave and why it was new wave, it is because they were not musicians. They were kids who used music – even if they couldn't play their instruments – to express themselves. The fundamental thing was a form of expression. And that's why it started getting into a different area from what was happening in other places. (Roman Kozak, *This Ain't No Disco: The Story Of CBGB*, p. 15)

The determination to celebrate non-musicianship was even stronger in UK punk and, indeed, the swift implosion that resulted was, for a nihilist genre, clearly not only fitting, but the whole point. In those terms the British punk revolution was more uncompromising and more complete than in the USA where the continuing fashion, especially outside New York, for ostentatious displays of technical excellence hindered the wholesale espousal of the new wave. Furthermore 'arty' bands who deliberately played down their musical ability had always been regarded with suspicion. The Velvet Underground, for example, never made the US album chart even though the critics consulted for the aforementioned *Rolling Stone* poll put 1967's *The Velvet Underground And Nico* at number 13.

Marquee Moon displays many of the hallmarks of the new wave as defined by Kristal: a terse, unadorned production (many of the tracks were recorded in one take), a brutal rhythm section, and whining, whinnying vocals. Predictably, it was ignored in America. But Verlaine's surreal, poetic lyrics and flowing guitar – seemingly uninfluenced by the giants of the instrument such as Clapton, Hendrix and Page – marked Television out as a band of considerable originality. On trend but also innovatory, Television hit on a blend that brought them success in Britain, where their 1977 tour, with Blondie as support, is still recalled with awe – including by the author, who was present at the Manchester show on 26 May.

But back in 1974, the band had received no reviews at all until June, when a piece appeared in the *Soho Weekly News*, written by one Patti Smith. Already established as a poet, painter and performance artist, Smith was a respected figure in New York and her endorsement was an important step for the band. For many years she had been romantically attached to the photographer Robert Mapplethorpe (who provided cover pictures for her own albums, and for *Marquee Moon*), but now Smith began to date Tom Verlaine, who played guitar on her debut single, 'Hey Joe', recorded the same month at New York's Electric Lady studio. As we saw in Chapter 2, its spoken intro was a dramatic take on the Patty Hearst saga, but in some ways the B-side, 'Piss Factory', was even more shocking – a compelling, high-speed, stream-of-consciousness rant about a mind-numbing job Smith had done in her teens:

> Sixteen and time to pay off
> I got this job in a piss factory inspecting pipe
> Forty hours thirty-six dollars a week
> But it's a paycheck, Jack.
> It's so hot in here, hot like Sahara
> You could faint in the heat
> But these bitches are just too lame to understand
> Too goddamned grateful to get this job
> To know they're getting screwed up the ass
> All these women they got no teeth or gum or cranium
> And the way they suck hot sausage
> But me well I wasn't sayin' too much neither
> I was moral school girl hard-working asshole
> I figured I was speedo motorcycle
> I had to earn my dough, had to earn my dough

While strictly speaking it may have lacked some of the musical features of new wave, 'Piss Factory' totally embodied its spirit and became, alongside 'Blank Generation', one of its first anthems. Although it was not a hit, Smith would go on to have chart success in both the US and UK, the first new wave artist to do so. No trend in pop/popular music had been led by a woman since Bessie Smith inspired the classic blues craze in the early 1920s but the new wave was shortly to have not one, but two, female figureheads.

*****

New York, new wave, new bands… and CBGB became the epicentre, attracting wannabes like a magnet. 1974 saw the formation of countless groups eager to be part of it all. One was Mink Deville, from far-off San Francisco, who started life as Billy de Sade and The Marquis before they gravitated to New York and became the house band at CBGB for three years; in 1977 they would have a UK hit with 'Spanish Stroll'. Another was The Artistics, formed by two students at the Rhode Island School of Design, David Byrne and Chris Frantz, with Frantz's girlfriend, Tina Weymouth, as their road manager. The three of them moved to New York and Weymouth learned to play bass; some months later, as support for The Ramones, they made their debut at CBGB with a new name – Talking Heads. They would become one of the most critically-acclaimed bands in America with no fewer than three entries in the *Rolling Stone 500 Greatest Album* list and, in 2011, a place in the same magazine's *100 Greatest Artists Of All Time.*

The Ramones themselves first played live at the Performance Studios, New York on 30 March 1974 and made their debut at CBGB on 16 August, playing ten numbers in less than 20 minutes. Their avowed ambition to get through their sets as quickly as possible by playing as quickly as possible may have contained an element of self-mockery but it was enormously influential on British punk – as was their uniform of black leather jackets, torn jeans and T-shirts and their consciously amateurish musicianship. Though influenced by the harsh, uncompromising sound of The Stooges and The MC5, The Ramones purveyed their own brand of the wall of noise with both style and humour:

> This was all in contrast to both the virtuosity and the slick stadium sound of mainstream rock and the glitter of glam. Rock journalist Danny Fields was so impressed he decided to manage them: "I borrowed money from my mother to buy them drums, so she's really responsible. I want her to get credit for starting the punk movement". (Kozak, *op.cit.*, p. 19)

According to bassist Dee Dee Ramone, The Ramones' first gig at CBGB was secured for them by two members of The Stilettos, Chris Stein and Deborah Harry. As noted above, both bands were managed by Terry Ork and, while entirely dissimilar in sound, neither took themselves too seriously. Featuring three female singers, The Stilettos specialised in pastiches of the then unfashionable girl group sound of the early 1960s but, like any band based on one jokey idea, their music had a very short shelf-life. Around the time of The Ramones' debut at the club, Stein and Harry were forming a new band, variously known as Angel, The Snake, Angel and The Snake and Blondie and The Banzai Babes. By October, they were simply known as Blondie.

Quite where the name Blondie came from has been a matter for debate. In one version, it came from wolf-whistling truck drivers who would shout 'Hey, Blondie!' at Harry. According to another, it derived from the well-known cartoon strip by Chic Young; as Rob Mackie (*The History Of Rock* magazine, Issue 115) has pointed out, this was

> apt for a group that used imagery from cartoons, B movies and tabloid headlines as inspiration for most of its early songs: "X

Offender", "A Shark In Jet's Clothing", "Kung Fu Girls" and "The Attack Of The Giant Ants".

All of the above tracks appeared on the band's debut album, *Blondie* (1976); sadly, we do not know what they sounded like in 1974. But judging from that release, they are likely to have been developing the sort of punchy yet melodic material that was to bring them massive success in the years to come.

Yet it wasn't just the music that made Blondie famous. Harry's image as a sort of latter-day Marilyn Monroe – with an alluring mixture of innocence and sensuousness – made her a sex symbol, not only within the new wave but across the whole music business. It may well have started as another pastiche but the subtlety was lost on a mainstream pop audience that thrived on unadulterated glamour. Thankfully Harry's talents as a vocalist and songwriter survived the trip, but it was a strange destination for a band who – unlike those acts who came to CBGB already formed – were, in Kristal's words, 'a real child' of the club – and of the new wave.

But glamour of a very different kind was the trademark of the band considered by many observers to have set the new wave in motion in the first place.

*****

Elements of the punk rock revolution were discernible well before the first shots were fired in 1974. The Doors, formed back in 1965, certainly had the attitude, and their stripped-down sound and doom-laden vocals would later re-surface in bands like The Stranglers and Joy Division. But their music was more to do with the death of the hippie dream or, more accurately, its transformation into a nightmare. The Stooges and The MC5 were nearer, as their 1970 albums *Fun House* and *Back In The USA* testify. The former was noise plus nihilism, the latter a string of short, high-speed tracks laced with bad taste. Both, as we have seen, influenced The Ramones.

But the pivotal band were The New York Dolls, whose music lay at the exact intersection between what had been and what was to come. As, essentially, a hard rock band, they drew on Led Zeppelin, Deep Purple and The Who, though pretty much every number was played at a breakneck tempo. That was not, however, what was different about them. Rather it was their stage-act that got them noticed – a combination of exaggerated, at times grotesque, posturing and an in-your-face sexuality that veered from the playful to the sinister. There was more than a hint of parody in all of this. Lead singer David Johansen mimicked Mick Jagger's voice, appearance and gyrations while bassist Arthur Kane's predilection for cross-dressing was, at least in part, a satire on David Bowie.

The location of The Dolls' live debut, on Christmas Eve 1971, could hardly have been more appropriate. The Endicott was a former luxury hotel which over the years had lost its lustre and was now one of the most infamous welfare hostels in New York, perfectly encapsulating the decadence, and danger, that surrounded the band. It was during their first visit to the UK that their drummer, Billy Murcia, was found dead in a bathtub – a tragic event that merely added to their notoriety. In a 1973 poll held by the American rock magazine *Creem*, they were voted both the best and the worst new band of the year. On a return trip to Britain, they were denounced by presenter Bob Harris as 'mock rock' following their appearance on the BBC TV show *The Old Grey Whistle Test.*

Dissatisfied with the sound on their debut album, The Dolls recruited George 'Shadow' Morton to produce the follow-up, *Too Much Too Soon*, which was released on 10 May 1974. But there is little evidence of the talent that ten years earlier had created 'Leader Of The Pack' and 'Remember' for the Shangri-Las. Instead, wildly distorted guitar squalls, hammering rhythms and Jaggeresque vocals dominate the record right from the start. Everything gets the same treatment, including ostensibly incongruous material like Archie Bell and The Drells' '(There's Gonna Be A) Show Down', written by Kenny Gamble and Leon Huff, or bluesman Sonny Boy Williamson II's 'Don't Start Me Talkin'', both of which are rendered unrecognisable. The Jay Hawks' 1956 comic opus, 'Stranded In The Jungle', fares better but is interwoven by a contemporary narrative, while 'Bad Detective', a backhanded tribute to Charlie Chan, lapses into surrealism.

But it is self-composed tracks like 'Babylon', 'Human Being' and, in particular, 'Who Are The Mystery Girls?' that really form the template for punk rock. Indeed, anyone listening only casually to these tracks could easily mistake them for the work of The Sex Pistols. This was no coincidence: just over a year later, The New York Dolls were being managed by Malcolm McLaren and getting their clothes from Vivienne Westwood.

*****

In September 1972 it was confirmed that the school leaving age in Britain was to be raised with effect from the following year. This meant that young people now had to stay in full-time education until they were sixteen years old (though those whose sixteenth birthday fell in late July or August were actually fifteen when they left – an anomaly that caused no end of trouble). Aside from improving the education of the nation's young people, this legislation had another happy consequence. In the summer of 1973, there were no unemployed school leavers. Those who, in previous years, would have been old enough to start work, or if unable to get a job claim supplementary benefit, were now compelled to stay on for a further year. Naturally there was, in some quarters, considerable reluctance to do so. Some young people voted with their feet and left anyway, even though no employer – legally, at any rate – could take them on. So for these dropouts the temptations of antisocial behaviour, including petty crime, loomed large.

In response to the problem, the Secretary of State for Education,

Margaret Thatcher, commissioned a review of the education welfare service, whose task was to identify truants and reintegrate them into school. The Employment and Training Act 1973 also imposed a duty on local authorities to provide a careers service, staffed with qualified professionals and with a remit to provide school students with impartial information, advice and guidance on the opportunities available in employment and further education.

But what these measures did not anticipate – and could not have anticipated – was that a worldwide recession was round the corner. The absence of school-leaver unemployment figures in 1973 had concealed a ticking time-bomb. By the end of 1974, jobs for school-leavers had begun to shrivel. As a clerical assistant in Manchester 's central careers office, part of my work was to provide managers with data comparing numbers of job vacancies currently available to young people with those received in the previous year; these figures made increasingly depressing reading. The youth unemployment rate was approaching 10%, double what it had been in 1972. Within a year the government were paying employers a subsidy to take on young people, a process that has continued, under various guises, until the present day.

As described in Chapter 7, the National Front exploited the opportunities such negative developments provided by holding a series of high profile marches and demonstrations, to which some young people – especially those from disadvantaged areas – were attracted. Furthermore, when Labour were returned to office in February 1974, new extreme right-wing groups began to flourish. Unison, for example, was formed by former NATO staff officer General Sir Walter Walker as a civilian volunteer force to deal with militant trade unions and Irish Republicans. By August, Walker was able to claim that 100,000 citizens had already joined up. The same month saw the publication of Colonel David Stirling's plans for another private army, GB 75, intended to combat both the unions and the government.

There was plenty of activity, too, at the other end of the ideological spectrum. The Workers Socialist League, for example, was formed in 1974 when 200 supporters of the British Leyland shop steward, Alan Thornett, were expelled by the Workers Revolutionary Party – itself founded only the previous year. Militant, then a faction of the Labour Party, was growing in influence and the International Socialists were about to morph into the Socialist Workers Party. Some groups made particular efforts to woo students: the International Marxists, for example, sold the underground magazine *Red Mole* and its successor, *Red Weekly*, on university campuses.

Rock festivals provided a sympathetic environment for such organisations. The US-based White Panthers, for example, were represented at the Windsor Free Festival, then in its third year and the brainchild of anarchist Ubi Dwyer and squatters' rights campaigner Sid Rawle (dubbed 'the king of the hippies' by the tabloid press). Held in Windsor Great Park in front of a crowd of 15,000, it was, according to one eyewitness, 'illegal, drug-happy and absurdly idealistic'. But what made the headlines in 1974 were the violent clashes between festival-goers and the 600 police officers who came to clear the site on 29 August. In the melee, more than 50 people were injured, including 22 police, and 300 arrests were made. Some commentators have seen Windsor as a forerunner of Glastonbury, though it is difficult to see the link between a free event with no basic amenities and today's immaculately organised extravaganza; but one thing is certain: the 1974 Windsor Free Festival marked the end of the great 1960s-style hippie pilgrimages.

Alongside the violence at political events and pop festivals came the hooliganism at football matches, a source of increasing concern in 1974. On 8 March the FA Cup Quarter-Final between Nottingham Forest and Newcastle United was halted after a pitch invasion by hundreds of fans, one of whom assaulted the Forest player, Dave Serella. At the UEFA Cup Final on 21 May Tottenham Hotspur supporters ripped up seats and threw them at Feyenoord fans before rampaging through the streets of Rotterdam. The incident so upset the Tottenham manager, Bill Nicholson, that it contributed to his decision to resign shortly afterwards.

Behaviour on the field was scarcely any better: at the (in this case inappropriately-named) FA Charity Shield on 10 August, Leeds United's Billy Bremner and Liverpool's Kevin Keegan, two of the most high-profile players in the country, were sent off for fighting. Two weeks later a seventeen-year-old Blackpool fan, Kevin Olsson, was stabbed to death at the back of the Spion Kop, Bloomfield Road, during his team's home match with Bolton Wanderers. And to complete a horrific opening month of the season, there were ferocious clashes between Cardiff City and Manchester United supporters on the 31st; recounting that day's events on the United fan website *strettynews.com*, Pete Molyneux confirms that 'Football hooliganism in the UK came of age in 1974'.

It all added up to a grim outlook for vast swathes of the country's young people and, inevitably, the nihilism that resulted was reflected in the music – nasty, brutish and short – which would soon be known as punk rock.

★★★★★

Malcolm McLaren had observed the links between pop culture and revolutionary politics as early as 1968. As a student at Croydon Art College, he became interested in Situationist International (SI), an association of avant-garde artists and intellectuals committed to radical social and political change. Part of SI's methodology was to organise 'happenings' designed to shock people – the middle classes in particular – out of their passive complacency. He had even participated in some of the happenings initiated by an offshoot of SI, King Mob. But 1960s culture did not really interest McLaren: what captivated him was the style and image of the British rock and roll singer, Billy Fury.

The Kings Road boutique Let It Rock which he opened in

November 1971 with his partner, Vivienne Westwood, specialised in 1950s fashions and was so successful that they were called on to design the costumes for *That'll Be The Day.* But when McLaren went to New York for the first time in August 1973, he saw the glamour and excitement of fifties rock and roll updated for a contemporary audience – by The New York Dolls. As Jon Savage has written:

> For McLaren, New York was like a jump-cut into the present. The city seemed boundless, unfolding a series of freedoms – from class, from stasis, from Puritanism – that had seemed a distant dream in England. With the New York Dolls, McLaren at last found himself in the world of celebrity – and he wanted more. (*England's Dreaming*, p. 62)

Just as crucially he came across Richard Hell with his new fashions – the torn T-shirts and safety pins – and his new music. Much later, he recalled:

> I remember telling the Sex Pistols, "Write a song like 'Blank Generation', but write your own bloody version, and their own version was 'Pretty Vacant'". (Legs McNeil and Gillian McCain, *Please Kill Me: The Uncensored Oral History of Punk*, p. 199)

To begin with, it was the T-shirts that permeated the Kings Road shop which in spring 1974 was, in honour of the rubber and leather ware that became its stock-in-trade, revamped and renamed Sex. During the refurbishment McLaren and Westwood were assisted by two teenagers, Warwick Nightingale and Glen Matlock. Along with guitarist Steve Jones and drummer Paul Cook, Nightingale was in a band called The Strand, which Matlock subsequently joined on bass. One year later, after dropping Nightingale and recruiting John Lydon aka Johnny Rotten on vocals, The Strand would become The Sex Pistols.

The Strand were keen to have McLaren as their manager and there is some evidence that he was interested in them. He even came up with a potential name. In autumn 1974 he worked with Westwood and Bernard Rhodes on a new T-shirt design which had 'Hates' printed on the left hand side and 'Loves' on the right. The former list includes one-time firebrands now see as Establishment lackeys (Mick Jagger, Michael Caine, Harold Pinter, Bryan Ferry), as well as political parties (the Liberals, the National Front) and mysterious references such as 'Elton John quote in *NME* 25 Sept re birthday spending'. The 'Loves' encompass notorious names like Christine Keeler, Ronnie Biggs and convicted IRA terrorists the Price sisters; musical iconoclasts like John Coltrane, Jimi Hendrix and Jim Morrison; and another intriguing quote – 'This country is run by a group of fascists so said Gene Vincent in a 1955 US radio interview'. Tucked in just before the latter are 'Kutie Jones and his SEX PISTOLS'.

Why Jones's name is singled out is an interesting question. Certainly McLaren seemed to like him – perhaps his lengthy criminal record gave him antihero status and/or made him especially vulnerable:

> Some time in November 1974, McLaren left for New York: "He said to me, 'Look after Steve'", says Rhodes, "meaning, 'He's got this sort of group, maybe we can do something'". (Savage, *op. cit.*, p. 83)

Once in New York, McLaren began to promote Sex merchandise but also, as an associate of the band, got involved in discussions about the future of The New York Dolls. Though established as a cult act, they had failed to make it big and, at the same time, were on the slippery path to drug and drink addiction; guitarist Sylvain Sylvain and singer David Johansen were also at loggerheads. Sylvain recalled that

> We had a meeting with [the Dolls' first manager] Marty Thau, myself, David and Malcolm about what to do with the band. Marty

> was devastated but Malcolm was enthusiastic: I always said the guy has a lot of power… Malcolm's investment was maybe eight hundred dollars. He called up the guy who ran the Hippodrome, he hated us, but Malcolm convinced him. He's like a preacher: if he gets you to believe, you will see the light. (*ibid.*, p. 87)

Despite kitting The Dolls out in red leather outfits designed by Westwood, McLaren's first (albeit unofficial) venture into band management proved unsuccessful and the band soon split up. Next time round, however, he would achieve the fame, and notoriety, he craved.

★★★★★

Malcolm McLaren was not the only one to experience a feeling of 'stasis' in the Britain of 1974. Boredom was a watchword among the teenage population, both school students (especially those forced to stay on an extra year) and the increasing numbers of young unemployed. But it also afflicted those who had grown up in the 1960s and seen things go slowly downhill ever since. Writer and musician CP Lee sums it up as follows: 'All I remember is a terminal ennui, a disassociation from stadium rock and a big feeling of disenchantment with everything'. In response Lee, with Jimmy Hibbert and Bob Harding, started to write comedy scripts for radio, eventually performing them live as Alberto Y Lost Trios Paranoias – a play on the name of early sixties world music act Alberto Y Los Trios Paraguayos.

The Albertos were in the noble tradition of rock satire as practised by the likes of Frank Zappa, The Bonzo Dog Doo Dah Band and The Fugs (whom they perhaps most closely resembled). Their sets were a non-stop series of parodies which, in Lee's words, 'indiscriminately sent up the music business'. But the business, nevertheless, developed a taste for The Albertos. *Melody Maker*'s Allan Jones gave a favourable review to their debut at the Marquee – where, somewhat unexpectedly, they had topped the bill, the French prog band Ange having been held up at customs – and one-nighters followed throughout the UK and Europe. In December 1974 Jones again referenced The Albertos as part of a *Melody Maker* article about life on the road, citing them as 'lurching from Salford to Southampton'.

The band were part of the Manchester musicians co-operative, Music Force, which had begun operations two years earlier and was linked to the newly-formed Workers Revolutionary Party. One of Music Force's key strategies was to open up new venues, a constant problem since the Manchester Corporation Act 1965 which had given the police sweeping powers to control, and curtail, live entertainment in pubs and clubs. The Albertos circumvented the legislation with what Lee describes as 'guerrilla gigs', spontaneously-organised events which might involve poets and film shows as well as music – 'half arts lab and half variety theatre' and just the thing to appeal to people suffering from stasis/boredom/ennui and looking for something different.

While Manchester musicians struggled for venues, London's pubs were, in the meantime, beginning to burst with bands also offering a very welcome alternative to mainstream rock. By then, most name bands had priced themselves out of the pub circuit but even had they been available, it is doubtful if they could have made as agreeable accompaniment to a pint of bitter as the energetic, no-nonsense outfits that now populated the capital's hostelries. The generic term 'pub rock', however, masks the variety of music being played.

Ducks Deluxe, for instance, included soul, R&B, blues and country in their repertoire. Boasting Martin Belmont, formerly of Brinsley Schwarz, on guitar, their prowess was such that they secured an appearance on John Peel's BBC radio programme, *Top Gear*, in April 1974. Unfortunately their eponymous debut album, released at the same time, does not convey the excitement of their live shows. Maybe they were trying too hard: the vocals, especially on the ballads 'Falling For That Woman' and 'Too Hot To Handle', are so affected as to verge on self-parody, as is the fake American accent on the Status Quo-like 'Don't Mind Rockin' Tonite'. The country-rock numbers 'Hearts On My Sleeve' and 'West Texas Trucking Board' work better but it is the jeering, throbbing 'Fireball' and 'Coast To Coast' that offer the clearest glimpse of the future.

Like Ducks Deluxe, Chilli Willi and The Red Hot Peppers included members of Brinsley Schwarz and (perhaps as a consequence) also did a nice line in country-rock. 1974's *Bongos Over Balham*, for example, opens with the affable, Nashville-flavoured 'We Get Along', and the up-tempo ' Breathe A Little' – featuring 'The Pepperettes' vocal group (Pentangle's Jacqui McShee, blues singer Jo Ann Kelly, jazz-rocker Carol Grimes and Sophie Israel) – is a delightful slice of western swing. 'Desert Island Woman', on the other hand, has the vocal harmonies and flowing guitar of West Coast rock, while 'Jungle Song' highlights harmonica, guitar and drums (played by Pete Thomas, later of The Attractions).

As for Brinsley Schwarz themselves, by 1974 they were on to their sixth album, *The New Favourites Of Brinsley Schwarz.* The band had done well to outlive the massive controversy with which they started their career when, four years earlier, their manager had flown a planeload of British journalists to New York to cover their appearance at the Fillmore East. The initiative was seen as an extreme and repellent example of media hype and for a time brought them unwanted notoriety, but eventually they settled down to life as the archetypical pub rock band.

Produced by Dave Edmunds, *New Favourites* is an attractive blend of blue-eyed soul and country-rock. No fewer than seven of the ten tracks are by the band's bassist, Nick Lowe, including the first version of the much-covered '(What's So Funny 'Bout) Peace, Love And Understanding'. Nothing afterwards quite matches this surging opus, though the Gram Parsons-like country waltz 'The Look That's In Your Eye Tonight' comes close. As with so many pub rock bands, it is the soul numbers that expose their vocal limitations: 'Ever Since

You're Gone' just about comes off but 'Tryin' To Live My Life Without You' entirely lacks the authority of the Otis Clay original.

Sensing that the next big thing was round the corner, new record labels began to appear with the express purpose of capturing the pub rock sound. One such was Anchor, founded in 1974 by Ian Ralfini in conjunction with the American company, ABC. Anchor's first release, AJ Webber's 'La La Song', got nowhere but they hit the jackpot with their second, the easy-paced, instantaneously catchy 'How Long' by Ace, which entered the UK singles chart on 9 November and made number 20. In the US – perhaps because of ABC's promotional muscle – it did even better, reaching number three in spring 1975.

Another Anchor group, Stretch, had a UK hit later that year with the funky 'Why Did You Do It' – a song about the bizarre chain of events that had engulfed the band, then known as Legs, in 1974. Their manager, Clifford Davis, believed he owned the name Fleetwood Mac and – though the actual Mac still existed – recruited members of Legs to tour America using it. Fans of the genuine Fleetwood Mac were told that John McVie and Bob Welch had left the band and that Mick Fleetwood and Christine McVie would be joining the tour at a later date. The truth was soon uncovered by Fleetwood Mac's road manager, the aptly-named John Courage, who hid the band's equipment away from the unwitting imposters, and the tour came to a premature end. The inevitable lawsuit followed, keeping the real Fleetwood Mac on the sidelines for over a year. There was, however, some compensation for the plastic Mac. As well as their hit as Stretch, they ended up backing a genuine (if former) member of the real band, Danny Kirwan, on his 1976 album, *Midnight In San Juan.*

★★★★★

Few pub rock bands survived the heady days of the mid-1970s. *Bongos Over Balham* was the last album by Chilli Willi and The Red Peppers, Brinsley Schwarz called it a day after *New Favourites*, and Ducks

Deluxe split up following a gig at the 100 Club on 1 July 1975. True, there have been revivals and reunions since then but the brief period when their vigorous brand of rock and roll ruled the roost had passed. In a sense, however, that was the point – what made their music so attractive was the almost universal inclination to get on, play a few fast, short, exciting numbers, and get off. Ephemerality was what it was all about.

But as with any idiom, some artists transcended its limitations while others used it as a springboard to the next level. Ian Dury could be placed in either category, or both. His band Kilburn and The High Roads were popular on the pub rock circuit but even at this early stage it was evident that Dury was a writer of wit and originality. In January 1974 Kilburn and The High Roads made an album, *Wotabunch!*, not released at the time because Raft Records, for whom it was made, went under shortly afterwards. It is a valuable document, not least because the band's sound is not as polished as on their 'official' debut, *Handsome*, and thus likely to be more akin to how they sounded live.

It is dominated by rock and roll pastiches in which the band's exuberance and Dury's witty, often dark lyrics make for a winning combination. 'Crippled With Nerves', for instance, is an affectionate parody of a rock and roll ballad with a suitably lurid tenor saxophone solo by Davey Payne, while 'Rough Kids' underpins Dury's street narrative with honky tonk piano, rock guitar and more dollops of sax. The album's centrepiece, in all senses, is 'Upminster Kid', the forerunner of 1977's 'Sweet Gene Vincent'. Here Dury reminisces about his youth as a Vincent lookalike – 'When I was fifteen, I had a black crepe jacket and sideboards to my chin' – but in the course of the song goes beyond the nostalgic narrative to evoke the grip that Vincent exerted on his imagination – 'Gene Vincent Craddock remembered the love of a rock and roll teen'/'Well, Gene Vincent Craddock, the people still move over when the Upminster Kid walks through'; so complete is the identification with his idol the dividing line between the two personas ceases to exist.

'The Badger And The Rabbit' and 'Mumble Rumble And The Cocktail Rock' are more straightforward, if equally idiosyncratic. The BBC subsequently filmed Kilburn and The High Roads performing the latter number at one of London's leading venues, the Hope and Anchor; though an unlikely sobriety pervades the proceedings, it is still a valuable window on the pub rock scene. A couple of tracks from *Wotabunch!* resurfaced on *Handsome.* 'The Roadette Song' is the colourful tale of a female roadie ('she can roll her shoulder, she can roll her arse'), later covered by Elvis Costello and Madness, while 'Pam's Moods', all of them evil, are recounted with mock-Jamaican accent and an anomalously sugary orchestral backdrop.

Ian Dury would find fame and fortune three years later but for now the leading pub rock band were unquestionably Dr Feelgood. Their debut album, *Down By The Jetty*, was recorded between July and November 1974 and embodies the virtues, and limitations, of the idiom. The clean, crisp sound is shorn of all elaboration, the delivery succinct, and the compositions – mainly by guitarist Wilko Johnson – brief and to the point. 'Roxette', for instance, has a pounding three-note riff belted out in unison by guitar, bass and drums and interwoven by Lee Brilleaux's terse vocals and wailing harmonica. 'She Does It Right' is fast and bluesy and though the pace slackens for the rueful 'The More I Give' ('the less I get from you'), the execution remains both concise and dynamic.

By the end of the album, however, the band's resources appear somewhat stretched; Johnson relieves Brilleaux with the occasional vocal but his singing is decidedly average and there is insufficient melodic or instrumental variation to sustain the interest. And the last two tracks could easily have been dispensed with. 'Oyeh!' is an undistinguished instrumental while the closing medley of (the curiously spelt) 'Bonie Moronie' and 'Tequilla' was recorded at Dingwall's Dance Hall and simply serves to remind the listener that this band was best experienced live.

Nevertheless *Down By The Jetty* was enormously influential, even in the USA, where it was introduced by drummer Clem Burke to the other members of Blondie, as well as to The Ramones and Richard Hell. In Britain, The Jam – prior to signing a recording contract – made a demo recording using one of its tracks, 'Cheque Book', and a copy of the album is shown on the cover of *Our Favourite Shop*, the 1985 album by The Style Council, another band led by Paul Weller. It is impossible to imagine that it did not have an impact, too, on the pub rock band formed in May 1974 and known as The 101ers. What is certain is that they were well aware of Eddie and The Hot Rods, since The 101ers' leader, Joe Strummer, later asserted that his band were superior to Dr Feelgood's fellow Canvey Islanders. The only evidence to support his claim lies in recordings made the following year, including the frantic 'Letsgetabitarockin' in which Strummer's high-velocity, barking vocals anticipate the sound of his next band, The Clash. The bridge from pub rock to punk rock is to be found right here.

★★★★★

The early months of 1974 were, especially in the Western world, shrouded by a pervasive and persistent sense of gloom. Much of it was the direct result of the oil crisis, which cut deep into the fabric of everyday life. And when inflation began to soar, it sparked off industrial unrest which in turn threatened the stability of governments across Europe. Elections in Britain and France produced new regimes: the fact that one country moved to the left and the other to the right was symptomatic of the confusion about what to do next. Searching questions were being asked of politicians – Did they actually have the power to prevent global calamities? And what could they do to deal with them?

But the oil crisis and the privations that followed merely compounded the malaise that was already in the air. In some cases, disaffection became insurrection. The rulers of Cyprus, Ethiopia and Portugal were overthrown – the latter a direct consequence of rebellions in Angola, Mozambique and Portuguese Guinea. In others, it was more like a creeping paralysis. In the United States, for example, all hopes that the Vietnam War might be coming to an end were dashed in January, when President Nguyen Van Thieu of South Vietnam announced that the year-long ceasefire was at an end. Rather than resume hostilities, however, President Richard Nixon chose to distance his country from the War, a gradual, lengthy and uncomfortable process. At the same time, mistrust of Nixon himself was intensifying with every new revelation unearthed by the Watergate investigations. Other news stories took second place to the unfolding drama and eventual denouement – the first-ever resignation of an American President.

As if this were not enough, the United States was plagued with violent incidents on the domestic front. Attempts to redress inequality by transporting children from poor areas to schools with more affluent intakes provoked a furious backlash. Police escorts provided to protect the buses from attack were themselves the target of bricks, bottles and other missiles and there were clashes in and around school premises. The Black Panther Party, viciously repressed by the FBI for the previous four years, seemed more interested in reprisals than the social programmes that had gained them widespread support within the African-American community. And, of course, there was the kidnapping and apparent indoctrination by the Symbionese Liberation Army of the heiress Patty Hearst, a bizarre sequence of events that culminated in the firebombing of the SLA's Los Angeles hideout.

Violence was a fact of life, too, in the UK. Prior to 1974, the troubles in Northern Ireland had been largely confined within the Six Counties and, in particular, to Derry and Belfast. But now the IRA's campaign spread to the UK mainland with the bombing of a motorway coach, a college and a number of pubs, including two in Birmingham's city centre on the same night, resulting in the deaths of 21 people. The extreme right-wing party, the National Front, was enjoying its best year to date in the polls, and responded by staging a series of provocative marches at which they clashed with groups representing the far left; during one such incident a Warwick University student, Kevin Gately, received a fatal blow to the head. And it was the worst year yet for football violence.

As ever, it was all reflected in popular culture and, especially in music. Many of the stars of the sixties were still around, though most would come to a creative dead-end during the year, or very soon afterwards. Some, notably Neil Young, were able to capture the despair of contemporary America; others, such as Randy Newman, brought a welcome satirical perspective. In the UK, artists like David Bowie offered withering social comment by allegorical means. More direct political polemic was to be found in the rebel music of Northern Ireland, of the Portuguese colonies and of Jamaica. In a vintage year for African-American music, the emphasis was on the personal rather than the political, but there were sufficient socially-aware releases to keep civil rights on the agenda.

Equally prevalent, however, were feelings of uncertainty about where music was going next. The legacy of the 1960s was finally exhausted with nothing, apparently, readily available to take its place. In that respect, too, music reflected the reaction, both in the UK and the USA, to the sequence of mind-numbing events. There was a sense of listlessness and inertia, of boredom – of the 'ennui' referred to by CP Lee and of the 'stasis' that Malcolm McLaren wanted to escape. Everything seemed to be on hold: the 'pause' button on the now ubiquitous cassette-player was firmly pressed down.

Yet before the end of the year, there was noticeable movement on all fronts. The recession would not be officially over until March 1975 but both the British and American governments were stabilising after the traumas that had all but engulfed them during the year. For President Ford, rising inflation and unemployment meant that things got worse before they got better, but by the end of 1974 the stock market crash had ended and there was a 2% rise in gross domestic product. The national mood was starting to lift as Watergate receded into history and, with it, America's involvement in Vietnam; three months later, after nearly 20 years, the War would be over altogether. Though the bussing controversy raged on, racial tensions were eased when Elaine Brown's accession as Black Panther Party leader signalled a return to community support, greater engagement with democratic politics and a decrease in violence.

In the UK, unemployment was also a concern but industrial unrest had died down and life had returned to normal. After their strong electoral showing, the National Front were now in decline and their provocative marches all but petered out. And there were signs of hope in Northern Ireland. The power-sharing Assembly had been a failure but the fact that political parties in the Six Counties had been prepared to work together was a positive step; moves towards reconciliation were further advanced when, on 20 December, the IRA announced a ceasefire. All of these developments would prove fragile – nothing in politics is permanent – but at least there was a sense of purposeful, and peaceful, progress on both sides of the Atlantic as the year came to a close.

Though it was not apparent at the time, 1974 was a year of transition across a whole spectrum of music. Jazz-rock gave way to jazz fusion, lovers rock transformed reggae and disco crossed over into the mainstream. Minimalism, itself at a zenith, inspired a whole new approach to composition and execution that made prog redundant and heralded new-age, ambient music and – ultimately – synthpop. Finally, in a sweeping rejection of the sights and sounds of the sixties, came the new wave in rock, generated in the clubs of New York and the pubs of London. Now there was no rewind, only fast forward.

Bibliography

Colin Barker (editor) – *Revolutionary Rehearsals* (Bookmarks, 1987)

British Hit Albums, 4th Edition (Guinness Publishing Ltd, 1990)

British Hit Singles and Albums, 19th Edition (Guinness World Records Limited, 2006)

Elaine Brown – *A Taste Of Power: A Black Woman's Story* (Anchor Books, 1994)

James Lincoln Collier – *Duke Ellington* (Pan, 1989 edition cited in this book)

Tim Pat Coogan – *Ireland In The Twentieth Century* (Arrow Books 2004, edition cited in this book)

Miles Davis with Quincy Troupe – *Miles: The Autobiography* (Picador, 1990 edition cited in this book)

Fred Emery – *Watergate* (Jonathan Cape, London, 1994)

Dona Cooper Hamilton and Charles V Hamilton – *The Dual Agenda* (Columbia University Press, 1997)

Stanley Karnow – *Vietnam: A History* (The Viking Press, New York, 1983)

Lewis M Killian – *The Impossible Revolution, Phase II: Black Power And The American Dream* (Random House, 1975)

Richard Killeen – *A Short History Of Modern Ireland* (Gill and Macmillan, Dublin, 2003)

Roman Kozak – *This Ain't No Disco: The Story Of CBGB* (Faber and Faber, 1988)

CP Lee – *When We Were Thin* (Hotun Press, 2007)

Joe Levy (editor) – *Rolling Stone: The 500 Greatest Albums Of All Time* (Wenner Books, 2005)

Nick Logan and Rob Finnis (editors) – *The New Musical Express Book Of Rock* (Star Books, 1975)

Nick Logan and Bob Woffinden (editors) – *The New Musical Express Book Of Rock 2* (Star Books, 1977)

Legs McNeil and Gillian McCain – *Please Kill Me: The Uncensored Oral History of Punk* (Grove Press, 1996)

Martin Meredith – *The State Of Africa* (The Free Press, 2006)
Ed Moloney – *A Secret History Of The IRA* (Penguin Books, 2007)
Ben Pimlott – *Harold Wilson* (Harper Collins, London, 1993)
Jon Savage – *England's Dreaming* (Faber and Faber, 2005 edition cited in this book)
Thomas Sowell – *Civil Rights: Rhetoric Or Reality?* (Quill Books, New York, 1984)
Martin C Strong – *The Great Rock Discography,* 7th edition (Canongate, Edinburgh, 2004)
Al J Venter – *Portugal's Guerrilla Wars In Africa* (Helion & Company, 2013)
Martin Walker – *The National Front* (Fontana Paperbacks, 1977)
Joel Whitburn – *The Billboard Book of USA Top 40 Albums* (Billboard Publications, 1987)
Joel Whitburn – *The Billboard Book of USA Top 40 Hits* (Billboard Publications, 1983)
Peter Woll – *American Government: Readings And Cases,* 7th edition (Little, Brown and Company, Boston, 1981)
Philip Ziegler – *Edward Heath* (Harper Press, 2011 edition cited in this book)

Notes and Acknowledgements

At various points in this book I have quoted from other authors, giving the name of the work concerned and the page number of the edition I have used. Publication details of these works can be found in the Bibliography. The sources of other material are as follows:

Chapter 1

'For such artists, the well was beginning to run dry'. This paraphrases a comment on the ageing rock stars of 1974 made to me by David K Williams at a book and record fair in Stockport, Greater Manchester, in October 2014.

The comments by Frank Snepp regarding the effect of Richard Nixon's resignation on the Vietnam War come from the documentary *Last Days In Vietnam*, directed by Rory Kennedy and broadcast on BBC 4 on 13 July 2015.

Chapter 2

The Source for the Gallup Poll figures cited is *www.gallup.com/poll/116677/presidential-approval-ratings*.

The Little Feat concert discussed is available on a bootleg entitled *Electrif Lycanthrope*. It is also available to listen to via SugarMegs.org (LittleFeat1974-09-19UltraSonicStudiosHEMPsteadNY).

Some of the material relating to the Patty Hearst case, including the quotes from Hearst and Rich Little, comes from the DVD *Guerrilla: The Taking Of Patty Hearst* (Docurama NVG-9738). The estimate of Randolph Apperson Hearst's wealth comes from his obituary in the 20 December 2000 edition of *The Guardian* newspaper.

Chapter 4

The ITV documentary *The Unknown Dead* is referred to in the *en.wikipedia.org* article on Haile Selassie, with a footnote sourcing the 12 September 2010 edition of *The Guardian.*

The performance by Celia Cruz (accompanied by The Fania All Stars) of 'Guantanamera' appears as one of the Extra Scenes on the DVD issue of *Soul Power* (The Masters of Cinema Series, # 87)

Chapter 5

David Bowie's description of his *Diamond Dogs* album comes from Nicholas Pegg's *The Complete David Bowie* (Titan Books, 2000), p. 289.

Chapter 6

The details of The Washingtonians' recordings are taken from the website *www.ellingtonia.com/discography*. Harry Carney's remark on the death of Duke Ellington is quoted on page 99 of Richard Cook's *Jazz Encyclopedia* (Penguin, 2005).

Chapter 7

Some of the material relating to loyalist music is derived from Bobbie Hanvey's essay *The Oul' Orange And Green*, published by the Arts Council of Northern Ireland.

The Danny Burns quote is an extract from the article about The Wolfhound on the website *www.theballadeers.com/ire.*

The details of the Birmingham pub bombings and the statement by Kieran Conway derive in part from the 9 December 2014 page of the Birmingham Mail website *www.birminghammail.co.uk.*

Chapter 8

The quote about the Windsor Free Festival is from an article on the event by Mark Hudson (*www.telegraph.co.uk/culture/music*).

General

DVD *That Was The Year: 1974* narrated by Robert Powell (Nugus/Martin Productions)

Information on records, when not obtained directly from the releases themselves, comes from:

- the Joel Whitburn and Guinness publications cited in the Bibliography
- *www.discogs.com*
- *www.wikipedia.org*
- *www.officialcharts.com*

As regards song lyrics, permission to quote has been obtained from the song publishers listed below. The publishers of the remaining songs from which I quote in this book have not responded to contact or cannot be traced.

'Kung Fu'
Words and music by Curtis Mayfield
©1974 (renewed) Warner-Tamerlane Publishing Corp. (BMI)

'There Were Roses' by Tommy Sands, published by Elm Grove Music.

Index

Names in parentheses are those to which the person or organisation are referred elsewhere. Page references in italics denote use in a quotation or diagram.

Music Index

The following records/compositions are referred to in this book. Albums are in italics.